GCSE
Core Science
Foundation Revision Guide

This book is for anyone doing **GCSE Core Science** at foundation level.

GCSE Core Science is all about **understanding how science works**. And not only that — understanding it well enough to be able to **question** what you hear on TV and read in the papers.

But you can't do that without a fair chunk of **background knowledge**. Hmm, tricky.

Happily this CGP book includes all the **science facts** you need to learn, and shows you how they work in the **real world**. And in true CGP style, we've explained it all as **clearly and concisely** as possible.

It's also got some daft bits in to try and make the whole experience at least vaguely entertaining for you.

What CGP is all about

Our sole aim here at CGP is to produce the highest quality books — carefully written, immaculately presented and dangerously close to being funny.

Then we work our socks off to get them out to you — at the cheapest possible prices.

Contents

SECTION 6 — MATERIALS AND REACTIONS

SECTION 7 — HEAT AND ENERGY

SECTION 8 — ELECTRICITY AND WAVES

SECTION 9 — RADIOACTIVITY AND SPACE

EXAM SKILLS

Published by Coordination Group Publications Ltd.

Editors:

Keri Barrow, Ellen Bowness, Gemma Hallam, Sarah Hilton, Sharon Keeley, Sam Norman, Ali Palin, Andy Park, Kate Redmond, Alan Rix, Edward Robinson, Rachel Selway, Ami Snelling, Claire Thompson, Julie Wakeling.

Contributors:

Mike Bossart, Mark A. Edwards, Sandy Gardner, Derek Harvey, Barbara Mascetti, John Myers, Richard Parsons, Adrian Schmit, Moira Steven, Mike Thompson, Jim Wilson.

ISBN: 978 1 84146 723 8

With thanks to Glenn Rogers for the proofreading.
With thanks to Laura Phillips and Katie Steele for the copyright research.
With thanks to Tom D. Thacher, M.D., for permission to reproduce the photograph on page 17.

With thanks to Science Photo Library for permission to reproduce the photographs used on pages 26, 39, 69, 74, 92, 101, 115, 119, 127 and 128.

Groovy website: www.cgpbooks.co.uk

Printed by Elanders Hindson Ltd, Newcastle upon Tyne.
Jolly bits of clipart from CorelDRAW®

Theories Come, Theories Go

SCIENTISTS ARE ALWAYS RIGHT — OR ARE THEY?

Well it'd be nice if that were so, but it just ain't — never has been and never will be.
Increasing scientific knowledge involves making mistakes along the way. Let me explain...

Scientists Come Up with Hypotheses — Then Test Them

1) Scientists try and explain things. Everything.

2) They start by observing or thinking about something they don't understand — it could be anything,
e.g. planets in the sky, a person suffering from an illness, what matter is made of... anything.

About 100 years ago, we
thought atoms looked like this.

3) Then, using what they already know (plus a bit of insight), they come up
with a hypothesis (a theory) that could explain what they've observed.
But a hypothesis is just a theory, a belief. And believing something is true
doesn't make it true — not even if you're a scientist.

4) So the next step is to try and convince other scientists that the hypothesis
is right — which involves using evidence. First, the hypothesis has to fit
the evidence already available — if it doesn't, it'll convince no one.

5) Next, the scientist might use the hypothesis to make a prediction — a crucial step. If the hypothesis
predicts something, and then evidence from experiments backs that up, that's pretty convincing.
This doesn't mean the hypothesis is true (the 2nd prediction, or the 3rd, 4th or 25th one might turn
out to be wrong) — but a hypothesis that correctly predicts something in the future deserves respect.

Other Scientists Will Test the Hypotheses Too

1) Now then... other scientists will want to use the hypothesis to make their own
predictions, and they'll carry out their own experiments. (They'll also try to
reproduce earlier results.) And if all the experiments in all the world back up the
hypothesis, then scientists start to have a lot of faith in it.

Then we thought
they looked like this.

2) However, if a scientist somewhere in the world does an experiment that doesn't fit
with the hypothesis (and other scientists can reproduce these results), then the
hypothesis is in trouble. When this happens, scientists have to come up with a new hypothesis
(maybe a modification of the old theory, or maybe a completely new one).

3) This process of testing a hypothesis to destruction is a vital part of the scientific process. Without the
'healthy scepticism' of scientists everywhere, we'd still believe the first theories that people came up
with — like thunder being the belchings of an angered god (or whatever).

If Evidence Supports a Hypothesis, It's Accepted — for Now

1) If pretty much every scientist in the world believes a hypothesis to be true because
experiments back it up, then it usually goes in the textbooks for students to learn.

2) Our currently accepted theories are the ones that have survived this 'trial by
evidence' — they've been tested many, many times over the years and
survived (while the less good ones have been ditched).

3) However... they never, never become hard and fast, totally indisputable fact.
You can never know... it'd only take one odd, totally inexplicable result, and
the hypothesising and testing would start all over again.

Now we think it's more like this.

You expect me to believe that — then show me the evidence...

If scientists think something is true, they need to produce evidence to convince others — it's all part of
testing a hypothesis. One hypothesis might survive these tests, while others won't — it's how things
progress. And along the way some hypotheses will be disproved — i.e. shown not to be true.
So, you see... not everything scientists say is true. It's how science works.

Bias and How to Spot It

Scientific results are often used to help people make a point (e.g. politicians, environmental campaigners... and so on). But results are sometimes presented in a biased way — and you need to be able to spot that.

You Don't Need to Lie to Make Things Biased

1) For something to be misleading, it doesn't have to be untrue. We tend to read scientific facts and assume that they're the 'truth', but there are many different sides to the truth. Look at this headline...

> **Scientists say 1 in 2 people are of above average weight**

Sounds like we're a nation of fatties. It's a scientific analysis of the facts, and almost certainly true.

2) But an average is a kind of 'middle value' of all your data.
Some readings are higher than average (about half of them, usually).
Others will be lower than average (the other half).

So the above headline (which made it sound like we should all lose weight) could just as accurately say:

> **Scientists say 1 in 2 people are of below average weight**

3) The point is... both headlines sound quite worrying, even though they're not. That's the thing... you can easily make something sound really good or really bad — even if it isn't. You can...

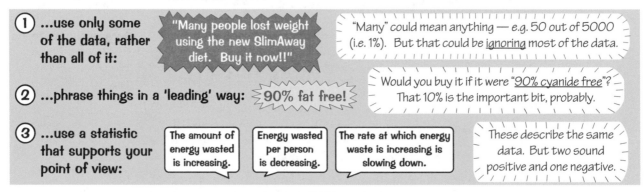

① ...use only some of the data, rather than all of it:

"Many people lost weight using the new SlimAway diet. Buy it now!!"

"Many" could mean anything — e.g. 50 out of 5000 (i.e. 1%). But that could be ignoring most of the data.

② ...phrase things in a 'leading' way:

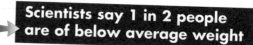 90% fat free!

Would you buy it if it were "90% cyanide free"? That 10% is the important bit, probably.

③ ...use a statistic that supports your point of view:

| The amount of energy wasted is increasing. | Energy wasted per person is decreasing. | The rate at which energy waste is increasing is slowing down. |

These describe the same data. But two sound positive and one negative.

Think About Why Things Might Be Biased

1) People who want to make a point can sometimes present data in a biased way to suit their own purposes (sometimes without knowing they're doing it).

2) And there are all sorts of reasons why people might want to do this — for example...

- Governments might want to persuade voters, other governments, journalists, etc. Evidence might be ignored if it could create political problems, or emphasised if it helps their cause.
- Companies might want to 'big up' their products. Or make impressive safety claims, maybe.
- Environmental campaigners might want to persuade people to behave differently.

3) People do it all the time. This is why any scientific evidence has to be looked at carefully. Are there any reasons for thinking the evidence is biased in some way?

- Does the experimenter (or the person writing about it) stand to gain (or lose) anything? (For example, are they being funded by a particular company or group?)
- Might someone have ignored some of the data for political or commercial reasons?
- Is someone using their reputation rather than evidence to help make their case?

Tell me what you want people to believe, and I'll find a statistic to help...

So scientific data and the person presenting it need to be looked at carefully. That doesn't mean the scientific data's always misleading, just that you need to be careful. The most credible argument will be the one that describes all the data that was found, and gives the most balanced view of it.

Science Has Limits

Science can give us amazing things — cures for diseases, space travel, heated toilet seats...
But science has its limitations — there are questions that it just can't answer.

Some Questions Are Unanswered by Science — So Far

1) We don't understand everything. And we never will. We'll find out more, for sure — as more
   hypotheses are suggested, and more experiments are done. But there'll always be stuff we don't know.

   For example, today we don't know as much as we'd like about climate change (global warming).
   Is climate change definitely happening? And to what extent is it caused by humans?

2) These are complicated questions, and at the moment scientists don't all agree on the answers.
   But eventually, we probably will be able to answer these questions once and for all.

3) But by then there'll be loads of new questions to answer.

Other Questions Are Unanswerable by Science

1) Then there's the other type... questions that all the experiments in the world won't help us answer
   — the "Should we be doing this at all?" type questions. There are always two sides...

2) Take embryo screening (which allows you to choose an embryo with particular characteristics).
   It's possible to do it — but does that mean we should?

3) Different people have different opinions. For example...

   • Some people say it's good... couples whose existing child needs a bone
     marrow transplant, but who can't find a donor, will be able to have another
     child selected for its matching bone marrow. This would save the life of their
     first child — and if they want another child anyway... where's the harm?

   • Other people say it's bad... they say it could have serious effects on the child. In the above example
     the new child might feel unwanted — thinking they were only brought into the world to help someone
     else. And would they have the right to refuse to donate their bone marrow (as anyone else would)?

4) This question of whether something is morally or ethically right or wrong can't be answered by more
   experiments — there is no "right" or "wrong" answer.

5) The best we can do is get a consensus from society — a judgement that most people are more or less
   happy to live by. Science can provide more information to help people make this judgement, and the
   judgement might change over time. But in the end it's up to people and their conscience.

Loads of Other Factors Can Influence Decisions Too

Here are some other factors that can influence decisions about science, and the way science is used:

Economic factors:
   • Companies very often won't pay for research unless there's likely to be a profit in it.
   • Society can't always afford to do things scientists recommend without cutting back
     elsewhere (e.g. investing heavily in alternative energy sources).

Social factors:
   • Decisions based on scientific evidence affect people — e.g. should fossil fuels be
     taxed more highly (to invest in alternative energy)? Should alcohol be banned (to
     prevent health problems)? Would the effect on people's lifestyles be acceptable...

Environmental factors:
   • Genetically modified crops may help us produce more food — but some
     people say they could cause environmental problems (see page 33).

Science is a "real-world" subject...

Science isn't just done by people in white coats in labs who have no effect on the outside world.
Science has a massive effect on the real world every day, and so real-life things like money, morals and
how people might react need to be considered. It's why a lot of issues are so difficult to solve.

The Nervous System

First thing on the menu is a page about the nervous system. The nervous system is what lets you react to what goes on around you, so you'd find life tough without it.

Sense Organs **Detect** Stimuli

A <u>stimulus</u> is a <u>change in your environment</u> which you may need to react to (e.g. a recently pounced tiger). You need to be constantly monitoring what's going on so you can respond if you need to.

1) You have five different <u>sense organs</u> — eyes, ears, nose, tongue and skin.

2) They all contain different <u>receptors</u>. Receptors are groups of cells which are <u>sensitive</u> to a <u>stimulus</u>. They change <u>stimulus energy</u> (e.g. light energy) into <u>electrical impulses</u>.

3) A stimulus can be <u>light</u>, <u>sound</u>, <u>touch</u>, <u>pressure</u>, <u>pain</u>, <u>chemical</u>, or a change in <u>position</u> or <u>temperature</u>.

> <u>Sense organs</u> and <u>Receptors</u>
> Don't get them mixed up:
>
> The <u>eye</u> is a <u>sense organ</u> — it contains <u>light receptors</u>.
>
> The <u>ear</u> is a <u>sense organ</u> — it contains <u>sound receptors</u>.

The <u>Five Sense Organs</u> and the <u>receptors</u> that each contains:

| 1) <u>Eyes</u> | <u>Light</u> receptors. |

| 2) <u>Ears</u> | <u>Sound</u> and "<u>balance</u>" receptors. |

| 3) <u>Nose</u> | <u>Smell</u> receptors — sensitive to chemical stimuli. |

4) <u>Tongue</u> <u>Taste</u> receptors:
— sensitive to bitter, salt, sweet and sour, plus the taste of savoury things like monosodium glutamate (MSG) — chemical stimuli.

5) <u>Skin</u>
Sensitive to <u>touch</u>, <u>pressure</u> and <u>temperature change</u>.

Sensory Neurones

The <u>nerve cells</u> that carry signals as <u>electrical impulses</u> from the <u>receptors</u> in the sense organs to the <u>central nervous system</u>.

The <u>Central Nervous System</u> <u>Coordinates a Response</u>

1) <u>The central nervous system</u> (CNS) is where all the information from the sense organs is <u>sent</u>, and where reflexes and actions are <u>coordinated</u>.

   The central nervous system consists of <u>the brain</u> and <u>spinal cord</u> only.

2) <u>Neurones</u> (nerve cells) <u>transmit the information</u> (as <u>electrical impulses</u>) very quickly to and from the CNS.

3) "<u>Instructions</u>" from the CNS are sent to the <u>effectors</u> (<u>muscles and glands</u>), which respond accordingly.

Motor Neurones

The <u>nerve cells</u> that carry signals to the <u>effector</u> muscles or glands.

Effectors

Muscles and glands are known as <u>effectors</u>. They respond in different ways — <u>muscles contract</u> in response to a nervous impulse, whereas <u>glands secrete hormones</u>.

<u>Your tongue's evolved for Chinese meals — sweet, sour, MSG...</u>

Listen up... the thing with GCSE Science is that it's not just a test of what you know — it's also a test of how well you can <u>apply</u> what you know. For instance, you might have to take what you know about a <u>human</u> and apply it to a <u>horse</u> (easy... sound receptors in its ears, light receptors in its eyes, etc.), or to a <u>snake</u> (so if you're told that certain types of snakes have <u>heat receptors</u> in nostril-like pits on their head, you should be able to work out what type of stimulus those pits are sensitive to). Thinking in an exam... gosh.

Reflexes

Your brain can <u>decide</u> how to respond to a stimulus <u>pretty quickly</u>.
But sometimes waiting for your brain to make a decision is just <u>too slow</u>. That's why you have <u>reflexes</u>.

Reflexes **Help** Prevent Injury

1) <u>Reflexes</u> are <u>automatic</u> responses to certain stimuli — they can reduce the chances of being injured.

2) For example, if someone shines a <u>bright light</u> in your eyes, your <u>pupils</u> automatically get smaller so that less light gets into the eye — this stops it getting <u>damaged</u>.

3) Or if you get a shock, your body releases the <u>hormone</u> adrenaline automatically — it doesn't wait for you to <u>decide</u> that you're shocked.

4) The route taken by the information in a reflex (from receptor to effector) is called a <u>reflex arc</u>.

The Reflex Arc Goes Through the Central Nervous System

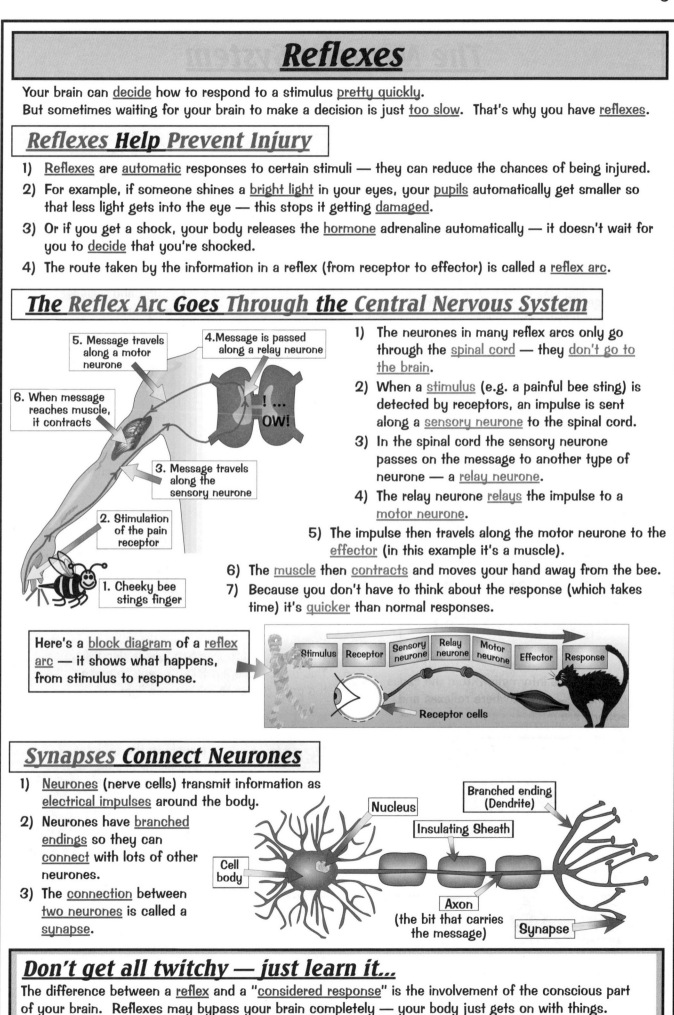

5. Message travels along a motor neurone

4. Message is passed along a relay neurone

6. When message reaches muscle, it contracts

! ... OW!

3. Message travels along the sensory neurone

2. Stimulation of the pain receptor

1. Cheeky bee stings finger

1) The neurones in many reflex arcs only go through the <u>spinal cord</u> — they <u>don't go to the brain</u>.

2) When a <u>stimulus</u> (e.g. a painful bee sting) is detected by receptors, an impulse is sent along a <u>sensory neurone</u> to the spinal cord.

3) In the spinal cord the sensory neurone passes on the message to another type of neurone — a <u>relay neurone</u>.

4) The relay neurone <u>relays</u> the impulse to a <u>motor neurone</u>.

5) The impulse then travels along the motor neurone to the <u>effector</u> (in this example it's a muscle).

6) The <u>muscle</u> then <u>contracts</u> and moves your hand away from the bee.

7) Because you don't have to think about the response (which takes time) it's <u>quicker</u> than normal responses.

Here's a <u>block diagram</u> of a <u>reflex arc</u> — it shows what happens, from stimulus to response.

| Stimulus | Receptor | Sensory neurone | Relay neurone | Motor neurone | Effector | Response |

Receptor cells

Synapses Connect Neurones

1) <u>Neurones</u> (nerve cells) transmit information as <u>electrical impulses</u> around the body.

2) Neurones have <u>branched endings</u> so they can <u>connect</u> with lots of other neurones.

3) The <u>connection</u> between <u>two neurones</u> is called a <u>synapse</u>.

Nucleus

Branched ending (Dendrite)

Insulating Sheath

Cell body

Axon (the bit that carries the message)

Synapse

Don't get all twitchy — just learn it...

The difference between a <u>reflex</u> and a "<u>considered response</u>" is the involvement of the conscious part of your brain. Reflexes may bypass your brain completely — your body just gets on with things.

The Eye

The eye's a good example of a sense organ...

Learn the Eye with All Its Labels:

1) The cornea refracts (bends) light into the eye.

2) The iris controls how much light enters the pupil (hole in the middle).

3) And the lens focuses the light onto the retina (the light-sensitive part — it's covered in light receptors called rods and cones).

   Rods are more sensitive in dim light but can't sense colour. Cones are sensitive to colours but are not so good in dim light.

   Red-green colour blindness is due to a lack of certain cone cells.

4) The optic nerve carries impulses from the receptors to the brain.

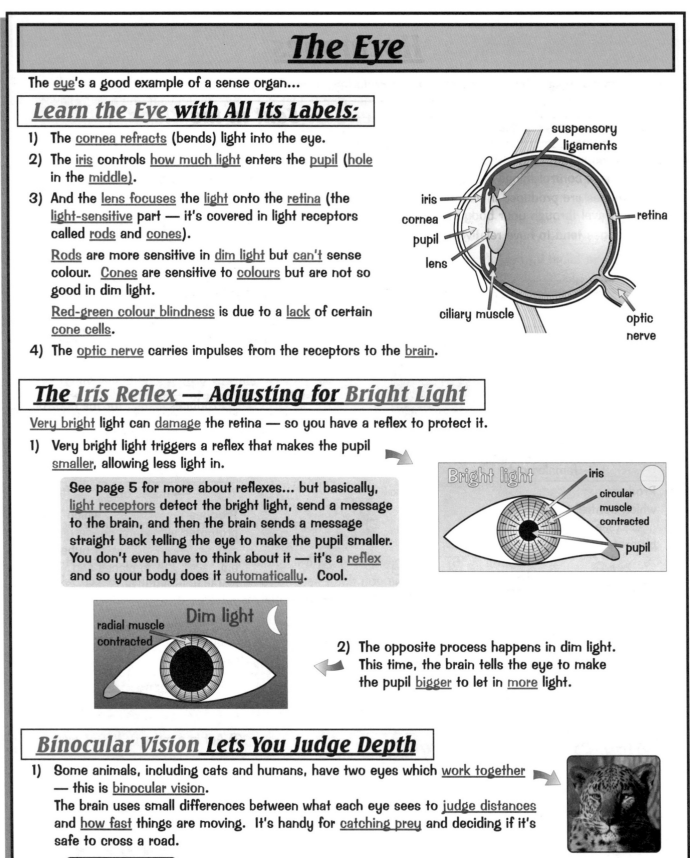

The Iris Reflex — Adjusting for Bright Light

Very bright light can damage the retina — so you have a reflex to protect it.

1) Very bright light triggers a reflex that makes the pupil smaller, allowing less light in.

   > See page 5 for more about reflexes... but basically, light receptors detect the bright light, send a message to the brain, and then the brain sends a message straight back telling the eye to make the pupil smaller. You don't even have to think about it — it's a reflex and so your body does it automatically. Cool.

2) The opposite process happens in dim light. This time, the brain tells the eye to make the pupil bigger to let in more light.

Binocular Vision Lets You Judge Depth

1) Some animals, including cats and humans, have two eyes which work together — this is binocular vision.
   The brain uses small differences between what each eye sees to judge distances and how fast things are moving. It's handy for catching prey and deciding if it's safe to cross a road.

2) Other animals, like turkeys and lizards, have monocular vision. Their eyes see totally separate views, meaning they have a wider field of vision, but can't easily judge depth or speed. The advantage of monocular vision is that the organisms are more likely to notice predators.

I think I'm a little long-sighted...

To see how important binocular vision is, cover one eye and try pouring water into a glass at arm's length. That's why you never see lizards or turkeys pouring themselves a drink — no binocular vision.

Hormones

The other way to send information around the body (apart from along nerves) is by using hormones.

Hormones Are Chemical Messengers Sent in the Blood

1) Hormones are chemicals released directly into the blood. They're carried in the blood to other parts of the body, but only affect particular cells (called target cells) in particular places. Hormones control things in organs and cells that need constant adjustment.

2) Hormones are produced in various glands, as shown on the diagram. They travel through your body at "the speed of blood".

3) Hormones tend to have relatively long-lasting effects.

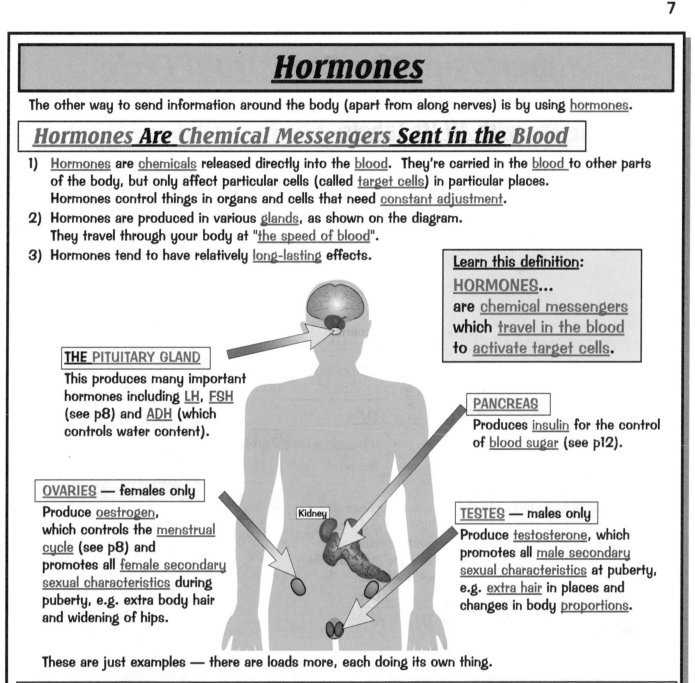

Learn this definition:
HORMONES...
are chemical messengers
which travel in the blood
to activate target cells.

THE PITUITARY GLAND
This produces many important hormones including LH, FSH (see p8) and ADH (which controls water content).

PANCREAS
Produces insulin for the control of blood sugar (see p12).

OVARIES — females only
Produce oestrogen, which controls the menstrual cycle (see p8) and promotes all female secondary sexual characteristics during puberty, e.g. extra body hair and widening of hips.

Kidney

TESTES — males only
Produce testosterone, which promotes all male secondary sexual characteristics at puberty, e.g. extra hair in places and changes in body proportions.

These are just examples — there are loads more, each doing its own thing.

Hormones and Nerves Do Similar Jobs, but There Are Differences

NERVES:
1) Very FAST message.
2) Act for a very SHORT TIME.
3) Act on a very PRECISE AREA.

HORMONES:
1) SLOWER message.
2) Act for a LONG TIME.
3) Act in a more GENERAL way.

So if you're not sure whether a response is nervous or hormonal, have a think...

1) If the response is really quick, it's probably nervous. Some information needs to be passed to effectors really quickly (e.g. pain signals, or information from your eyes telling you about the lion heading your way), so it's no good using hormones to carry the message — they're too slow.

2) But if a response lasts for a long time, it's probably hormonal. For example, when you get a shock, a hormone called adrenaline is released into the bloodstream (causing the fight-or-flight response, where your body is hyped up ready for action). You can tell it's a hormonal response (even though it kicks in pretty quickly) because you feel a bit wobbly for a while afterwards.

Nerves, hormones — no wonder revision makes me tense...

Hormones control various organs and cells in the body, though they tend to control things that aren't immediately life-threatening. For example, they take care of most things to do with sexual development, pregnancy, birth, breast-feeding, blood sugar levels, water content... and so on. Pretty amazing really.

Puberty and the Menstrual Cycle

Hormones control almost everything to do with <u>sex</u> and <u>reproduction</u>.

Hormones **Promote** Sexual Characteristics at Puberty

At puberty your body starts releasing <u>sex hormones</u> — <u>testosterone</u> in men and <u>oestrogen</u> in women. These trigger off the <u>secondary sexual characteristics</u>:

In men
1) <u>Extra hair</u> on face and body.
2) <u>Muscles develop</u>.
3) <u>Penis and testicles</u> enlarge.
4) <u>Sperm</u> production.
5) <u>Deepening</u> of <u>voice</u>.

In women
1) <u>Extra hair</u> on underarms and pubic area.
2) <u>Hips widen</u>.
3) Development of <u>breasts</u>.
4) <u>Egg release</u> and <u>periods start</u>.

The Menstrual Cycle Has Four Stages

Stage 1
<u>Day 1 is when the bleeding starts</u>.
The uterus lining breaks down for about four days.

Stage 2
<u>The lining of the womb builds up again</u>, from day 4 to day 14, into a thick spongy layer full of blood vessels, ready to receive a fertilised egg.

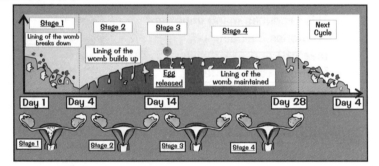

Stage 3   <u>An egg is developed and then released</u> from the ovary at day 14.

Stage 4   <u>The wall is then maintained</u> for about 14 days, until day 28. If no fertilised egg has landed on the uterus wall by day 28, the spongy lining starts to break down and the whole cycle starts again.

Hormones Control the Different Stages

There are <u>three main hormones</u> involved:

1) **FSH** (Follicle-Stimulating Hormone):
   1) Produced by the <u>pituitary gland</u>.
   2) Causes an <u>egg to mature in one of the ovaries</u>.
   3) Stimulates the <u>ovaries to produce oestrogen</u>.

2) Oestrogen:
   1) Produced in the <u>ovaries</u>.
   2) Causes <u>pituitary</u> to produce <u>LH</u>.
   3) <u>Inhibits</u> the further release of <u>FSH</u>.

3) LH (Luteinising Hormone):
   1) Produced by the <u>pituitary gland</u>.
   2) Stimulates the <u>release of an egg</u> at around the middle of the menstrual cycle.

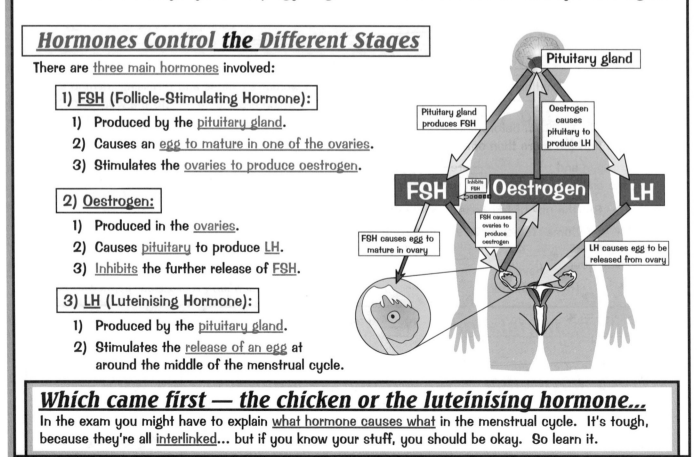

Which came first — the chicken or the luteinising hormone...

In the exam you might have to explain <u>what hormone causes what</u> in the menstrual cycle. It's tough, because they're all <u>interlinked</u>... but if you know your stuff, you should be okay. So learn it.

Controlling Fertility

The hormones FSH, oestrogen and LH can be used to change artificially how fertile a woman is.

Hormones Can Be Used to Reduce Fertility...

1) The hormone oestrogen can be used to prevent the release of an egg — so oestrogen can be used as a method of contraception.

2) The pill is an oral contraceptive that contains oestrogen.

3) If oestrogen is taken every day, it inhibits the production of FSH. After a while egg development and production stop and stay stopped.

Advantages
1) The pill's over 99% effective at preventing pregnancy.
2) It reduces the risk of getting some types of cancer.

Disadvantages
1) It isn't 100% effective — there's still a very slight chance of getting pregnant.
2) It can cause side effects like headaches, nausea, irregular menstrual bleeding, and fluid retention.
3) It doesn't protect against sexually transmitted infections (STIs).

...or Increase It

1) Some women have levels of FSH that are too low to cause their eggs to mature. This means that no eggs are released and the women can't get pregnant.

2) The hormone FSH can be taken by these women to stimulate egg production in their ovaries.

Advantage
It helps a lot of women to get pregnant when previously they couldn't... pretty obvious.

Disadvantages
1) It doesn't always work.
2) Too many eggs could be stimulated, resulting in unexpected multiple pregnancies (twins, triplets etc.).

IVF Can Also Help Couples to Have Children

IVF ("in vitro fertilisation") involves collecting eggs from the woman's ovaries and fertilising them in a lab using the man's sperm. These are then grown into embryos, which are transferred to the woman's uterus.

1) Hormones are given before egg collection to stimulate egg production (so more than one egg can be collected).

2) Oestrogen and progesterone are often given to make implantation of the embryo into the uterus more likely to succeed.

But the use of hormones in IVF can cause problems for some women...

1) Some women have a very strong reaction to the hormones — including abdominal pain, vomiting and dehydration.

2) There have been some reports of an increased risk of cancer due to the hormonal treatment (though others have reported no such risk — the position isn't really clear at the moment).

Too many initials to learn — FSH, IVF, STIs, CIA, DVD...

It's not just scientists who have an opinion on whether these hormonal treatments are good or bad... The teachings of several religions are interpreted by some people as being against contraception (though this often includes other methods too — not just hormone-based contraception). Some people also think that contraception increases promiscuous and irresponsible behaviour, since people know they are very unlikely to get pregnant (though they'd still be at risk of being infected by a sexually transmitted infection (STI)). It's one of those situations where science can't really provide all the answers.

Homeostasis

Homeostasis involves balancing body functions to maintain a "constant internal environment".
Hormones are sometimes (but not always) involved.

Homeostasis is Maintaining a Constant Internal Environment

Conditions in your body need to be kept steady so that cells can function properly. This involves
balancing inputs (stuff going into your body) with outputs (stuff leaving). For example...

1) Levels of CO_2 — your cells constantly produce CO_2 (see page 14), which you need to get rid of.

2) Levels of oxygen — you need to replace the oxygen that your cells use up.

3) Water content — you need to keep a balance between the water you gain (in drink and food, and from
    respiration) and the water you pee, sweat and breathe out.

4) Body temperature — you need to get rid of excess body heat when you're hot, but retain heat when
    the environment is cold.

Water Is Lost from the Body in Various Ways

Water is taken into the body as food and drink and is lost from the body in these ways:

1) through the SKIN as SWEAT...

2) via the LUNGS in BREATH...

3) via the kidneys as URINE.

Some water is also lost in faeces (poo).

The balance between sweat and urine can depend on what you're doing, or what the weather's like...

On a COLD DAY, or when you're NOT EXERCISING, you don't
sweat much, so you'll produce more urine, which will be pale
(since the waste carried in the urine is more diluted).

On a HOT DAY, or when you're EXERCISING,
you sweat a lot, and so you will produce less
urine, but this will be more concentrated (and
hence a deeper colour). You will also lose
more water through your breath when you
exercise because you breathe faster.

Ion Content Is Regulated by the Kidneys

1) Ions (e.g. sodium, Na^+) are taken into the body in food,
    then absorbed into the blood.

2) If the food contains too much of any kind of ion then the
    excess ions need to be removed. E.g. a salty meal will
    contain far too much Na^+.

3) Some ions are lost in sweat (which tastes salty, you'll have
    noticed).

4) The kidneys will remove the excess from the blood — this is
    then got rid of in urine.

Kidneys

If you do enough revision, you can avoid negative feedback...

Negative feedback is a fancy sounding name for a not-very-complicated idea. It's common sense really.
For example, if you looked sad, I'd try and cheer you up. And if you looked really happy, I'd probably
start to annoy you by flicking the backs of your ears. It stops things getting out of balance, I think.

Homeostasis

Homeostasis is a fancy word, but it covers lots of things, so maybe that's fair enough.

Body Temperature is Kept at About 37 °C

1) The human body works best at about 37 °C.
   This is the temperature your body tries to maintain.
2) A part of the brain acts as your own personal thermostat — it receives messages about body temperature.
3) To keep you at the right temperature your body does these things:

When You're TOO HOT:

1) Hairs lie flat.
2) Lots of sweat is produced — when it evaporates it transfers heat from you to the environment, cooling you down (see p93).
3) More blood flows near the skin, so heat can be lost to the surroundings.
4) You can take off layers of clothing to help you cool down.

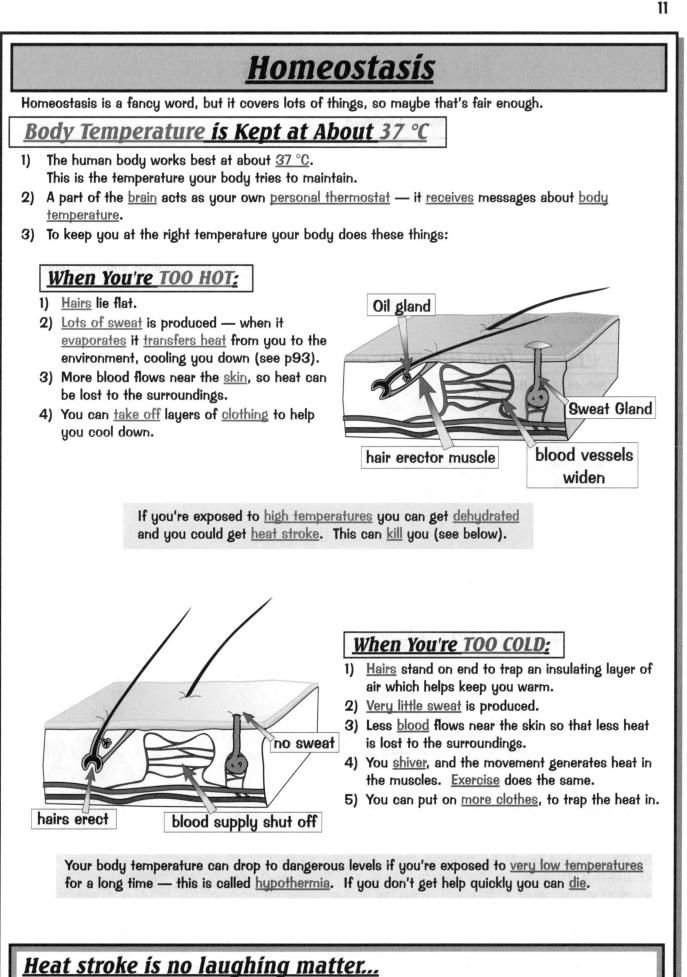

Oil gland

Sweat Gland

hair erector muscle

blood vessels widen

If you're exposed to high temperatures you can get dehydrated and you could get heat stroke. This can kill you (see below).

When You're TOO COLD:

1) Hairs stand on end to trap an insulating layer of air which helps keep you warm.
2) Very little sweat is produced.
3) Less blood flows near the skin so that less heat is lost to the surroundings.
4) You shiver, and the movement generates heat in the muscles. Exercise does the same.
5) You can put on more clothes, to trap the heat in.

no sweat

hairs erect

blood supply shut off

Your body temperature can drop to dangerous levels if you're exposed to very low temperatures for a long time — this is called hypothermia. If you don't get help quickly you can die.

Heat stroke is no laughing matter...

If you're in really high temperatures for a long time you can get heat stroke — sweating stops, since you get so dehydrated, and there's a big rise in your body temperature. If you don't cool down you can die. Fortunately, good old British drizzle means that heat stroke needn't worry most of us. Lucky old us.

Insulin and Diabetes

Insulin is a hormone which controls how much sugar there is in your blood.

Insulin Controls Blood Sugar Levels

1) Eating foods rich in carbohydrates puts a lot of glucose (a type of sugar) into the blood from the gut.

2) The normal metabolism of cells removes glucose from the blood.

3) Vigorous exercise removes much more glucose from the blood.

4) Obviously, to control the level of blood glucose there has to be a way to add or remove glucose from the blood. And this is it:

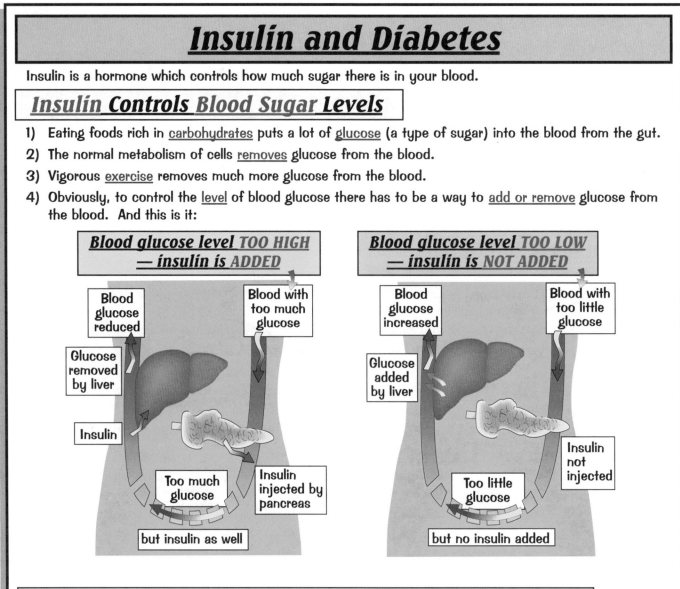

Blood glucose level TOO HIGH — insulin is ADDED

Blood glucose reduced

Blood with too much glucose

Glucose removed by liver

Insulin

Too much glucose

Insulin injected by pancreas

but insulin as well

Blood glucose level TOO LOW — insulin is NOT ADDED

Blood glucose increased

Blood with too little glucose

Glucose added by liver

Insulin not injected

Too little glucose

but no insulin added

Diabetes — the Pancreas Stops Making Enough Insulin

1) Diabetes (type 1) is a disease in which the pancreas doesn't produce enough insulin. The result is that a person's blood sugar can rise to a level that can kill them.

Remember, insulin reduces blood sugar levels.

2) The problem can be controlled in two ways:

   i) Avoiding foods rich in carbohydrates (which turn to glucose when digested).

   ii) Injecting insulin into the blood before meals (especially if the meal is high in carbohydrates). This makes the liver remove the glucose from the blood as soon as it enters it from the gut.

Insulin is Made Using Genetically Engineered Bacteria

1) Insulin used by diabetics used to come from cows and pigs. The cows and pigs were slaughtered and their insulin was extracted and purified.

2) This can't produce enough insulin to keep up with the demand though. Also, the insulin isn't quite the same as the human form, which means the immune system often attacks it, reducing its efficiency.

3) So... bacteria are now genetically modified to include the human insulin gene (see page 33). They produce a pure form of human insulin which isn't rejected by the immune system — and they can produce as much as is needed.

And people used to think the pancreas was just a cushion... (true)

Hormones control a lot of your body's functions. So if one of these functions isn't being done quite right, it might be possible to fix it by injecting suitable hormones — just like with diabetes. Clever.

Revision Summary for Section 1

Congratulations, you've made it to the end of the first section. I reckon that section wasn't too bad. There's some pretty interesting stuff there — nerves, hormones, homeostasis... what more could you want? Actually, I know what more you could want... some questions to make sure you know it all.

1) List the five sense organs and the receptors that each one contains.

2) What do the letters CNS stand for? What does the CNS do? What does it consist of?

3) Where would you find the following receptors in a dog: a) smell b) taste c) light d) pressure e) sound.

4) What is the purpose of a reflex action?

5) Describe the pathway of a reflex arc from stimulus to response.

6) Draw a diagram of a typical neurone, labelling all its parts.

7) Describe the iris reflex. Why is this important?

8) Define "hormone".

9) Give two examples of hormones, saying where they're made and what they do.

10) List three differences between nerves and hormones.

11)* Here's a table of data about response times.
a) Which response (A or B) is carried by nerves?
b) Which is carried by hormones?

Response	Reaction time (s)	Response duration (s)
A	0.005	0.05
B	2	10

12) What secondary sexual characteristics does testosterone trigger in males? And oestrogen in females?

13) Draw a timeline of a 28-day menstrual cycle. Label the four stages of the cycle and label when the egg is released.

14) What roles do oestrogen, FSH and LH play in the menstrual cycle?

15) State two advantages and two disadvantages of using the contraceptive pill.

16) Which hormone is used to stimulate egg production in fertility treatment?

17) Describe how IVF is carried out.

18) What is meant by homeostasis?

19) Describe how the amount and concentration of urine you produce varies depending on how much exercise you do and how hot it is.

20) Describe how body temperature is reduced when you're too hot. What happens if you're cold?

21) Briefly describe the relationship between food, exercise, blood glucose and insulin.

22) Define diabetes and explain two ways in which it can be controlled.

* Answers on page 140

Section 1 — Nerves and Hormones

Respiration and Blood

Respiration does <u>NOT</u> mean breathing in and out. <u>Respiration</u> actually goes on in <u>every cell</u> in your body.

Respiration *is the Process of Releasing Energy from Glucose*

1) Respiration is the process of <u>releasing energy</u> from <u>glucose</u>.
2) This energy is used to do things like contracting <u>muscles</u> and maintaining a steady <u>body temperature</u>...
3) There are <u>two types</u> of respiration — <u>aerobic</u> and <u>anaerobic</u>.

Aerobic Respiration *Needs Plenty of Oxygen*

1) <u>Aerobic respiration</u> happens when there's <u>plenty of oxygen</u> available. ("<u>Aerobic</u>" means "<u>with oxygen</u>".)
2) This is the most efficient way to release <u>energy</u> from <u>glucose</u>, and is the type of respiration that you use <u>most of the time</u>.

> Glucose + Oxygen ➞ Carbon dioxide + Water (+ ENERGY)

Anaerobic Respiration *Does Not Use Oxygen At All*

1) When you do really <u>vigorous exercise</u>, your body can't supply enough <u>oxygen</u> to your muscles for aerobic respiration. Your muscles have to start <u>respiring anaerobically</u> as well.
2) "<u>Anaerobic</u>" just means "<u>without</u> oxygen".
3) It's <u>NOT</u> the best way to convert glucose into energy because it releases much <u>less energy</u>. Also, <u>lactic acid</u> is produced (which builds up in the muscles, making them <u>painful</u> and <u>fatigued</u>). But at least you can keep on using your muscles.

> Glucose ➞ Lactic Acid (+ ENERGY)

<u>Unfit</u> people have to resort to <u>anaerobic</u> respiration <u>quicker</u> than fit people do.

The Oxygen *for Respiration is Carried by the* Blood

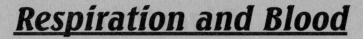

1) Blood is <u>pumped</u> around the body by the contractions of the <u>heart</u>.
2) The blood leaves the heart and flows through <u>arteries</u>. These split into thousands of tiny capillaries, which take blood to every cell in the body. The blood then flows back to the heart through veins.
3) Blood pressure (measured in millimetres of mercury, mmHg) is at its <u>highest</u> when the heart <u>contracts</u> — this is the <u>systolic pressure</u>. When the heart <u>relaxes</u>, the pressure is at its <u>lowest</u> — the <u>diastolic pressure</u>.

Diagram labels: brain, aorta, lungs, pulmonary artery, pulmonary vein, vena cava, heart, liver, gut, kidneys, from lower limbs, to lower limbs

Red Blood Cells *Carry the Oxygen*

1) Oxygen is carried by red blood cells.
2) They have a doughnut shape to give a <u>large surface area</u> for absorbing <u>oxygen</u>.
3) They contain a substance called <u>haemoglobin</u>.
4) In the <u>lungs</u>, haemoglobin combines with <u>oxygen</u>. In body tissues the oxygen is released.

I reckon aerobics classes should be called anaerobics instead...

There's other stuff in your blood as well — e.g. <u>white blood cells</u> (which help fight disease — see p24), <u>platelets</u> (which help your blood clot), and <u>plasma</u> (the liquid that all the different bits and bobs float around in). But it's the red blood cells that carry the oxygen — remember that.

Digestion

Digestion is the breaking down of the nutrients in your food, so that they can be absorbed.

Big Molecules are Broken Down into Smaller Ones

1) The aim of the game is to get all the nutrients from your food into your blood.

2) First the big lumps of food are physically digested so they can pass easily through the digestive system. This basically means chewing it in the mouth and churning it about in the stomach.

3) Then you use chemical digestion to break down the molecules further.

4) This involves using enzymes — biological catalysts that break down the big molecules into smaller ones.

There are Three Main Types of Digestive Enzyme

1) CARBOHYDRASES break down big carbohydrates (e.g. STARCH) into SIMPLE SUGARS.

They're present in two places:
1) The mouth
2) The small intestine

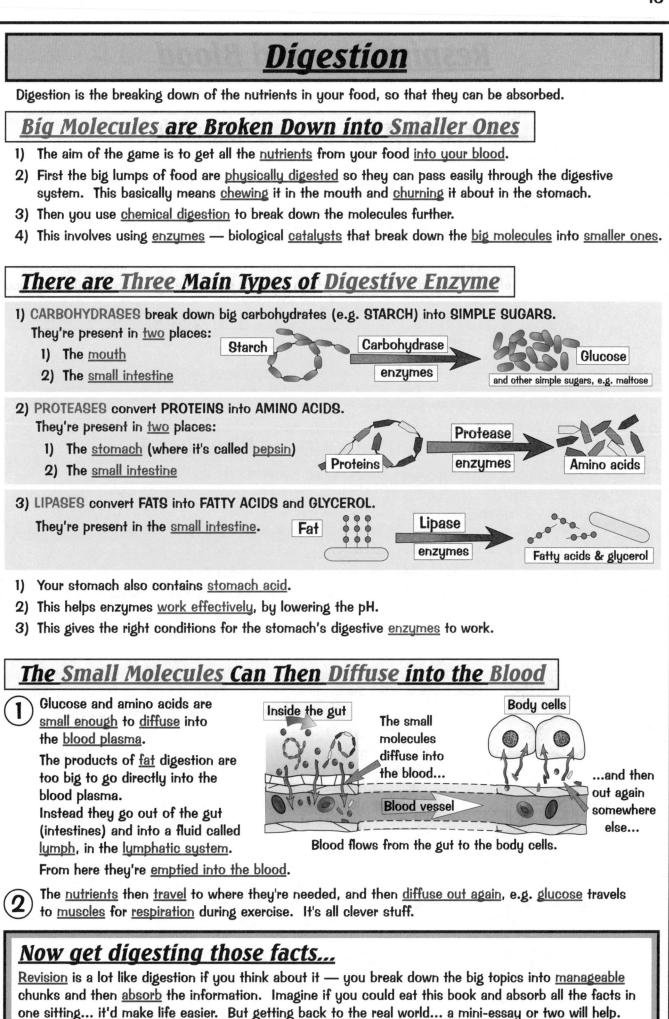

Starch → Carbohydrase enzymes → Glucose and other simple sugars, e.g. maltose

2) PROTEASES convert PROTEINS into AMINO ACIDS.

They're present in two places:
1) The stomach (where it's called pepsin)
2) The small intestine

Proteins → Protease enzymes → Amino acids

3) LIPASES convert FATS into FATTY ACIDS and GLYCEROL.

They're present in the small intestine.

Fat → Lipase enzymes → Fatty acids & glycerol

1) Your stomach also contains stomach acid.

2) This helps enzymes work effectively, by lowering the pH.

3) This gives the right conditions for the stomach's digestive enzymes to work.

The Small Molecules Can Then Diffuse into the Blood

(1) Glucose and amino acids are small enough to diffuse into the blood plasma.

The products of fat digestion are too big to go directly into the blood plasma.
Instead they go out of the gut (intestines) and into a fluid called lymph, in the lymphatic system.
From here they're emptied into the blood.

Inside the gut — The small molecules diffuse into the blood... Blood vessel — Body cells ...and then out again somewhere else...

Blood flows from the gut to the body cells.

(2) The nutrients then travel to where they're needed, and then diffuse out again, e.g. glucose travels to muscles for respiration during exercise. It's all clever stuff.

Now get digesting those facts...

Revision is a lot like digestion if you think about it — you break down the big topics into manageable chunks and then absorb the information. Imagine if you could eat this book and absorb all the facts in one sitting... it'd make life easier. But getting back to the real world... a mini-essay or two will help.

Diet and Exercise

Why is it some people can eat loads and not put on weight, while others only have to look at a chocolate bar and they're a pound heavier...

A Balanced Diet Does a Lot to Keep You Healthy

1) For good health, your diet must provide the energy you need (but not more) — see below.

2) But that's not all. You also need to have the right balance of foods as well.
   You need: ...enough carbohydrates and fats to keep warm and provide energy,
   ...enough protein for growth, cell repair and cell replacement,
   ...enough fibre to keep everything moving smoothly through your digestive system,
   ...and tiny amounts of various vitamins and minerals to keep your skin, bones, blood and everything else generally healthy.

   > You can calculate the recommended daily allowance (RDA) of protein:
   > RDA (g) = 0.75 × body mass (kg)

3) People whose diet is badly out of balance are said to be malnourished (not the same as starvation). Malnourished people can be fat or thin, or unhealthy in other ways.

People's Energy Needs Vary Because of Who They Are...

1) You need energy to fuel the chemical reactions in the body that keep you alive. These reactions are called your metabolism, and the speed at which they occur is your metabolic rate.

2) Muscle needs more energy than fatty tissue, which means (all other things being equal) people with a higher proportion of muscle to fat in their bodies will have a higher metabolic rate.

3) However, overweight people are likely to have a higher metabolic rate than people who aren't — the bigger you are, the more energy your body needs to be supplied with.

4) Men tend to have a slightly higher rate than women — they're generally slightly bigger and have a larger proportion of muscle. Other genetic factors may also have some effect.

5) And regular exercise can boost your resting metabolic rate because it builds muscle.

...and Because of What They Do

1) When you exercise, you obviously need more energy — so your metabolic rate goes up during exercise and stays high for some time after you finish.

2) So people who have more active jobs need more energy on a daily basis — builders require more energy per day than office workers, for instance. The table below shows the average kilojoules burned per minute when doing different activities.

Activity	kJ/min
Sleeping	4.5
Watching TV	7
Jogging (5 mph)	40
Climbing stairs	77
Swimming	35

3) The temperature can also affect your metabolic rate. When it's cold, your body has to produce more heat (which requires energy) — this increases your metabolic rate.

4) All these factors have an effect on the amount of energy your diet should contain. If you do little exercise and it's hot outside, you're going to need less energy than if you're constantly on the go in a cold country.

Diet tip — the harder you revise the more calories you burn...

Exercise is important as well as diet — people who exercise regularly are usually fitter than people who don't. But being fit isn't the same as being healthy — e.g. you can be fit as a fiddle and slim, but malnourished at the same time because your diet isn't balanced.

Diet Problems

Health problems due to the wrong kind of diet are different in different parts of the world. In some countries the problem is too much of the wrong kind of food, in others the problem is not having enough.

In Developed Countries the Problem Is Too Much Food

1) In developed countries, obesity is becoming a serious problem.

2) Hormonal problems can lead to obesity, though the usual cause is a bad diet, overeating and a lack of exercise.

3) Health problems that can arise as a result of obesity include:
arthritis (inflammation of the joints), diabetes (inability to control blood sugar levels), high blood pressure and heart disease. It's also a risk factor for some kinds of cancer.

4) The National Health Service spends loads each year treating obesity-related conditions.

5) And more is lost to the economy generally due to absence from work.

In Developing Countries the Problem Is Often Too Little

1) In developing countries, some people suffer from lack of food. This can be a lack of one or more specific types of food (malnutrition), or not enough food of any sort (starvation). Young children, the elderly and women tend to be the worst sufferers.

2) The effects of malnutrition vary. But problems commonly include slow growth (in children), fatigue, poor resistance to infection, and irregular periods in women.

3) Eating too little protein can cause a condition called kwashiorkor.
Diets in many parts of the world are deficient in protein, especially in poorer developing countries, as protein-rich foods are often too expensive to buy.

A kwashiorkor sufferer

Photo courtesy of Tom D. Thacher, MD.

Body Mass Index Indicates If You're Under- or Overweight

Body mass index (BMI) is calculated from a person's height and weight.

$$BMI = \frac{body\ mass}{(height)^2} \quad \begin{array}{l}(kg)\\(m)\end{array}$$

A BMI between 18.5 and 24.9 is considered normal. A BMI above 30 is often taken to mean that the person is obese (though BMI isn't always reliable).

High Cholesterol and Salt Levels Are Risk Factors for Heart Disease

1) Cholesterol is a fatty substance that's essential for good health. It's found in every cell in the body.

2) But a high cholesterol level in the blood causes an increased risk of various problems — like coronary heart disease. This is due to blood vessels getting clogged with fatty cholesterol deposits.

3) The liver is really important in controlling the amount of cholesterol in the body. It makes new cholesterol, and removes it from the blood so that it can be eliminated from the body.

The amount the liver makes depends on your diet and inherited factors.

4) Eating too much salt may cause high blood pressure for about 30% of the UK population. However, it's not always easy to keep track of how much salt you eat — most of the salt you eat is probably in processed foods. The salt you sprinkle on your food makes up quite a small proportion.

5) And just to complicate things, on food labels, salt is usually listed as sodium.

Obesity is an increasingly weighty issue nowadays...

You need to understand exactly what "risk factor" actually means. If you have a risk factor, it means you're more likely to suffer from a disease, but not that you're guaranteed to. For example, a smoker with high cholesterol and high blood pressure is 30 times more likely to develop heart disease than someone without these risk factors. But it's not a guarantee... statistics don't do guarantees.

Health Claims

It's sometimes hard to figure out if health claims or adverts are true or not.

New Day, New Food Claim — It Can't All Be True

1) To get you to buy a product, advertisers aren't allowed to make claims that are untrue — that's illegal.

2) But they do sometimes make claims that could be misleading or difficult to prove (or disprove).

   For example, some claims are just vague (calling a product "light" for instance — does that mean low calorie, low fat, something else...).

   Alternatively, they might call a breakfast cereal "low fat", and that'd be true.
   But that could suggest that other breakfast cereals are high in fat — when in fact they're not.

3) And every day there's a new food scare in the papers (eeek — we're all doomed).
   Or a new miracle food (phew — we're all saved).

4) It's not easy to decide what to believe and what to ignore. But these things are worth looking for:

   a) Is the report a scientific study, published in a reputable journal?
   b) Was it written by a qualified person (not connected with the food producers)?
   c) Was the sample of people asked/tested large enough to give reliable results?
   d) Have there been other studies which found similar results?

   A "yes" to one or more of these is a good sign.

Not All Diets Are Scientifically Proven

With each new day comes a new celebrity-endorsed diet. It's a wonder anyone's overweight.

1) One way to promote a new diet is to say, "Celebrity A has lost x pounds using it".

2) But effectiveness in one person doesn't mean much. Only a large survey can tell if a diet is more or less effective than just eating less and exercising more.

3) Weight loss is a complex process. Just like with food claims, the best thing to do is look at the evidence in a scientific way.

It's the Same When You Look at Claims About Drugs

Claims about the effects of drugs (both medical and illegal ones) also need to be looked at critically. But at least here the evidence is usually based on scientific research.

STATINS
1) There's evidence that drugs called statins lower blood cholesterol and lower the risk of heart disease in diabetic patients.
2) The research was done by government scientists with no connection to the manufacturers. And the sample was big — 6000 patients.
3) Other studies have since backed up these findings.

But research findings are not always so clear cut...

CANNABIS
1) Many scientists have looked at whether cannabis use causes brain damage and mental health problems or leads to further drug taking.
2) The results vary, and are sometimes interpreted differently.
3) Basically, until more definite scientific evidence is found, no one's sure.

"Brad Pitt says it's great" is NOT scientific proof...

Learn what to look out for before you put too much faith in what you read. Then buy my book — 100% of the people I surveyed (i.e. both of them) said it had no negative effect whatsoever on their overall wellbeing!

Drugs

Drugs alter what goes on in your body. Your body's essentially a seething mass of chemical reactions — drugs can interfere with these reactions, sometimes for the better, sometimes not.

Drugs Can be Beneficial or Harmful, Legal or Illegal

1) Drugs are substances which alter the chemical reactions in the body.

2) Some drugs are medically useful, such as antibiotics (e.g. penicillin).

3) But many drugs are dangerous if misused (this goes for both illegal drugs and legal ones). That could mean problems with either your physical or mental health.

4) This is why you can buy some drugs over the counter at a pharmacy, others are restricted so you can only get them on prescription (your doctor decides if you should have them), and others are illegal.

5) Some people get addicted to some drugs — this means they have a physical need for that drug, and if they don't get it they get withdrawal symptoms. (Many legal drugs are addictive — e.g. caffeine. Caffeine withdrawal symptoms include irritability and shaky hands.)

6) Tolerance develops with some drugs — the body gets used to having it and so you need a higher dose to give the same effect. This can happen with legal drugs (e.g. alcohol), and illegal drugs (e.g. heroin).

7) Some drugs are illegal — usually because they're considered to be dangerous. In the UK, illegal drugs are classified into three main categories — Classes A, B and C. Which class a drug is in depends on how dangerous it is thought to be — Class A drugs are the most dangerous.

- CLASS A drugs include heroin, LSD, ecstasy and cocaine.
- CLASS B drugs include amphetamines (speed). (Amphetamines are class A if prepared for injection.)
- CLASS C drugs include cannabis, anabolic steroids and tranquillisers.

Drugs Can Affect Your Behaviour

1) A lot of drugs affect your nervous system. Drugs can interfere with the way signals are sent around your body from receptors to the brain, and from the brain to muscles (see page 4).

2) The effects of drugs on the nervous system can alter behaviour, which can be dangerous for either the person who took the drug, or for others.

3) For example, driving and operating machinery aren't safe if you've taken certain drugs — e.g. alcohol, tranquillisers or cannabis (see page 21 for more info about alcohol).

4) Some drugs (e.g. alcohol) can also affect people's judgement. This could mean someone just 'losing their inhibitions' — relaxing a bit at a party, for instance.

5) But it could mean they take more risks — e.g. sharing needles and having unprotected sex are more likely to happen under the influence of drink or drugs. This increases the risk of infections like HIV.

6) Drug abuse can also affect your immune system — making infections more likely.

Sedatives and Stimulants Affect the Nervous System

1) Sedatives (or depressants) — e.g. alcohol, barbiturates, solvents, temazepam. These cause slow reactions and poor judgement of speed and distances.

2) Stimulants — e.g. nicotine, ecstasy, caffeine. These do the opposite of depressants — they make you feel more alert and awake.

Drugs can kill you or cure you (or anything in between)...

Many people take drugs of some kind, e.g. caffeine, headache tablets, alcohol, hayfever medicine or an inhaler for asthma. Most of these are okay if you're careful with them and don't go mad. It's misuse that can get you into trouble (e.g. a paracetamol overdose can kill you). Read the packet.

Medical Drugs

Drugs have medical uses too, obviously. But before they can be used, they have to be tested...

Medical Drugs Have to Be Thoroughly Tested

New drugs are constantly being developed. But before they can be given to the general public, they have to go through a thorough testing procedure. This is what usually happens...

1 Computer models are often used in the early stages — these simulate a human's response to a drug. This can identify promising drugs to be tested in the next stage (but sometimes it's not as accurate as actually seeing the effect on a live organism).

2 Drugs are then developed further by testing on human tissues in the lab. However, you can't use human tissue to test drugs that affect whole or multiple body systems, e.g. testing a drug for blood pressure must be done on a whole animal because it has an intact circulatory system.

3 The next step is to develop and test the drug using live animals. The law in Britain states that any new drug must be tested on two different live mammals. Some people think it's cruel to test on animals, but others believe this is the safest way to make sure a drug isn't dangerous before it's given to humans.

But some people think that animals are so different from humans that testing on animals is pointless.

4 After the drug has been tested on animals it's tested on human volunteers in a clinical trial — this should determine whether there are any side effects.

Developing New Drugs is Expensive

1) New drugs are often very sophisticated, and it can take many years to develop and test a drug to the stage where it can be put into use.

2) Most potential drugs are rejected during the trials.

3) This means that new drugs tend to cost a lot.

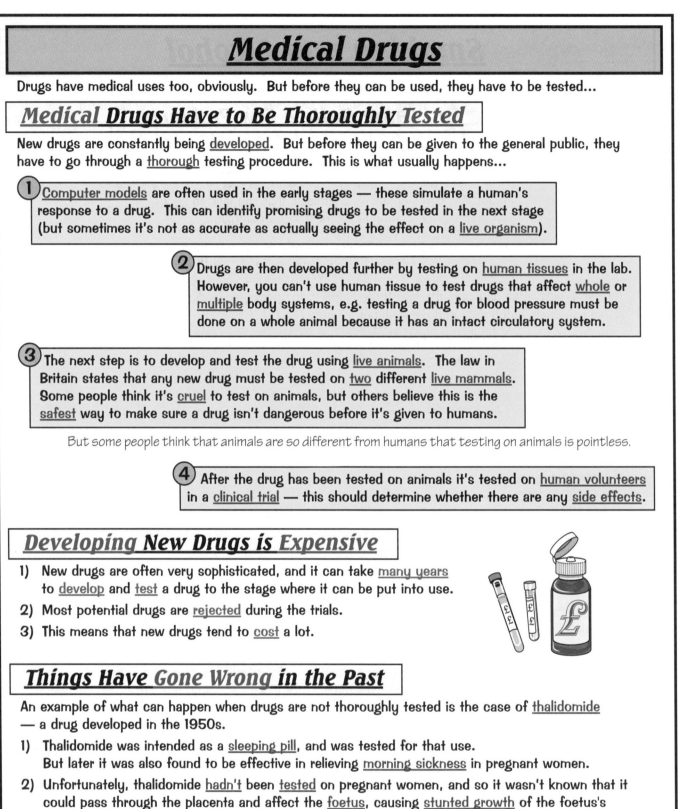

Things Have Gone Wrong in the Past

An example of what can happen when drugs are not thoroughly tested is the case of thalidomide — a drug developed in the 1950s.

1) Thalidomide was intended as a sleeping pill, and was tested for that use. But later it was also found to be effective in relieving morning sickness in pregnant women.

2) Unfortunately, thalidomide hadn't been tested on pregnant women, and so it wasn't known that it could pass through the placenta and affect the foetus, causing stunted growth of the foetus's arms and legs. In some cases, babies were born with no arms or legs at all.

3) About 10 000 babies were affected by thalidomide, and only about half of them survived.

4) The drug was banned, and more rigorous testing procedures were introduced.

5) Thalidomide has recently been reintroduced — as a treatment for leprosy, AIDS and certain cancers. But it can't be used on pregnant women.

A little learning is a dangerous thing...

Thalidomide was an attempt to improve people's lives which then caused some pretty tragic knock-on effects. Could the same thing happen today? Well, maybe not the exact same thing, but there's no such thing as perfect knowledge — you can never eliminate risk completely.

Smoking and Alcohol

Two drugs that have a massive impact on people and society are both <u>legal</u>.

Smoking Tobacco Can Cause Quite a Few Problems

1) Tobacco smoke contains <u>carbon monoxide</u> — this <u>combines</u> with <u>haemoglobin</u> in blood cells, meaning the blood can carry <u>less oxygen</u>.
   In pregnant women, this can deprive the <u>foetus</u> of oxygen, leading to the baby being born <u>underweight</u>.

2) Tobacco smoke also contains carcinogens — chemicals that can lead to <u>cancer</u>.
   Lung cancer is way more common among smokers than non-smokers.
   Lung cancer kills <u>most</u> of the people who get it.

3) Smoking also causes <u>disease</u> of the <u>heart</u> and <u>blood vessels</u> (leading to <u>heart attacks</u> and <u>strokes</u>).
   It also causes damage to the <u>lungs</u> (leading to diseases like <u>emphysema</u> and <u>bronchitis</u>).

4) The <u>tar</u> in cigarettes damages the <u>cilia</u> (little hairs) in the passages leading to your lungs (see p24).
   These hairs help catch <u>dust</u> and <u>bacteria</u> before they reach the lungs.
   When these cilia are damaged, <u>chest infections</u> are more likely.

5) And to top it all off, smoking tobacco is <u>addictive</u> —
   due to the <u>nicotine</u> in tobacco smoke.

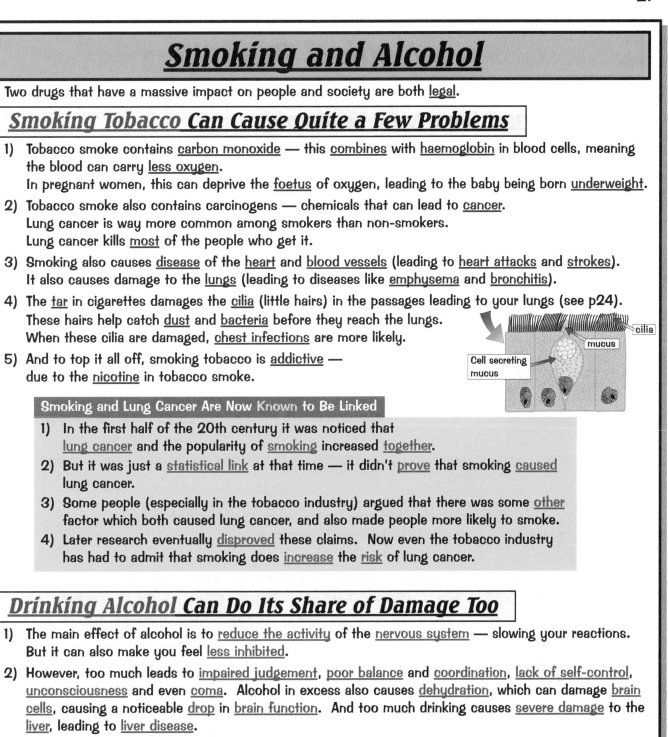

Smoking and Lung Cancer Are Now Known to Be Linked

1) In the first half of the 20th century it was noticed that <u>lung cancer</u> and the popularity of <u>smoking</u> increased <u>together</u>.

2) But it was just a <u>statistical link</u> at that time — it didn't <u>prove</u> that smoking <u>caused</u> lung cancer.

3) Some people (especially in the tobacco industry) argued that there was some <u>other</u> factor which both caused lung cancer, and also made people more likely to smoke.

4) Later research eventually <u>disproved</u> these claims. Now even the tobacco industry has had to admit that smoking does <u>increase</u> the <u>risk</u> of lung cancer.

Drinking Alcohol Can Do Its Share of Damage Too

1) The main effect of alcohol is to <u>reduce the activity</u> of the <u>nervous system</u> — slowing your reactions. But it can also make you feel <u>less inhibited</u>.

2) However, too much leads to <u>impaired judgement</u>, <u>poor balance</u> and <u>coordination</u>, <u>lack of self-control</u>, <u>unconsciousness</u> and even <u>coma</u>. Alcohol in excess also causes <u>dehydration</u>, which can damage <u>brain cells</u>, causing a noticeable <u>drop</u> in <u>brain function</u>. And too much drinking causes <u>severe damage</u> to the <u>liver</u>, leading to <u>liver disease</u>.

3) There are <u>social</u> costs too. Alcohol is linked with loads of murders, stabbings and domestic assaults.

These Two Legal Drugs Have a Massive Impact

1) <u>Alcohol</u> and <u>tobacco</u> have a bigger impact in the UK than illegal drugs, as <u>so many</u> people take them.

2) The National Health Service spends loads on treating people with <u>lung diseases</u> caused by <u>smoking</u> (or passive smoking). Add to this the cost to businesses of people missing days from work, and the figures get pretty scary.

3) The same goes for <u>alcohol</u>. The costs to the NHS are huge, but are pretty small compared to the costs related to <u>crime</u> (police time, damage to people/property) and the <u>economy</u> (lost working days etc.).

Drinking and smoking — it's so big and clever...

So it's legal drugs that have the most impact on the country as a <u>whole</u> — when you take everything into consideration. Should the <u>Government</u> do more to reduce the number of people who smoke — or is it up to individual <u>people</u> what they do with their lives... there's no easy answer to that one.

Solvents and Painkillers

Two other groups of drugs you need to know about are solvents and painkillers.

Solvents Affect the Lungs and Neurones

1) Solvents are found in lighter fuel, spray paints, aerosols, thinners and dry cleaning fluids. They're useful chemicals, but can be misused as drugs (by inhaling the fumes).

2) Solvents act on the nervous system — like alcohol, they're depressants.

3) Solvent abuse can cause all sorts of harm. In the long term often, solvent abuse can cause brain damage.

4) Most solvents also irritate the lungs and the breathing passages.

Paracetamol is a Painkiller

1) Paracetamol is a medicine that can relieve mild to moderate pain, and reduce fever.

2) Paracetamol is generally pretty safe, but an overdose can be deadly. Paracetamol overdose causes horrendous liver damage. If it isn't treated quickly (and I mean really quickly) it's very dangerous. And paracetamol's especially dangerous after alcohol, so it's not a good idea for hangovers.

3) A paracetamol overdose is particularly dangerous because the damage sometimes isn't apparent for 4-6 days after the drug's been taken. By that time, it's too late — there's nothing doctors can do to repair the damage. Dying from liver failure takes several days, and involves heavy-duty pain.

4) Paracetamol in normal doses won't damage the liver (though accidental overdoses are quite common).

Opiates and Cannabinoids are Used as Painkillers

Some types of painkillers can only be used under medical supervision.

Opiates

- Opiates include opium, morphine and codeine — they're all painkillers.
- Morphine's used by doctors — it's very effective.
- But just like heroin, morphine's very addictive, and so it's illegal without a prescription.

Cannabis

- Cannabis has been used as a medicine for centuries, but it's now illegal.
- For years, no one really knew what cannabis did inside the body — this was because research was tricky (due to legal restrictions).
- Recent research seems to suggest that cannabinoids do provide benefit for some patients (though for most people, there's probably something better available).

Different Painkillers Work in Different Ways

1) Aspirin and ibuprofen work by inhibiting the formation of chemicals which cause swelling and make the endings of nerves that register pain more sensitive.

2) Paracetamol seems to work in a similar way to aspirin and ibuprofen, but scientists aren't really sure.

3) Opiates work by interfering with the mechanism by which 'pain-sensing' nerve cells transmit messages. They also act on the brain to stop it sensing the pain.

You can learn this — take the pain, take the pain...

Isn't it amazing that we're still not sure how paracetamol works... Apparently the pain-reducing effects of paracetamol were just discovered by accident. That's science for you — a series of accidents which add together to make amazing discoveries. Learn all the stuff, test yourself, and learn it again if need be.

Causes of Disease

An <u>infectious</u> disease is a disease that can be <u>transmitted</u> from one person to another — either <u>directly</u> (person to person), or <u>indirectly</u> (where some kind of <u>carrier</u> is involved, e.g. mosquitoes spread malaria, and certain bacteria are passed on in food or water). But obviously <u>not all</u> diseases are infectious.

Infectious Diseases <u>are Caused by</u> Pathogens

1) <u>Pathogens</u> are <u>microorganisms</u> (<u>microbes</u>) that cause <u>disease</u>.

2) They include some <u>bacteria</u>, <u>protozoa</u> (certain single-celled creatures), <u>fungi</u> and <u>viruses</u>.

3) All pathogens are <u>parasites</u> — they live off their host and give nothing in return.

4) Microorganisms can <u>reproduce very fast</u> inside a host organism.

Bacteria <u>and</u> Viruses <u>are Very</u> Different

...but they can both multiply quickly inside your body — they love the warm conditions.

1. Bacteria Are Very Small Living Cells

1) Bacteria are <u>very small cells</u> (about 1/100th the size of your body cells), which can reproduce rapidly inside your body.

2) They make you <u>feel ill</u> by doing <u>two</u> things:
   a) <u>damaging your cells</u>,
   b) <u>producing toxins</u> (poisons).

3) But... some bacteria are <u>useful</u> if they're in the <u>right place</u>, like in your digestive system.

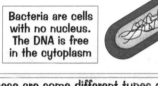

Bacteria are cells with no nucleus. The DNA is free in the cytoplasm

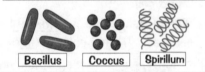

These are some different types of bacteria

| Bacillus | Coccus | Spirillum |

TB (tuberculosis) is caused by bacteria.

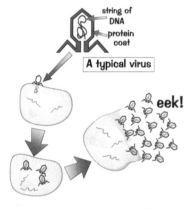

string of DNA
protein coat

A typical virus

eek!

2. Viruses Are Not Cells — They're Much Smaller

1) Viruses are <u>not cells</u>. They're <u>tiny</u>, about 1/100th the size of a bacterium.

2) They <u>replicate themselves</u> by <u>invading your cells</u> and using the <u>cells' machinery</u> to produce many <u>copies</u> of themselves.

3) The cell will usually then <u>burst</u>, releasing all the new viruses.

4) This <u>cell damage</u> is what makes you feel ill.

Other Health Disorders <u>Can be Caused in Various</u> Ways

1) <u>Vitamin deficiency</u> e.g. you can get scurvy if you don't get enough <u>vitamin C</u>.

2) <u>Mineral deficiency</u> e.g. a lack of <u>iron</u> in the diet can lead to <u>anaemia</u>. Iron is needed to make the protein <u>haemoglobin</u> (which carries <u>oxygen</u> in the red blood cells).

3) <u>Genetic inheritance</u> of disorders (see p32), e.g. <u>red-green colour blindness</u> (sufferers find it hard to distinguish between red and green) and <u>haemophilia</u> (a blood clotting disorder).

4) <u>Body disorders</u> are caused by body cells not working properly, e.g. <u>diabetes</u> (see p12) and <u>cancer</u>.

Smiling's infectious — but I dunno what the pathogen is...

A lot of microorganisms <u>won't</u> do you any harm — it's just the pathogens that you want to steer clear of — so don't eat rotten meat, etc. Your body's actually got loads of microorganisms inside it, all over it, everywhere. As has your home (even if it's just been cleaned). It's a fact of life — get used to it.

The Body's Defence Systems

Your body is constantly fighting off attack from all sorts of nasties — yep, things really are out to get you. The body has <u>three</u> lines of defence to stop things causing disease.

The First Line of Defence Stops Pathogens Entering the Body

The first line of defence consists mostly of <u>physical barriers</u> — they stop <u>foreign bodies</u> getting in.

1) The SKIN

<u>Undamaged skin</u> is a very effective barrier against microorganisms.

And if it gets <u>damaged</u>, blood <u>clots</u> quickly to <u>seal cuts</u>.

2) The RESPIRATORY SYSTEM

The nasal passage and windpipe are lined with <u>mucus</u> and <u>cilia</u> which catch <u>dust</u> and <u>microbes</u> before they reach the lungs.

cilia
mucus
goblet cell (secreting mucus)
nucleus

3) The EYES

<u>Eyes</u> produce (in <u>tears</u>) a chemical called <u>lysozyme</u> which <u>kills bacteria</u> on the surface of the eye.

This is a <u>chemical barrier</u> — not a physical one.

The Second Line of Defence is Non-Specific White Blood Cells

1) Anything that gets through the first line of defence and into the body should be picked up by a type of white blood cell.

2) These detect things that are '<u>foreign</u>' to the body, e.g. microbes. They <u>engulf microbes</u> and <u>digest them</u>.

3) They're <u>non-specific</u> — they attack anything that's not meant to be there.

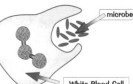

microbes
White Blood Cell

4) The white blood cells also trigger an <u>inflammatory response</u>. <u>Blood flow</u> to the infected area is <u>increased</u> (making the area <u>red</u> and <u>hot</u>). And <u>plasma</u> leaks into the damaged tissue (which makes the area <u>swell up</u>) — this is all so that the right cells can get to the area to <u>fight</u> the infection.

The Third Line of Defence is Specific White Blood Cells

1. Some Produce Antibodies

1) Every invading cell has unique molecules (called <u>antigens</u>) on its surface.

2) When certain white blood cells come across an <u>antigen</u> it doesn't recognise, they will start to produce <u>antibodies</u> to lock on to the invading cells and mark them out for destruction.

3) The antibodies produced are specific to that type of antigen — they won't lock on to any others.

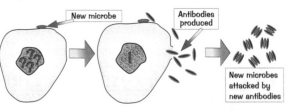

New microbe
Antibodies produced
New microbes attacked by new antibodies

4) Antibodies are then produced <u>rapidly</u> and flow round the body.

5) Some of these white blood cells stay around in the blood after the original infection has been fought. They can reproduce very fast if the <u>same</u> antigen enters the body for a <u>second</u> time. That's why you're immune to <u>most</u> diseases if you've already had them.

2. Some Produce Antitoxins These counter toxins produced by <u>invading microbes</u>.

Cilia and mucus — biological self-defence...

The <u>first</u> line of defence stops nasty bugs getting in, while the <u>other two</u> fight infections once they're inside the body. It's amazingly clever, the human <u>immune system</u> — with all its different strategies to deal with invading organisms. But that's evolution for you, I guess...

Vaccinations

Vaccinations changed the way we deal with disease. Not bad for a little jab.

Immunisation — Protects *from* Future Infections

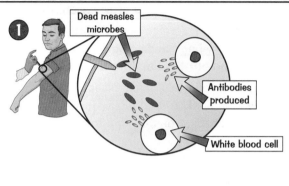

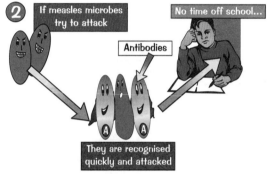

1) When you're infected with a new <u>microorganism</u>, it takes your white blood cells a few days to <u>learn</u> how to deal with it. But by that time, you can be pretty <u>ill</u>.

2) <u>Immunisation</u> involves injecting <u>dead</u> or <u>inactive</u> microorganisms. These carry <u>antigens</u>, which cause your body to produce <u>antibodies</u> to attack them — even though the microorganism is <u>harmless</u> (since it's dead or inactive).

3) If live microorganisms of the same type appear after that, the white blood cells can <u>rapidly</u> mass-produce antibodies to help kill off the pathogen. Cool.

4) Vaccinations "wear off" over time. So <u>booster</u> injections can be given to increase levels of antibodies again.

Immunity can be *Active* or *Passive*

There are two kinds of immunity from disease — <u>active immunity</u> and <u>passive immunity</u>. Immunisation is classed as <u>active immunity</u>:

- <u>Active</u> immunity is where the immune system <u>makes its own antibodies</u>. It includes becoming <u>naturally immune</u> (see previous page) and <u>artificially immune</u> (<u>immunisation</u>). Active immunity is usually <u>permanent</u>.

- <u>Passive</u> immunity is where you use <u>antibodies made by another organism</u> (e.g. antibodies are passed from mother to baby through breast milk). Passive immunity is only <u>temporary</u>.

Immunisation Has *Changed the Way We Fight Disease*

1) Vaccinations mean we don't have to deal with a problem once it's happened — we can <u>prevent</u> it happening in the first place. Vaccines have helped <u>control</u> lots of infectious diseases that were once <u>common</u> in the UK (e.g. polio, measles, whooping cough, rubella, mumps, tetanus, TB...).

2) Vaccination is now used all over the world. <u>Smallpox</u> no longer occurs at all, and <u>polio</u> infections have fallen by 99%.

Prevention is better than cure...

Science isn't just about doing an experiment, finding the answer and telling everyone about it — scientists often disagree. Not that long ago different scientists had different opinions on the <u>MMR</u> vaccine — and argued about its safety. Many different studies were done before scientists concluded it was safe.

Treating Disease — Past and Future

The way we fight disease has changed loads over the last few decades. Thankfully.

Semmelweiss Cut Deaths by Using Antiseptics

1) In the 1840s Ignaz Semmelweiss saw that women were dying in huge numbers after childbirth from a disease called puerperal fever.

2) He believed that doctors were spreading the disease on their unwashed hands. By telling doctors entering his ward to wash their hands in an antiseptic solution, he cut the death rate dramatically.

3) Semmelweiss didn't understand about how bacteria cause disease. This meant he couldn't prove why his idea worked, and his methods were dropped when he left the hospital (allowing death rates to rise once again — d'oh).

4) Nowadays we know that basic hygiene is essential in controlling disease (though recent reports have found that a lack of it in some modern hospitals has helped the disease MRSA spread — see below).

Antibiotics Changed the Way We Fight Infections

1) Antibiotics were an incredibly important (but accidental) discovery.

2) Some killer diseases (e.g. pneumonia and tuberculosis) suddenly became much easier to treat.

3) However, antibiotics don't destroy viruses.

4) Viruses reproduce using your own body cells, which makes it very difficult to develop drugs that destroy just the virus without killing the body's cells.

5) Flu and colds are caused by viruses. Usually you just have to wait for your body to deal with the virus, and relieve the symptoms if you start to feel really grotty.

6) There are some antiviral drugs available, but they're usually reserved for very serious viral illnesses (such as AIDS and hepatitis).

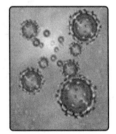

Flu virus. Lovely.

We Face New and Scary Dangers All the Time

1) For the last few decades, humans have been able to deal with bacterial infections using antibiotics.

2) But there'd be a real problem if a virus or a strain of bacterium evolved so that it was both deadly and could easily pass from person to person.

3) Flu viruses, for example, evolve quickly — so this is quite possible.

4) If this happened, precautions could be taken to stop the virus spreading in the first place. However, this is hard nowadays — millions of people travel by plane every day.

5) And vaccines and antiviral drugs could be developed (but these take time to mass produce).

A pandemic is when a disease spreads all over the world.

6) But in the worst-case scenario, a flu pandemic (e.g. one evolved from bird flu) could kill billions of people all over the world.

Antibiotic resistance is inevitable...

Antibiotic resistance is scary. Bacteria reproduce quickly, and so are pretty fast at evolving to deal with threats (e.g. antibiotics). If we were back in the situation where we had no way to treat bacterial infections, we'd have a nightmare. So do your bit, and finish your courses of antibiotics.

Revision Summary for Section 2

That was a long(ish) section, but kind of interesting, I reckon. These questions will show what you know and what you don't... if you get stuck, have a look back to remind yourself. But before the exam, make sure you can do all of them without any help — if you can't, you know you're definitely <u>not ready</u>.

1) What is "aerobic respiration"? Give the word and symbol equations for it.

2) Explain the term "anaerobic respiration".

3) Name the three main types of digestive enzyme and explain what they do.

4) Name five essential nutrients the body needs and what they're used for.

5)* Put these people in order of how much energy they would likely need from their food (from highest to lowest): a) mechanic, b) professional runner, c) secretary.

6) What's the difference between 'fit' and 'healthy'? Can you be one without being the other?

7) Name five health problems that are associated with obesity.

8) What is cholesterol?

9) State the formula for working out someone's BMI. What is BMI useful for?

10) Why can it be tricky to know how much salt you're eating?

11) Name four things that you could consider when trying to decide if a health claim is believable.

12) Define the terms prescription and addiction.

13) Describe the four stages of drug testing.

14) Name a drug that was not tested thoroughly enough and describe the consequences of its use.

15) Describe four different illnesses that smoking can cause.

16) How do carbon monoxide, carcinogens and tar in tobacco smoke each affect the body?

17) Alcohol is a depressant drug. Describe the symptoms of drinking too much alcohol.

18)* Here is a graph of Mark's blood alcohol concentration against time.
   a) When did Mark have his first alcoholic drink?
   b) When did Mark have his second alcoholic drink?
   c) The legal limit for driving in the UK is 80 mg of alcohol per 100 ml of blood. Would Mark have been legally allowed to drive at 9pm?

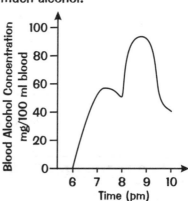

19) Describe one of the effects that inhaling solvents can cause.

20) What kinds of pain is paracetamol used to relieve? Why shouldn't you exceed the recommended dose?

21) Name two types of painkiller that can only be used under medical supervision.

22) How do aspirin and ibuprofen work? What about opiates?

23) Name the four types of microorganism that can cause disease.

24) Name three parts of the body which make up the first line of defence against pathogens.

25) What is the body's second line of defence against pathogens?

26) Explain how immunisation stops you getting infections.

27) Why don't antibiotics work against the flu?

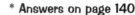

Variation in Plants and Animals

The word 'variation' sounds far too fancy for its own good. All it means is how animals or plants of the same species look or behave slightly differently from each other. You know, a bit taller or a bit fatter or a bit more scary-to-look-at etc. There are two kinds of variation — genetic and environmental.

Genetic Variation is Caused by Genes (Surprise)

1) All animals (including humans) are bound to be slightly different from each other because their genes are slightly different.

2) Genes are the code which determines how your body turns out — they control your inherited traits, e.g. eye colour. We all end up with a slightly different set of genes. The exceptions to this rule are identical twins, because their genes are exactly the same.

Most Variation in Animals is Due to Genes and Environment

1) Most variation in animals is caused by a mixture of genetic and environmental factors.

2) Almost every single aspect of a human (or other animal) is affected by our environment in some way, however small. In fact it's a lot easier to list the factors which aren't affected in any way by environment:

If you're not sure what "environment" means, think of it as "upbringing" instead.

> 1) **Eye colour,**
> 2) **Hair colour** in most animals (in humans, vanity plays a big part),
> 3) **Inherited disorders** like haemophilia, cystic fibrosis, etc.,
> 4) **Blood group.**

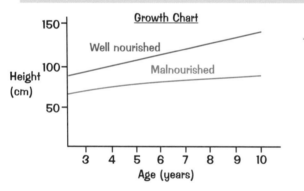

Growth Chart

Well nourished

Malnourished

Height (cm)

Age (years)

3) Environment can have a large effect on human growth even before someone's born. For example, a baby's weight at birth can be affected by the mother's diet.

4) And having a poor diet whilst you're growing up can stunt your growth — another environmental variation.

Environmental Variation in Plants is Much Greater

Plants are strongly affected by:
1) sunlight, 2) moisture level, 3) temperature, 4) the mineral content of the soil.

For example, plants may grow twice as big or twice as fast due to fairly modest changes in environment such as the amount of sunlight or rainfall they're getting, or how warm it is or what the soil is like.

Think about it — if you give your pot plant some plant food (full of lovely minerals), then your plant grows loads faster. Farmers and gardeners use mineral fertilisers to improve crop yields.

Environmental variation — like sun and scattered showers...

So there you go... the "nature versus nurture" debate (*Are you like you are because of the genes you're born with, or because of the way you're brought up?*) summarised in one page. And the winner is... well, both of them really. Your genes are pretty vital, but then so is your environment. What an anticlimax.

DNA and Genes

If you're going to get anywhere with this topic you have to make sure you know exactly what DNA is, what and where chromosomes are, and what and where a gene is. If you don't get that sorted out first, then anything else you read about them won't make a lot of sense to you — will it.

Whether you're talking about animals or plants, this basic stuff about genes is pretty much the same...

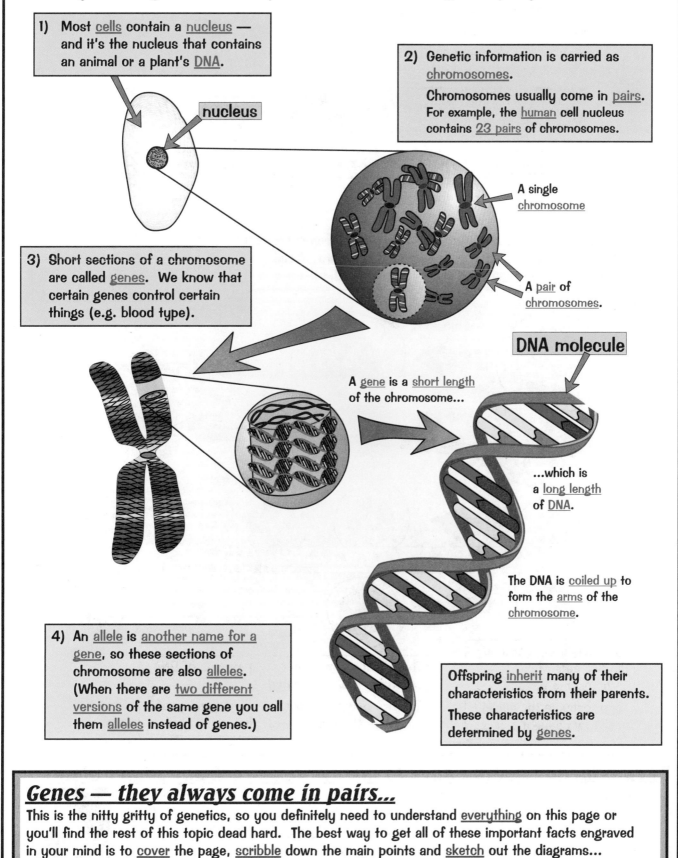

1) Most cells contain a nucleus — and it's the nucleus that contains an animal or a plant's DNA.

nucleus

2) Genetic information is carried as chromosomes.

Chromosomes usually come in pairs. For example, the human cell nucleus contains 23 pairs of chromosomes.

A single chromosome

A pair of chromosomes.

3) Short sections of a chromosome are called genes. We know that certain genes control certain things (e.g. blood type).

DNA molecule

A gene is a short length of the chromosome...

...which is a long length of DNA.

The DNA is coiled up to form the arms of the chromosome.

4) An allele is another name for a gene, so these sections of chromosome are also alleles. (When there are two different versions of the same gene you call them alleles instead of genes.)

Offspring inherit many of their characteristics from their parents.

These characteristics are determined by genes.

Genes — they always come in pairs...

This is the nitty gritty of genetics, so you definitely need to understand everything on this page or you'll find the rest of this topic dead hard. The best way to get all of these important facts engraved in your mind is to cover the page, scribble down the main points and sketch out the diagrams...

Section 3 — Genetics and Evolution

Asexual Reproduction

Cells can split in two — nice trick if you can do it.

Asexual Reproduction **Produces** Identical Offspring

1) Cells can split to form two identical copies of themselves.
   This goes on in all <u>plants</u> and <u>animals</u> (including you).

2) This process is used for growth, repair and asexual reproduction.

3) Some organisms can also <u>reproduce</u> in this way, e.g. spider plants, strawberries and potatoes.
   This is known as <u>asexual</u> reproduction. Here's a <u>definition</u>:

> In <u>asexual reproduction</u> there is only <u>one</u> parent, and the offspring therefore
> have <u>exactly the same genes</u> as the parent (i.e. they're <u>clones</u> — see p35).

The Offspring Are Genetically Identical to the Parent Cell

The really riveting part here is how the <u>chromosomes split</u> inside the cell. Enjoy...

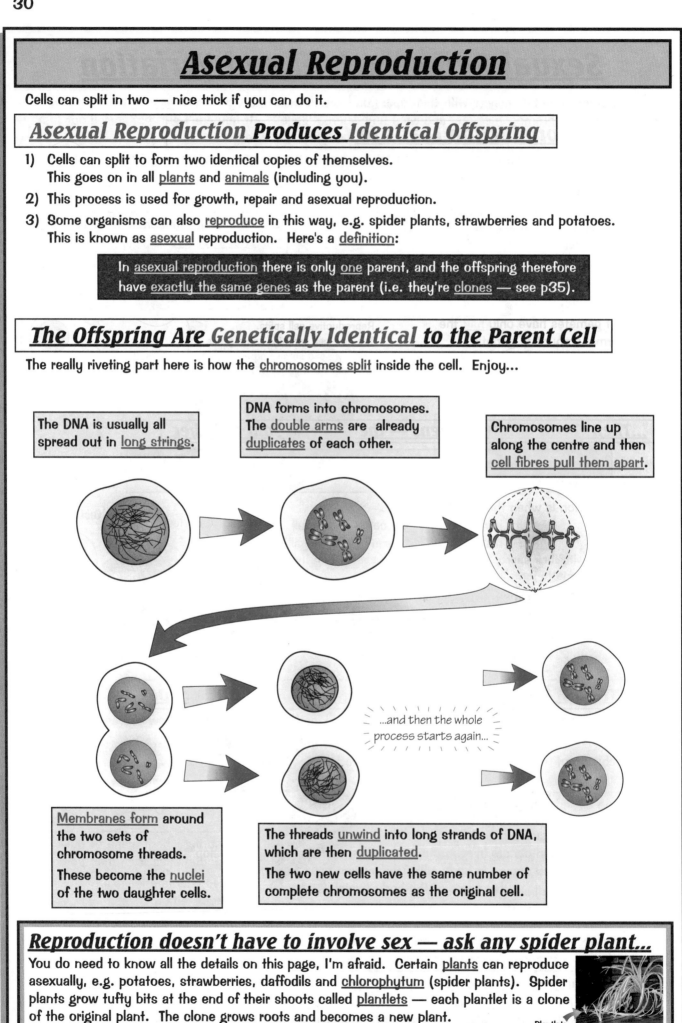

The DNA is usually all spread out in <u>long strings</u>.

DNA forms into chromosomes. The <u>double arms</u> are already <u>duplicates</u> of each other.

Chromosomes line up along the centre and then <u>cell fibres pull them apart</u>.

...and then the whole process starts again...

<u>Membranes form</u> around the two sets of chromosome threads. These become the <u>nuclei</u> of the two daughter cells.

The threads <u>unwind</u> into long strands of DNA, which are then <u>duplicated</u>. The two new cells have the same number of complete chromosomes as the original cell.

Reproduction doesn't have to involve sex — ask any spider plant...

You do need to know all the details on this page, I'm afraid. Certain <u>plants</u> can reproduce asexually, e.g. potatoes, strawberries, daffodils and <u>chlorophytum</u> (spider plants). Spider plants grow tufty bits at the end of their shoots called <u>plantlets</u> — each plantlet is a clone of the original plant. The clone grows roots and becomes a new plant.

Plantlets

Section 3 — Genetics and Evolution

Sexual Reproduction and Variation

If you thought reproduction by mitosis was exciting, you'll love this...

Sexual Reproduction Leads to Genetic Variation

First, Gametes are Formed — Sperm Cells and Egg Cells...

1) Gametes are sperm cells and egg cells.

2) They're formed in the ovaries or testes from reproductive cells.

3) Gametes contain some genes from your dad and some from your mum.

4) But gametes have only half the normal amount of genetic information — 23 chromosomes, not the full 46.

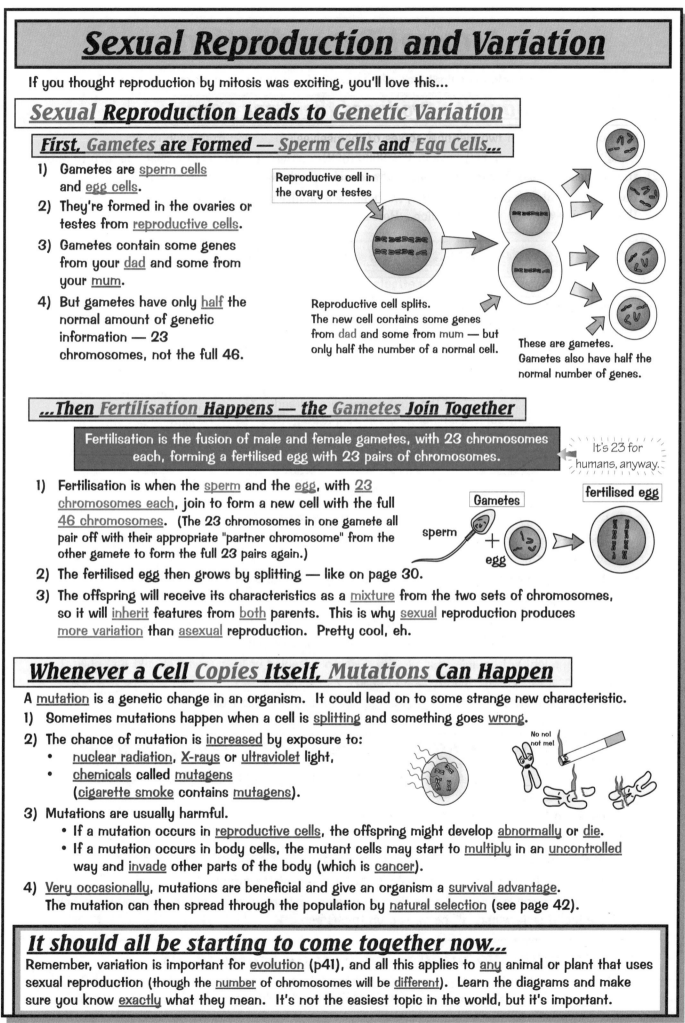

Reproductive cell in the ovary or testes

Reproductive cell splits. The new cell contains some genes from dad and some from mum — but only half the number of a normal cell.

These are gametes. Gametes also have half the normal number of genes.

...Then Fertilisation Happens — the Gametes Join Together

Fertilisation is the fusion of male and female gametes, with 23 chromosomes each, forming a fertilised egg with 23 pairs of chromosomes.

It's 23 for humans, anyway.

1) Fertilisation is when the sperm and the egg, with 23 chromosomes each, join to form a new cell with the full 46 chromosomes. (The 23 chromosomes in one gamete all pair off with their appropriate "partner chromosome" from the other gamete to form the full 23 pairs again.)

Gametes

sperm
+
egg

fertilised egg

2) The fertilised egg then grows by splitting — like on page 30.

3) The offspring will receive its characteristics as a mixture from the two sets of chromosomes, so it will inherit features from both parents. This is why sexual reproduction produces more variation than asexual reproduction. Pretty cool, eh.

Whenever a Cell Copies Itself, Mutations Can Happen

A mutation is a genetic change in an organism. It could lead on to some strange new characteristic.

1) Sometimes mutations happen when a cell is splitting and something goes wrong.

2) The chance of mutation is increased by exposure to:
   - nuclear radiation, X-rays or ultraviolet light,
   - chemicals called mutagens (cigarette smoke contains mutagens).

No no! not me!

3) Mutations are usually harmful.
   - If a mutation occurs in reproductive cells, the offspring might develop abnormally or die.
   - If a mutation occurs in body cells, the mutant cells may start to multiply in an uncontrolled way and invade other parts of the body (which is cancer).

4) Very occasionally, mutations are beneficial and give an organism a survival advantage. The mutation can then spread through the population by natural selection (see page 42).

It should all be starting to come together now...

Remember, variation is important for evolution (p41), and all this applies to any animal or plant that uses sexual reproduction (though the number of chromosomes will be different). Learn the diagrams and make sure you know exactly what they mean. It's not the easiest topic in the world, but it's important.

Genetic Disorders

When a single gene controls the inheritance of a characteristic, you can work out the odds of getting it...

Alleles Are Different Versions of the Same Gene

1) Most of the time you have two of each gene (i.e. two alleles) — one from each parent.

2) If the alleles are different you have instructions for two different versions of a characteristic (e.g. blue eyes or brown eyes), but you only show one version of the two (e.g. brown eyes).

3) The version of the characteristic that appears is caused by the dominant allele. The other allele is said to be recessive.

Genetic Disorders are Caused by Faulty Alleles

A faulty allele could have either of these effects...

1) The faulty gene could directly cause a genetic disorder.

> Cystic fibrosis, haemophilia, red-green colour blindness (and many other disorders) are all caused by faulty genes.

2) The faulty gene may not cause a problem directly, but it could mean a predisposition to certain health problems — meaning it's more likely (though not definite) that you'll suffer from them in the future.

> For example, some genes predispose people to getting breast cancer.

Knowing About Genetic Disorders Opens Up a Whole Can of Worms

Knowing there are inherited conditions in your family raises difficult issues:

- Should all family members be tested to see if they're carriers?
  Some people might prefer not to know, but is this fair on any partners or future children they might have?

- Is it right for someone who's at risk of passing on a genetic condition to have children?
  Is it fair to put them under pressure not to, if they decide they want children?

- It's possible to test a foetus for some genetic conditions while it's still in the womb.
  But if the test is positive, is it right to terminate the pregnancy?
  The family might not be able to cope with a sick or disabled child, but why should that child have a lesser right to life than a healthy child?
  Some people think abortion is always wrong under any circumstances.

Gene Therapy is being Developed to Treat Genetic Disorders

1) Cystic fibrosis is a genetic disorder — it results in the body producing a lot of thick sticky mucus in the air passages and in the pancreas.

2) Scientists are trying to cure this using gene therapy.
   Gene therapy means correcting faulty genes — usually a healthy copy of the gene is added.

> 1) At the moment scientists are trying to cure cystic fibrosis (CF) with gene therapy.
>
> 2) There are still problems — for example, at the moment the effect wears off after a few days.
>
> 3) However, since this kind of gene therapy involves only body cells (and not reproductive cells), the faulty gene would still be passed on to children.

Unintentional mooning — caused by faulty jeans...

On a related note... the Human Genome Project aimed to map all the genes in a human (see p34). This has now been completed, and the results could help with future gene therapies. Exciting stuff.

Genetic Engineering

Scientists can now <u>add</u>, <u>remove</u> or <u>change</u> an organism's <u>genes</u> to alter its characteristics.

Genetic Engineering <u>Uses</u> Enzymes <u>to Cut and Paste</u> Genes

The basic idea is to move <u>useful genes</u> from one organism's chromosomes into the cells of another.

1) A useful gene is "<u>cut</u>" from one organism's chromosome using <u>enzymes</u>.

2) <u>Enzymes</u> are then used to <u>cut</u> another organism's chromosome and to <u>insert</u> the useful gene.

3) For example, the human insulin gene can be inserted into <u>bacteria</u> to <u>produce human insulin</u>:

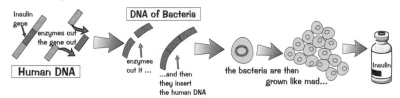

Genes <u>can be</u> Transferred <u>into</u> Animals <u>and</u> Plants

The same method can be used to <u>transfer useful genes</u> into <u>animals</u> and <u>plants</u> shortly after <u>fertilisation</u>. This has (or could have) some really <u>useful applications</u>.

1) <u>Genetically modified (GM) plants</u> have been developed that are <u>resistant to viruses</u> and <u>herbicides</u> (chemicals used to kill weeds).

    And <u>long-life</u> tomatoes can be made by changing the gene that causes the fruit to ripen.

2) Genes can also be inserted into <u>animal embryos</u> so that the animal grows up to have more <u>useful characteristics</u>.

    For example, <u>sheep</u> have been genetically engineered to produce substances (e.g. drugs) in their <u>milk</u> that can be used to treat <u>human diseases</u>.

3) <u>Genetic disorders</u> like cystic fibrosis are caused by faulty genes. Scientists are trying to cure these disorders by <u>inserting working genes</u> into sufferers. This is called <u>gene therapy</u> — see page 32.

But Genetic Engineering is a <u>Controversial Topic...</u>

Genetic engineering is an <u>exciting new area in science</u> which has the <u>potential</u> for solving many of our problems (e.g. treating diseases, more efficient food production etc.). But not everyone likes it.

1) Some people <u>strongly believe</u> that we shouldn't go <u>tinkering about with genes</u> because it's <u>not natural</u>.

2) There are also <u>worries</u> that changing an organism's genes might <u>accidentally</u> create unplanned <u>problems</u> — which could then get passed on to <u>future generations</u>.

There Are Pros <u>and</u> Cons <u>with</u> GM Crops

1) Some people say that growing GM crops will affect the number of <u>weeds</u> and <u>flowers</u> (and therefore <u>wildlife</u>) that usually lives in and around the crops — <u>reducing</u> farmland <u>biodiversity</u>.

2) Not everyone is convinced that GM crops are <u>safe</u>. People are worried they may develop <u>allergies</u> to the food — although there's probably no more risk for this than for eating usual foods.

3) A big concern is that <u>transplanted genes</u> may get out into the <u>natural environment</u>. For example, the <u>herbicide resistance</u> gene may be picked up by weeds, creating a new '<u>superweed</u>' variety.

4) On the plus side, GM crops can <u>increase the yield</u> of a crop, making more food.

5) People living in developing nations often lack <u>nutrients</u> in their diets. GM crops could be <u>engineered</u> to contain nutrients that are <u>missing</u>. For example, they're testing 'golden rice' that contains beta-carotene — lack of this substance can cause <u>blindness</u>.

6) GM crops are already being used elsewhere in the world (not the UK), often <u>without any problems</u>.

If only there was a gene to make revision easier...

It's up to the <u>Government</u> to weigh up all the <u>evidence</u> before <u>making a decision</u> on how this knowledge is used. All scientists can do is make sure the Government has all the information it needs.

The Human Genome Project

Some people have called the Human Genome Project "more exciting than the first moon landing", or "the search for the <u>Holy Grail of science</u>". Maybe they should get out more.

The Idea was to Map the 25 000 (or so) Human Genes

The big idea was to <u>find every single human gene</u> — all <u>25 000 genes</u> that curl up to form the 23 chromosomes (the other 23 have the same genes — but maybe different versions). Well... they've <u>found them all</u> — and now they're trying to figure out what each one <u>does</u>.

> In the exam, they'll probably ask you to say what's <u>good</u> about it, what's <u>bad</u> about it, or <u>both</u>.

The Good Stuff — Improving Medicine and Forensic Science

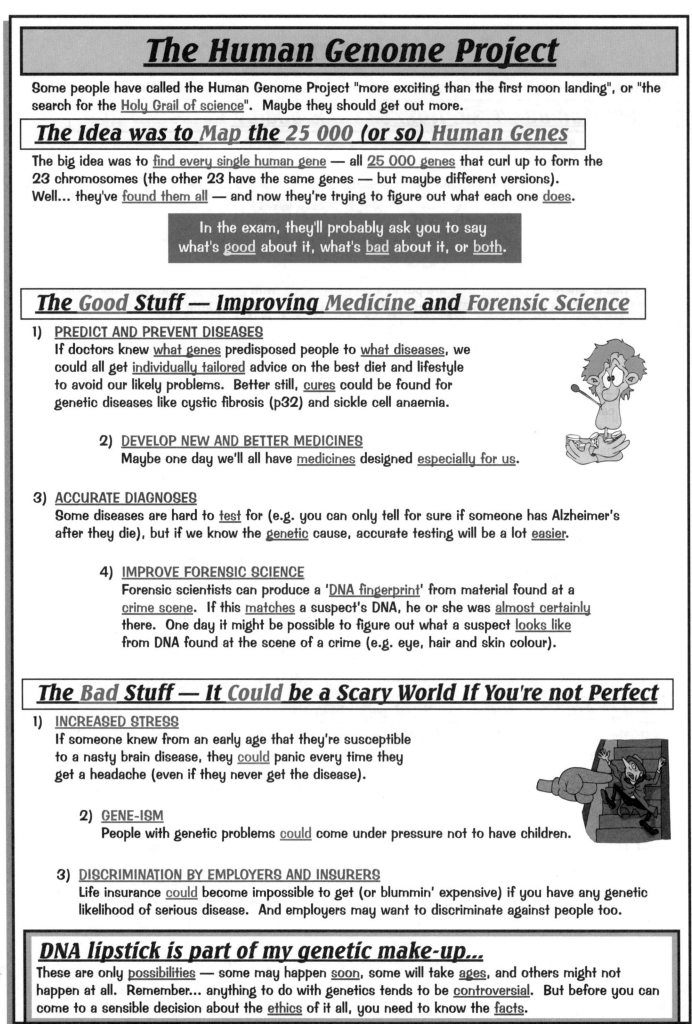

1) <u>PREDICT AND PREVENT DISEASES</u>
   If doctors knew <u>what genes</u> predisposed people to <u>what diseases</u>, we could all get <u>individually tailored</u> advice on the best diet and lifestyle to avoid our likely problems. Better still, <u>cures</u> could be found for genetic diseases like cystic fibrosis (p32) and sickle cell anaemia.

   2) <u>DEVELOP NEW AND BETTER MEDICINES</u>
      Maybe one day we'll all have <u>medicines</u> designed <u>especially for us</u>.

3) <u>ACCURATE DIAGNOSES</u>
   Some diseases are hard to <u>test</u> for (e.g. you can only tell for sure if someone has Alzheimer's after they die), but if we know the <u>genetic</u> cause, accurate testing will be a lot <u>easier</u>.

   4) <u>IMPROVE FORENSIC SCIENCE</u>
      Forensic scientists can produce a '<u>DNA fingerprint</u>' from material found at a <u>crime scene</u>. If this <u>matches</u> a suspect's DNA, he or she was <u>almost certainly</u> there. One day it might be possible to figure out what a suspect <u>looks like</u> from DNA found at the scene of a crime (e.g. eye, hair and skin colour).

The Bad Stuff — It Could be a Scary World If You're not Perfect

1) <u>INCREASED STRESS</u>
   If someone knew from an early age that they're susceptible to a nasty brain disease, they <u>could</u> panic every time they get a headache (even if they never get the disease).

   2) <u>GENE-ISM</u>
      People with genetic problems <u>could</u> come under pressure not to have children.

3) <u>DISCRIMINATION BY EMPLOYERS AND INSURERS</u>
   Life insurance <u>could</u> become impossible to get (or blummin' expensive) if you have any genetic likelihood of serious disease. And employers may want to discriminate against people too.

DNA lipstick is part of my genetic make-up...

These are only <u>possibilities</u> — some may happen <u>soon</u>, some will take <u>ages</u>, and others might not happen at all. Remember... anything to do with genetics tends to be <u>controversial</u>. But before you can come to a sensible decision about the <u>ethics</u> of it all, you need to know the <u>facts</u>.

Cloning

Nature already makes clones (see page 30). This page is about how humans make them.

Plants Can Be Cloned from Cuttings and by Tissue Culture

CUTTINGS

1) Gardeners can take cuttings from good parent plants, and then plant them to produce clones of the parent plant.
2) These plants can be produced quickly and cheaply.

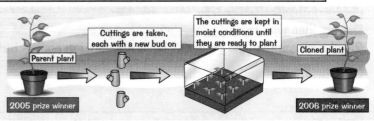

Parent plant | Cuttings are taken, each with a new bud on | The cuttings are kept in moist conditions until they are ready to plant | Cloned plant
2005 prize winner | 2006 prize winner

TISSUE CULTURE

This is where a few plant cells are put in a growth medium with hormones, and they then grow into clones of the parent. You can make new plants very quickly, in very little space, all year round.

The disadvantage to both these methods is a 'reduced gene pool' (see below).

You Can Make Animal Clones Using Embryo Transplants

Farmers can produce cloned offspring from their best bull and cow — using embryo transplants.

1) Sperm cells are taken from a prize bull, and egg cells from a prize cow.
2) The sperm are then used to fertilise the egg cell. This is then split many times (to form clones).
3) These cloned embryos can then be implanted into lots of other cows where they grow into genetically identical calves.

4) The advantage of this is that hundreds of "ideal" offspring can be produced every year from the best bull and cow.
5) The big disadvantage is a reduced gene pool.

A "reduced gene pool" means fewer alleles in a population — which will happen if you breed from the same plants or animals all the time. If a population are all closely related and a new disease appears, all the plants or animals could be wiped out — there may be no allele in the population giving resistance to the disease.

Oh Eck!

Adult Cell Cloning is Another Way to Make a Clone...

1) Adult cell cloning is the technique that was used to create Dolly — the world-famous cloned sheep.

2) Dolly was made by taking a sheep egg cell and removing its genetic material.

3) A complete set of chromosomes from the cell of an adult sheep was then inserted into the 'empty' egg cell.

4) This eventually grew into a sheep that was genetically identical to the original adult.

Egg cell | Adult body cell
Nucleus removed | + | Nucleus removed
Embryo
Implanted into surrogate mother | Stem cells harvested
Live animal | Stem cells for treating disease

Episode Two — Attack of Dolly the Sheep...

Cloning can be a controversial topic — especially when it's to do with cloning animals (and especially humans). Is it healthy scientific progress, or are we trying to 'play God'?

Photosynthesis

Bit of a deviation from the 'genetics' theme here... but try not to worry about that too much.

Photosynthesis Produces Glucose from Sunlight

Photosynthesis uses energy from the Sun to change carbon dioxide and water into glucose and oxygen.

Carbon dioxide + water $\xrightarrow[\text{chlorophyll}]{\text{LIGHT}}$ glucose + oxygen

(Photosynthesis and respiration are opposite processes — see p14 for respiration.)

Glucose is Converted into Other Substances

GLUCOSE is SOLUBLE, which makes it good for transporting to other places in the plant. It's also a small molecule — so it can diffuse in and out of cells easily. Here's how plants use the glucose they make:

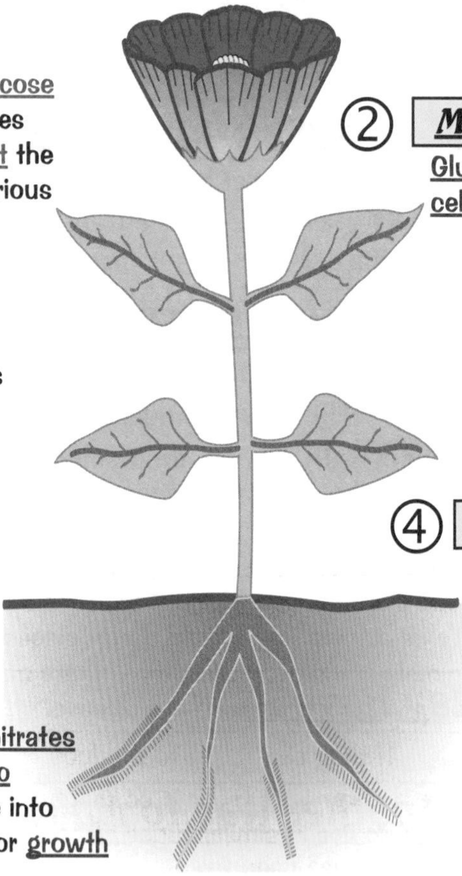

① **For Respiration**

Plants use some of the glucose for respiration. This releases energy so they can convert the rest of the glucose into various other useful substances.

② **Making Cell walls**

Glucose is converted into cellulose for making cell walls.

③ **Stored in Seeds**

Glucose is turned into fats and oils for storing in seeds.
Sunflower seeds, for example, contain a lot of oil — we get cooking oil and margarine from them.

④ **Stored as Starch**

Glucose is turned into starch and stored in roots, stems and leaves, ready for use when photosynthesis isn't happening, like at night.

⑤ **Making Proteins**

Glucose is combined with nitrates from the soil to make amino acids, which are then made into proteins. These are used for growth and repair.

Three Factors Control the Rate of Photosynthesis

1) LIGHT

If there's not enough light, the rate of photosynthesis will slow down.

2) CARBON DIOXIDE

As with light, if there's not enough carbon dioxide, the rate of photosynthesis will slow down.

3) TEMPERATURE

As the temperature increases, so does the rate of photosynthesis.

Convert this page into stored information...

Photosynthesis is important. All the energy we get from eating comes from it. When we eat plants, we're consuming the energy they've made, and when we eat meat, we're eating animals who got their energy from eating plants, or from eating animals that have eaten other animals who have... and so on.

Ecosystems and Species

An <u>ecosystem</u> is all the <u>different organisms</u> living together in a <u>particular environment</u>. Sounds cosy.

Artificial Ecosystems _Can be_ Carefully Controlled

1) There are <u>two types of ecosystem</u> you need to know about:

> A <u>NATURAL ECOSYSTEM</u> is one where humans <u>don't control the processes</u> going on within it.
> An <u>ARTIFICIAL ECOSYSTEM</u> is one where humans <u>deliberately</u> promote the growth of certain living organisms and get rid of others which threaten their well-being.

2) Humans <u>might</u> affect <u>natural ecosystems</u> in some way, but they <u>don't take deliberate steps</u> to decide what animals and plants should be there. So a woodland is an example of a natural ecosystem.

3) <u>Artificial ecosystems</u> are most common in money-making enterprises, e.g. <u>farms</u> and <u>market gardens</u>.

Estimate _Population Sizes_ in an Ecosystem Using a Quadrat

A <u>quadrat</u> is a square frame enclosing a known area. You just place it on the ground, and look at what's inside it. To estimate <u>population size</u>:

1) Count all the organisms in a <u>1 m² quadrat</u>.
2) Multiply the number of organisms by the <u>total area</u> (in m²) of the habitat.
3) Er, that's it. Bob's your uncle.

A quadrat

Unrelated _Species May Have_ Similar Features

1) Organisms are of the <u>same species</u> if they can <u>breed</u> to produce <u>fertile offspring</u>.
2) Similar species often share a <u>recent common ancestor</u>, so they're <u>closely related</u>. They often look very <u>alike</u> and tend to live in similar types of <u>habitat</u>, e.g. whales and dolphins.
3) This isn't always the case though — closely related species may look <u>very different</u> if they've evolved to live in <u>different habitats</u>, e.g. llamas and camels.
4) Species that are <u>very different genetically</u> may also end up looking alike. E.g. dolphins and sharks look pretty similar and swim in a similar way. But they're totally different species — dolphins are <u>mammals</u> and sharks are <u>fish</u>.

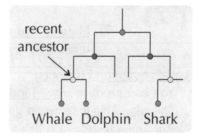

recent ancestor

Whale Dolphin Shark

Ecosystems — aren't they used in submarines...

It's possible to breed lions and tigers together... it's true — they produce <u>hybrids</u> called tigons and ligers. They look a bit like lions and a bit like tigers... as you'd expect. In the same way, a bat is (I think) just a hybrid of a bird and a cat. And a donkey is the result of breeding a dog and a monkey.

Energy and Biomass

Ecosystems — communities of things living side by side in harmony... before eating each other.

Pyramids of Biomass Show Weight

1) Biomass is how much the creatures at each level of a food chain would weigh if you put them together.

2) The pyramid of biomass below shows the food chain of a mini meadow ecosystem. The dandelions are the provider (starting point) — they're eaten by the rabbits (primary consumers), which are eaten by the fox (secondary consumer)... and so on.

3) If you weighed them, all the dandelions would have a big biomass and the hundreds of fleas would have a very small biomass. Biomass pyramids are always a pyramid shape.

4) Each time you go up one level, the mass of organisms goes down. It takes a lot of food from the level below to keep any one animal alive.

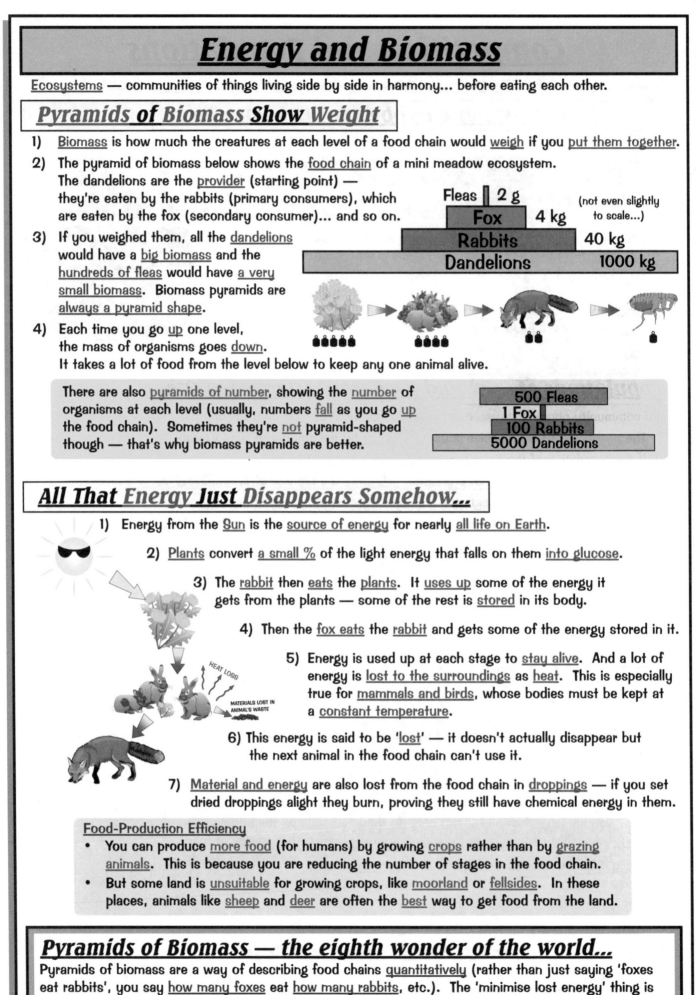

Fleas | 2 g
Fox | 4 kg
Rabbits | 40 kg
Dandelions | 1000 kg

(not even slightly to scale...)

There are also pyramids of number, showing the number of organisms at each level (usually, numbers fall as you go up the food chain). Sometimes they're not pyramid-shaped though — that's why biomass pyramids are better.

500 Fleas
1 Fox
100 Rabbits
5000 Dandelions

All That Energy Just Disappears Somehow...

1) Energy from the Sun is the source of energy for nearly all life on Earth.

2) Plants convert a small % of the light energy that falls on them into glucose.

3) The rabbit then eats the plants. It uses up some of the energy it gets from the plants — some of the rest is stored in its body.

4) Then the fox eats the rabbit and gets some of the energy stored in it.

5) Energy is used up at each stage to stay alive. And a lot of energy is lost to the surroundings as heat. This is especially true for mammals and birds, whose bodies must be kept at a constant temperature.

6) This energy is said to be 'lost' — it doesn't actually disappear but the next animal in the food chain can't use it.

7) Material and energy are also lost from the food chain in droppings — if you set dried droppings alight they burn, proving they still have chemical energy in them.

HEAT LOSS

MATERIALS LOST IN ANIMAL'S WASTE

Food-Production Efficiency

• You can produce more food (for humans) by growing crops rather than by grazing animals. This is because you are reducing the number of stages in the food chain.

• But some land is unsuitable for growing crops, like moorland or fellsides. In these places, animals like sheep and deer are often the best way to get food from the land.

Pyramids of Biomass — the eighth wonder of the world...

Pyramids of biomass are a way of describing food chains quantitatively (rather than just saying 'foxes eat rabbits', you say how many foxes eat how many rabbits, etc.). The 'minimise lost energy' thing is what gives you battery farming... if you stop the poor hens running around, less energy is lost. Hmm...

Competition and Populations

Organisms have to compete for resources in the environment where they live.

Population Size is Limited by Available Resources

Population size is limited by:

1) The total amount of food or nutrients available (plants don't eat, but they get minerals from the soil).

2) The amount of water available.

3) The amount of light available (this applies only to plants really).

4) The quality and amount of shelter available.

Animals and plants of the same species and of different species will COMPETE against each other for these resources. They all want to survive and reproduce.

Similar organisms will be in the closest competition — they'll be competing for the same ecological niche.

Populations of Prey and Predators Affect Each Other

In a community containing prey and predators (as most of them do of course):

1) The population of any species is usually limited by the amount of food available.

2) If the population of the prey increases, then so will the population of the predators.

3) However as the population of predators increases, the number of prey will decrease.

4) So the number of prey affects the number of predators, which affects the number of prey... and so on.

Parasites and Mutualistic Relationships

The survival of some organisms can depend almost entirely on the presence of other species.

1) PARASITES live off a host. They take what they need to survive, without giving anything back. This often harms the host — which makes it a win-lose situation.

- Tapeworms absorb lots of nutrients from the host, causing them to suffer from malnutrition.
- Fleas are parasites. Dogs gain nothing from having fleas (unless you count hundreds of bites).

2) MUTUALISM is a relationship where both organisms benefit — so it's a win-win relationship.

- 'Cleaner species' are fantastic. E.g. oxpeckers live on the backs of various large mammals. Not only do they eat pests on the buffalo, like ticks, flies and maggots (providing the oxpeckers with a source of food), but they also alert the animal to any predators that are near, by hissing.

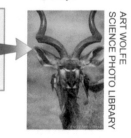

Revision stress — don't let it eat you up...

In the exam you might get asked about the distribution of any animals or plants. Just think about what the organisms would need to survive. And remember, if things are in limited supply then there's going to be competition. And the more similar the needs of the organisms, the more they'll have to compete.

Fossils

Fossils are ace... I saw dinosaur fossils at a museum once. Dinosaur fossils... cool or what.

Fossils Provide Lots of Evidence for Evolution

A fossil is any trace of an animal or plant that lived long ago. They show how today's species have changed and developed over millions of years. There are three ways fossils can be formed:

1) From gradual replacement by minerals (Most fossils happen this way.)

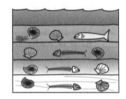

Things like teeth, shells, bones... which don't decay easily, can last ages when buried. They're eventually replaced by minerals, forming a rock-like substance shaped like the original hard part. The fossil stays distinct inside rock, and is eventually dug up.

2) From casts and impressions

Sometimes, fossils form when an organism's buried in a soft material like clay. The clay hardens around it and the organism decays, leaving a cast of itself. Things like footprints can be pressed into these materials when soft, leaving an impression when it hardens.

3) From preservation in places where no decay happens

The whole original plant or animal may survive for thousands of years:

  a) In amber — no oxygen or moisture for the decay microbes.

  Insects are often found fully preserved in amber, which is a clear yellow "stone" made of fossilised resin that ran out of an ancient tree millions of years ago, engulfing the insect.

  b) In glaciers — too cold for the decay microbes to work.

  A woolly mammoth was found fully preserved in a glacier somewhere several years ago (at least that's what I heard, though I never saw any pictures of it so maybe it was a hoax, I'm not really sure, but anyway in principle one could turn up any time...)

  c) In waterlogged bogs — too acidic for decay microbes.

  A 10 000 year old man was found in a bog a few years ago. He was dead, and a bit squashed but otherwise quite well preserved, although it was clear he'd been murdered.

The Fossil Record is Incomplete

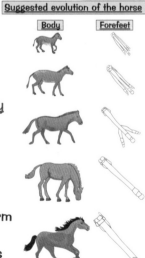

Suggested evolution of the horse

Body   Forefeet

1) Fossils found in rock layers tell us two things:
   i) What the creatures and plants looked like.
   ii) How long ago they existed.
      (Generally, the deeper the rock, the older the fossil.)

2) The fossil record is incomplete (there are 'missing links'). This is because very few dead plants or animals actually turn into fossils. Most just decay away.

3) The fossil record of the horse provides strong evidence for the theory of evolution (see next page). If you look at fossilised bones, you can put together a family tree of the horse — showing how modern horses have evolved.

   Over many generations, the middle toe has got slowly bigger and bigger to form the familiar hoof of today's horse, and the animals have got generally larger.

   But making an accurate family tree is tricky. Not all the similar-looking fossils found are ancestors of today's horses — some were 'evolutionary dead-ends'.

Don't get bogged down by all this information...

The fossil record provides good evidence for evolution, but it can't prove it. But proving a theory of something that happens over millions of years was never going to be straightforward, I guess.

Evolution

The theory of evolution states that one of your (probably very distant) ancestors
was a blob in a swamp somewhere. Something like that, anyway.

The Theory of Evolution is Cool

1) This suggests that all the animals and plants on Earth gradually 'evolved' over millions of
years, rather than just suddenly popping into existence. Makes sense.

2) Life on Earth began as simple organisms from which all the more complex organisms evolved.
And it only took about 3 000 000 000 years.

There are Lots of Modern Examples of Evolution

1) Peppered Moths Adapted Their Colour

Peppered moths are often seen on the bark of trees. Until the 19th
century, the only ones found in England were light in colour. Then some
areas became polluted and the soot darkened the tree trunks. A black
variety of moth was found. The moths had adapted to stay camouflaged.

2) Bacteria Adapt to Beat Antibiotics

Bacteria adapt to become resistant to our bacteria-fighting weapons — antibiotics.

1) If someone gets ill they might be given an antibiotic which kills 99% of the bacteria.

2) The 1% that survive are resistant so if they're passed on to somebody else, the antibiotic won't help them.

Nowadays bacteria are getting resistant at such a rate the development of antibiotics can't keep up. Eeek!

3) Rats Adapt to Beat Poison

The poison warfarin was widely used to control the rat population. However, a certain gene gives rats
resistance to it, so rats which carry it are more likely to survive and breed. This gene has become more
and more frequent in the rat population, so warfarin isn't as much use any more.

Environmental Change Can Cause Extinction

1) If a species can't evolve quickly enough, it's in trouble.

2) The dinosaurs and woolly mammoths became extinct, and it's only fossils that tell us they ever existed.

> There are three ways a species can become extinct:
> 1) The environment changes more quickly than the species can adapt.
> 2) A new predator or disease kills them all.
> 3) They can't compete with another (new) species for food.

3) As the environment changes, it'll favour certain characteristics (see p42).

4) Over many generations those features will be present in more of the population.
In this way, the species constantly adapts to its changing environment.

5) But if the environment changes too fast the whole species may become extinct.

Did you know exams evolved from the Spanish Inquisition...

...well that's not really true. But it is true that humans and apes both evolved from a common ancestor.
Scientists reckon that 5-8 million years ago the species separated and one population evolved into
humans and the other into apes — so you're a distant relation (250 000th cousin, maybe) of a chimp.

Natural Selection

OK... Charles Darwin realised that evolution took place, and developed a theory about how it actually happened. He called it the theory of <u>natural selection</u>. This is how he came up with it...

Natural Selection Explains How Evolution Can Occur

1) <u>Charles Darwin</u> came up with the idea of <u>natural selection</u>.
2) He noticed that species tend to be <u>well-adapted</u> to the <u>environment</u> they live in.
3) He argued that organisms that are <u>better adapted</u> have a <u>better chance of survival</u>, and are therefore more likely to <u>breed</u> successfully — passing on their <u>characteristics</u> to the next generation.
4) So if an organism is born with a <u>useful</u> characteristic (either due to the normal <u>shuffling up</u> of mum and dad's genes, or due to <u>mutations</u>), that characteristic has a good chance of being <u>passed on</u>. Whereas if a mutation leads to a <u>disadvantage</u>, the organism may well <u>die</u> before it can breed.
5) So '<u>good</u>' characteristics <u>accumulate</u>, '<u>bad</u>' ones are <u>lost</u>. And this is how animals <u>adapt</u>. For example:

Organisms with Certain Characteristics Will Survive Better

FOX!

Here's an example... once upon a time maybe all rabbits had <u>short ears</u> and managed OK. Then one day out popped a rabbit with <u>big ears</u> who could hear better and was always the first to dive for cover at the sound of a predator. Pretty soon he's fathered a whole family of rabbits with <u>big ears</u>, all diving for cover before the other rabbits, and before you know it there are only <u>big-eared</u> rabbits left — because the rest just didn't hear trouble coming quick enough.

This is how populations <u>adapt</u> to changes in their environment (an organism doesn't actually change when it's alive — changes only occur from generation to generation).

Over many generations the <u>characteristic</u> that <u>increased survival</u> becomes <u>more common</u> in the population. If members of a species are separated somehow, and evolve in different ways to adapt to different conditions, then over time, you can end up with totally <u>different species</u>.

Darwin's Theory Wasn't Popular at First

1) Darwin's theory <u>caused some trouble</u> at the time — it was the first plausible explanation for our own existence <u>without</u> the need for a "Creator".
2) This was <u>bad news</u> for the religious authorities of the time, who tried to ridicule old Charlie's ideas. The idea that humans and monkeys had a common ancestor was hard for people to accept, and easy to take the mick out of. But, as they say, "<u>the truth will out</u>".
3) Some <u>scientists weren't keen</u> either, at first. Darwin didn't provide a proper explanation of exactly <u>how</u> individual organisms passed on their survival characteristics to their offspring.
4) Later, the idea of <u>genetics</u> was understood (p29) — which <u>did</u> explain how characteristics are inherited.

Natural selection... sounds like vegan chocolates...

This is a good example of how scientific theories come about — someone <u>observes</u> something and then tries to <u>explain</u> it. Their theory will then be <u>tested</u> by other scientists using <u>evidence</u> — if the theory passes these tests, it gains in credibility. If not, it's <u>rejected</u>. Natural selection <u>hasn't</u> been rejected yet.

Adaptation

Animals and plants survive in many different <u>environments</u> — from <u>hot deserts</u> to <u>cold polar regions</u>, and pretty much everywhere in between. They can do this because they've <u>adapted</u> to their environment.

Desert Animals *Have* Adapted *to Save Water*

Animals that live in <u>hot</u>, <u>dry</u> conditions need to <u>keep cool</u> and use <u>water</u> efficiently.

LARGE SURFACE AREA COMPARED TO VOLUME   This lets desert animals <u>lose more body heat</u> — which helps to stop them overheating.

EFFICIENT WITH WATER
1) Desert animals <u>lose less water</u> by producing small amounts of <u>concentrated urine</u>.
2) They also make very little <u>sweat</u>.

GOOD IN HOT, SANDY CONDITIONS
1) Desert animals have very thin layers of <u>body fat</u> to help them <u>lose</u> body heat. Camels keep nearly all their fat in their <u>humps</u>.
2) <u>Large feet</u> spread their <u>weight</u> across soft sand — making getting about easier.
3) A <u>sandy colour</u> gives good <u>camouflage</u>.

Arctic Animals *Have* Adapted *to* Reduce Heat Loss

Animals that live in <u>really cold</u> conditions need to <u>keep warm</u>.

SMALL SURFACE AREA COMPARED TO VOLUME   Animals living in <u>cold</u> conditions have a <u>compact</u> (rounded) shape to keep their <u>surface area</u> to a minimum — this <u>reduces heat loss</u>.

WELL INSULATED
1) They also have a thick layer of <u>blubber</u> for <u>insulation</u> — this also acts as an <u>energy store</u> when food is scarce.
2) <u>Thick hairy coats</u> keep body heat in, and <u>greasy fur</u> sheds water.

GOOD IN SNOWY CONDITIONS
1) Arctic animals have <u>white fur</u> to match their surroundings — for <u>camouflage</u>.
2) <u>Big feet</u> help by <u>spreading weight</u> — which stops animals sinking into the snow or breaking thin ice.

Some *Plants* **Have** Adapted *to Living in a* Desert

Desert-dwelling plants make best use of what little water is available.

MINIMISING WATER LOSS
1) Cacti have <u>spines instead of leaves</u> — to <u>reduce water loss</u>.
2) They also have a <u>small surface area</u> compared to their size (about 1000 times smaller than normal plants), which also <u>reduces water loss</u>.
3) A cactus <u>stores water</u> in its thick stem.

MAXIMISING WATER ABSORPTION   Some cacti have <u>shallow</u> but <u>extensive roots</u> to <u>absorb</u> water quickly over a large area. Others have <u>deep roots</u> to access <u>underground water</u>.

Some *Plants* **and** *Animals* **Are** Adapted *to* Deter Predators

There are various <u>special features</u> used by animals and plants to help <u>protect</u> them against being <u>eaten</u>.
1) Some plants and animals have <u>armour</u> — like roses (with <u>thorns</u>), cacti (with <u>sharp spines</u>) and tortoises (with <u>hard shells</u>).
2) Others produce <u>poisons</u> — like bees and poison ivy.
3) And some have amazing <u>warning colours</u> to scare off predators — like wasps.

Cactus spines — nasty.

In a nutshell, it's horses for courses...

It's <u>no accident</u> that animals and plants look like they do. So by looking at an animal's <u>characteristics</u>, you should be able to have a pretty good guess at the kind of <u>environment</u> it lives in — or vice versa. Why does it have a large/small surface area... what are those spines for... why is it green... and so on.

Revision Summary for Section 3

There's a lot to remember from this section and quite a few of the topics are controversial, e.g. cloning, genetic engineering, and so on. You need to know all sides of the story, as well as all the facts... so, here are some questions to help you. If you get any wrong, go back and learn the stuff.

1) What are the two types of variation? Describe their relative importance for plants and animals.

2) List four features of animals which aren't affected at all by the environment, and three which are.

3) Draw a set of diagrams showing the relationship between: cell, nucleus, chromosomes, genes, DNA. Describe what genes do.

4) How many pairs of chromosomes do human cells have?

5) What is asexual reproduction?

6) What are gametes? How many chromosomes does a human gamete have?

7) How does sexual reproduction produce genetic variation?

8) What is a mutation? Name three things that can increase the likelihood of genetic mutations.

9) What is an allele?

10) Describe two ways in which a faulty gene could lead to health problems.

11) What's the basic idea behind gene therapy?

12) Give a good account of the important stages of genetic engineering.

13) State two examples of useful applications of genetic engineering.

14) Why are some people concerned about genetic engineering?

15) What is the Human Genome Project? Write down four good things and three bad things about it.

16) How would you make a plant clone using tissue culture? What are the pros and cons?

17) Explain the steps involved in adult cell cloning.

18) Write down the word equation for photosynthesis. Give three uses of glucose in plants.

19) What three factors affect the rate of photosynthesis?

20) How could you estimate a population size in a habitat using a quadrat?

21) Explain two reasons why different species may look similar.

22) Why are pyramids of biomass always pyramid shaped?

23) How much energy and biomass pass from one trophic level to the next? Where does the rest go?

24) Name three things that: a) plants compete for, b) animals compete for.

25) Explain how the sizes of prey and predator populations depend on each other.

26) What is the difference between a parasitic and a mutualistic relationship? Give an example of each.

27) What is a fossil? Describe the three ways that fossils can form. Give an example of each type.

28) Why are fossils important to our understanding of dinosaurs?

29) Why is the fossil record incomplete?

30) What's the theory of evolution?

31) Describe three examples of evolution that we have noticed happening recently.

32) Give three reasons why some species become extinct.

33) How did Darwin explain evolution? Why was his theory controversial?

34) Name four ways in which a desert animal may be adapted to its environment. And two ways a desert plant may be adapted.

35) Explain how an animal that lives in the Arctic might be adapted to its environment.

36) State three ways that plants and animals might be adapted to deter predators.

Atoms

Hello, good evening and welcome to Chemistry. This section covers all of Chemistry's essential <u>gory details</u> — about <u>atoms</u>, <u>their innards</u>, and <u>what they get up to</u> with each other when no one's looking.

Structure of the Atom *— There's Nothing to It*

The structure of atoms is quite simple. Just learn and enjoy, my friend.

The Nucleus

1) It's in the <u>middle</u> of the atom.

2) It contains <u>protons</u> and <u>neutrons</u>. (It's the <u>number of protons</u> in an atom that decides what element it is.)

3) The nucleus has an overall <u>positive charge</u> because protons are positively charged while neutrons have no charge.

4) Almost the <u>whole mass</u> of the atom is <u>concentrated</u> in the <u>nucleus</u>. But size-wise it's <u>tiny</u> compared to the atom as a whole.

The Electrons

1) They move <u>around</u> the nucleus in energy levels called <u>shells</u>. (Each shell is only allowed a <u>certain number of electrons</u>.)

2) They have a <u>negative charge</u> (electrons and protons have equal but opposite charges).

3) They're <u>tiny</u> compared to the nucleus (they have <u>virtually no mass</u>). But as they move around they cover a <u>lot of space</u>. (The size of their orbits determines <u>how big</u> the atom is.)

Number of Protons Equals *Number of Electrons*

1) Neutral atoms have <u>no charge</u> overall.

2) This is because the <u>number of protons</u> always <u>equals</u> the <u>number of electrons</u> in a <u>neutral atom</u>, and the <u>charge</u> on the <u>electrons</u> is the <u>same</u> size as the charge on the <u>protons</u>, but <u>opposite</u>.

3) The number of neutrons isn't fixed but is usually <u>about the same</u> as the number of protons.

Know Your Particles

1) <u>Protons</u> are <u>heavy</u> and <u>positively charged</u>.

2) <u>Neutrons</u> are <u>heavy</u> and <u>neutral</u> (no charge).

3) <u>Electrons</u> are <u>tiny</u> and <u>negatively charged</u>.

PARTICLE	RELATIVE MASS	RELATIVE CHARGE
Proton	1	+1
Neutron	1	0
Electron	$\frac{1}{2000}$	−1

Each Element has an *Atomic Number* and a *Mass Number*

1) The <u>atomic number</u> says how many <u>protons</u> there are in an atom, and is unique to that element.

2) The atomic number <u>also</u> tells you the number of <u>electrons</u>.

3) The <u>mass number</u> is the total number of <u>protons and neutrons</u> in the atom. So if you want to find the number of <u>neutrons</u> in an atom, just <u>subtract</u> the <u>atomic number</u> from the <u>mass number</u>.

MASS NUMBER
Total number of
protons and neutrons. →**16**

ATOMIC NUMBER
(or PROTON NUMBER) →**8 O**
Number of protons, which is equal to
the number of electrons.

Basic atom facts — they don't take up much space...

Atoms are <u>tiny</u>. But the atom's <u>nucleus</u> is <u>REAL tiny</u>. An atom might measure 0.1 nanometres across — that's 0.000 000 000 1 metres, or a hundred-millionth of a centimetre. Wow. That's little.

Elements, Compounds and Mixtures

There are only about 100 or so different kinds of atoms, which doesn't sound too bad.
But they can join together in loads of different combinations, which makes life more complicated.

Elements Consist of One Type of Atom Only

Quite a lot of everyday substances are elements. An element contains only one kind of atom.

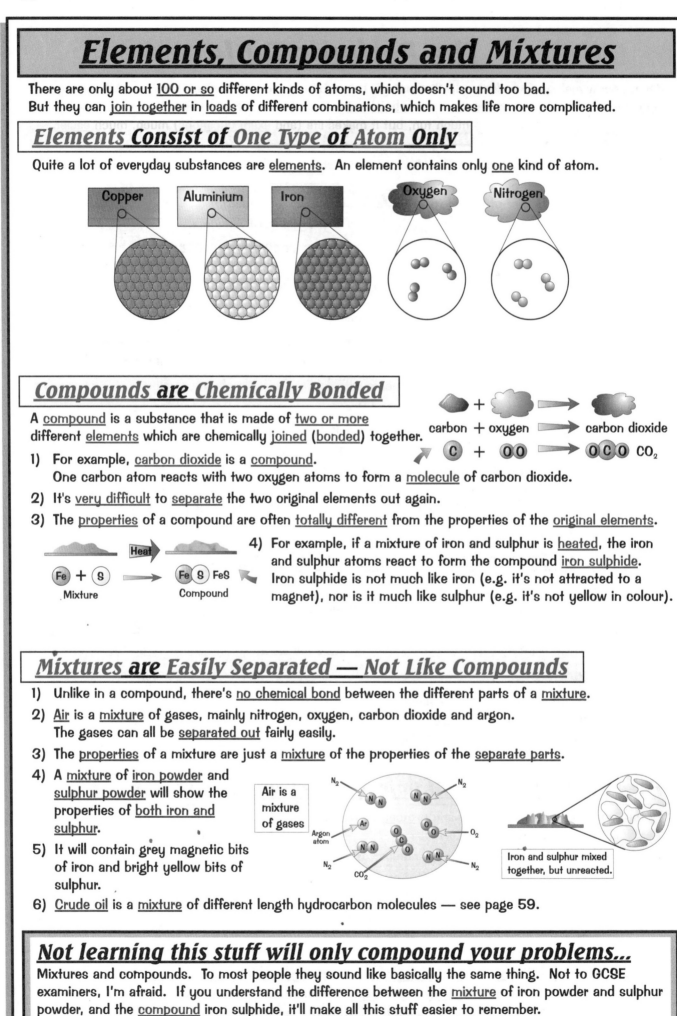

Compounds are Chemically Bonded

A compound is a substance that is made of two or more different elements which are chemically joined (bonded) together.

carbon + oxygen ⟹ carbon dioxide

C + OO ⟹ OCO CO$_2$

1) For example, carbon dioxide is a compound.
   One carbon atom reacts with two oxygen atoms to form a molecule of carbon dioxide.

2) It's very difficult to separate the two original elements out again.

3) The properties of a compound are often totally different from the properties of the original elements.

Fe + S → Fe S FeS
Mixture   Compound

4) For example, if a mixture of iron and sulphur is heated, the iron and sulphur atoms react to form the compound iron sulphide. Iron sulphide is not much like iron (e.g. it's not attracted to a magnet), nor is it much like sulphur (e.g. it's not yellow in colour).

Mixtures are Easily Separated — Not Like Compounds

1) Unlike in a compound, there's no chemical bond between the different parts of a mixture.

2) Air is a mixture of gases, mainly nitrogen, oxygen, carbon dioxide and argon.
   The gases can all be separated out fairly easily.

3) The properties of a mixture are just a mixture of the properties of the separate parts.

4) A mixture of iron powder and sulphur powder will show the properties of both iron and sulphur.

5) It will contain grey magnetic bits of iron and bright yellow bits of sulphur.

Air is a mixture of gases

Argon atom

Iron and sulphur mixed together, but unreacted.

6) Crude oil is a mixture of different length hydrocarbon molecules — see page 59.

Not learning this stuff will only compound your problems...

Mixtures and compounds. To most people they sound like basically the same thing. Not to GCSE examiners, I'm afraid. If you understand the difference between the mixture of iron powder and sulphur powder, and the compound iron sulphide, it'll make all this stuff easier to remember.

The Periodic Table

Chemistry would be <u>really messy</u> if it was all <u>big lists</u> of names and properties. So instead they've come up with a kind of <u>shorthand</u> for the names, and made a beautiful table to organise the elements — like a big <u>filing system</u>. Might not be much fun, but it makes life (and <u>exam questions</u>) much, much <u>easier</u>.

Atoms Can be Represented by Symbols

Atoms of each element can be represented by a <u>one or two letter symbol</u> — it's a type of <u>shorthand</u> that saves you the bother of having to write the full name of the element.

Some make <u>perfect sense</u>, e.g.

C = carbon   Li = lithium   Mg = magnesium

Others seem to make about as much sense as an apple with a handle.

E.g.   Na = sodium   Fe = iron   Pb = lead

The Periodic Table Puts Elements with Similar Properties Together

1) The periodic table is laid out so that elements with <u>similar properties</u> form <u>columns</u>.

2) These <u>vertical columns</u> are called <u>groups</u> and Roman numerals are often used for them.

3) If you know the <u>properties</u> of <u>one element</u>, you can <u>predict</u> properties of <u>other elements</u> in that group.

4) For example the <u>Group 1</u> elements are Li, Na, K, Rb, Cs and Fr. They're all <u>metals</u> and they <u>react the same way</u>. E.g. they all react with water to form an <u>alkaline solution</u> and <u>hydrogen gas</u>.

5) You can also make predictions about <u>reactivity</u>. E.g. in Group 1, the elements react <u>more vigorously</u> as you go <u>down</u> the group. And in Group 7, <u>reactivity decreases</u> as you go down the group.

6) There are <u>100ish elements</u>, which all materials are made of. If it wasn't for the periodic table <u>organising everything</u>, you'd have a <u>heck of a job</u> remembering all those properties. It's <u>ace</u>.

I'm in a chemistry band — I play the symbols...

Scientists keep making <u>new elements</u> and feeling well chuffed with themselves. The trouble is, these new elements only last for <u>a fraction of a second</u> before falling apart. You <u>don't</u> need to know the properties of each group of the periodic table, but if you're told, for example, that fluorine (Group 7) forms <u>two-atom molecules</u>, it's a fair guess that chlorine, bromine, iodine and astatine <u>do too</u>.

Balancing Equations

All chemical reactions can be shown using an <u>equation</u>. Unfortunately, getting equations right takes a bit of practice. So make sure you <u>get</u> a bit of practice — don't just skate over them.

Atoms Aren't Lost or Made in Chemical Reactions

1) During chemical reactions, things <u>don't</u> appear out of nowhere and things <u>don't</u> just disappear.

2) You still have the <u>same atoms</u> at the <u>end</u> of a chemical reaction as you had at the <u>start</u>. They're just <u>arranged</u> in different ways.

3) <u>Balanced symbol equations</u> show the atoms at the <u>start</u> (the <u>reactant</u> atoms) and the atoms at the <u>end</u> (the <u>product</u> atoms) and how they're arranged. For example:

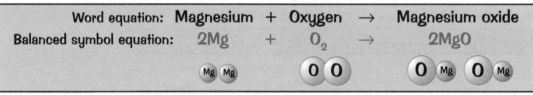

Word equation: Magnesium + Oxygen → Magnesium oxide

Balanced symbol equation: $2Mg$ + O_2 → $2MgO$

Balancing the Equation — Match Them Up One by One

1) There must always be the <u>same</u> number of atoms of each element on <u>both sides</u> — they can't just <u>disappear</u>.

2) You <u>balance</u> the equation by putting numbers <u>in front</u> of the formulas where needed. Take this equation for reacting sulphuric acid (H_2SO_4) with sodium hydroxide (NaOH) to get sodium sulphate (Na_2SO_4) and water (H_2O):

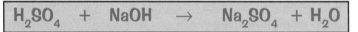

$$H_2SO_4 \; + \; NaOH \; \rightarrow \; Na_2SO_4 + H_2O$$

The <u>formulas</u> are all correct but the numbers of some atoms <u>don't match up</u> on both sides. E.g. there are 3 H's on the left, but only 2 on the right.

3) You <u>can't change formulas</u> like H_2O to H_3O. You can only put numbers <u>in front of them</u>.

Method: Balance Just ONE Type of Atom at a Time

The more you practise, the quicker you get, but all you do is this:

1) Find an element that <u>doesn't balance</u> and <u>pencil in a number</u> to try and sort it out.
2) <u>See where it gets you</u>. It may create <u>another imbalance</u> — if so, just pencil in <u>another number</u> and see where that gets you.
3) Carry on chasing <u>unbalanced</u> elements and it'll <u>sort itself out</u> pretty quickly.

<u>I'll show you</u>...

In the equation above you soon notice we're short of H atoms on the RHS (Right-Hand Side).

1) The only thing you can do about that is make it $2H_2O$ instead of just H_2O:

$$H_2SO_4 \; + \; NaOH \; \rightarrow \; Na_2SO_4 + 2H_2O$$

2) But that now causes too many H atoms and O atoms on the RHS, so to balance that up you could try putting 2NaOH on the LHS (Left-Hand Side):

$$H_2SO_4 \; + \; 2NaOH \; \rightarrow \; Na_2SO_4 + 2H_2O$$

3) And suddenly there it is! <u>Everything balances</u>. And you'll notice the Na just sorted itself out.

Balancing equations — weigh it up in your mind...

REMEMBER WHAT THOSE NUMBERS MEAN: A number in <u>front</u> of a formula applies to the <u>entire</u> <u>formula</u>. So, $3Na_2SO_4$ means three lots of Na_2SO_4. The little numbers in the <u>middle</u> or at the <u>end</u> of a formula <u>only</u> apply to the atom <u>immediately before</u>. So the 4 in Na_2SO_4 just means 4 O's, not 4 S's.

Group 1 — The Alkali Metals

Alkali metals are in the left-hand column of the periodic table. They're all very reactive.
Lithium, sodium and potassium are stars of the show here.

Group 1 Elements React Vigorously in Water

1) When lithium, sodium or potassium are put in water, they react vigorously.

2) The reaction makes an alkaline solution (which would change universal indicator to blue or purple)
— this is why Group 1 is known as the alkali metals.

3) As you go down Group 1, the elements get more reactive.

4) You can see this in the rate of reaction with water.

REACTIONS WITH WATER

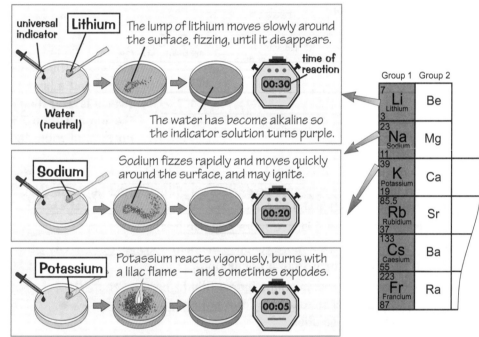

universal indicator   **Lithium**   The lump of lithium moves slowly around the surface, fizzing, until it disappears.

Water (neutral)   The water has become alkaline so the indicator solution turns purple.

time of reaction   00:30

Sodium   Sodium fizzes rapidly and moves quickly around the surface, and may ignite.   00:20

Potassium   Potassium reacts vigorously, burns with a lilac flame — and sometimes explodes.   00:05

Group 1	Group 2
7 Li Lithium 3	Be
23 Na Sodium 11	Mg
39 K Potassium 19	Ca
85.5 Rb Rubidium 37	Sr
133 Cs Caesium 55	Ba
223 Fr Francium 87	Ra

5) Lithium takes longer than sodium or potassium to react, so it's the least reactive.

6) Potassium takes the shortest time to react of these three elements, so it's the most reactive.

The elements in GROUP 1 get MORE REACTIVE as the
ATOMIC NUMBER INCREASES.

Reaction with Water Produces Hydrogen Gas

1) The reaction of the alkali metals with water produces hydrogen — this is what you can see fizzing.

2) A lighted splint will indicate the hydrogen by making the notorious "squeaky pop" as the H_2 ignites.

3) These reactions can be written down as chemical equations — e.g. for sodium the equation is...

In words: sodium + water → sodium hydroxide + hydrogen

In symbols: $2Na_{(s)} + 2H_2O_{(l)} \rightarrow 2NaOH_{(aq)} + H_{2(g)}$

Notorious Squeaky Pop — a.k.a. the Justin Timberlake test...

Alkali metals are ace. They're so reactive you have to store them in oil — because otherwise
they'd react with the air. AND they fizz in water and burn and explode and everything. Cool.

Group 7 — The Halogens

The halogens are in the last but one column of the periodic table.

HALOGEN — Seven Letters — Group 7

1) The elements in Group 7 of the periodic table are called the halogens.
2) Halogens are really useful and many everyday things contain them, e.g. toothpaste and the non-stick coating on frying pans.
3) But on their own, they're poisonous.
4) Chlorine's good because it kills bacteria. It's used in bleach and swimming pools.
5) The properties of the elements in Group 7 change gradually as you go down the group (i.e. as the atomic number increases). Look at the table below.

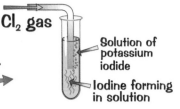

Group 7 Elements	Atomic number	Colour	Physical state at room temperature	Boiling point
Fluorine	9	yellow	gas	−188 °C
Chlorine	17	green	gas	−34 °C
Bromine	35	red-brown	liquid	59 °C
Iodine	53	dark grey	solid	185 °C

6) As the atomic number of the halogens increases, the elements have a darker colour and a higher boiling point (which is why they go from gases at the top of Group 7 to solids at the bottom, at room temperature).

More Reactive Halogens will Displace Less Reactive Ones

1) The higher up Group 7 an element is, the more reactive it is.
2) A displacement reaction is where a more reactive element "pushes out" (displaces) a less reactive element from a compound.
3) For example, chlorine is more reactive than iodine (it's higher up Group 7). So chlorine reacts with potassium iodide to form potassium chloride, and the iodine gets left in the solution.

$Cl_2(g) + 2KI(aq) \rightarrow I_2(aq) + 2KCl(aq)$
$Cl_2(g) + 2KBr(aq) \rightarrow Br_2(aq) + 2KCl(aq)$

These are the equations for chlorine displacing iodine and bromine. They might give you a different example in the exam, but the equations are all quite similar.

Halogen atoms like to pair up — so you need to write Cl_2, Br_2, etc.

The Halogens React with Metals to Form Salts

Halogens react with most metals, including iron and aluminium, to form salts (also called metal halides).

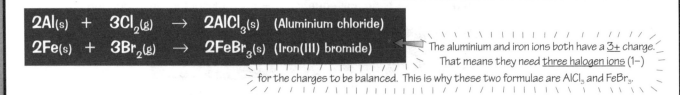

$2Al(s) + 3Cl_2(g) \rightarrow 2AlCl_3(s)$ (Aluminium chloride)
$2Fe(s) + 3Br_2(g) \rightarrow 2FeBr_3(s)$ (Iron(III) bromide)

The aluminium and iron ions both have a 3+ charge. That means they need three halogen ions (1−) for the charges to be balanced. This is why these two formulae are $AlCl_3$ and $FeBr_3$.

They're great, the halogens — you have to hand it to them...

Well, I think halogens are just slightly less grim than the alkali metals. At least they change colour and go from gases to liquid to solid. Learn the boring facts anyway. And smile.

Group 0 — The Noble Gases

The noble gases — stuffed full of every honourable virtue.
And located on the far right-hand side of the periodic table.

Group 0 Elements are All Inert, Colourless Gases

1) Group 0 elements are called the noble gases and include the elements helium, neon and argon (plus a few others).

2) The noble gases were only discovered just over 100 years ago — it took so long to find them because they have properties that make them hard to observe...

3) All elements in Group 0 are colourless gases at room temperature.

4) They are also more or less inert — this means they don't react with much at all.

5) Luckily the noble gases all have a dead handy property that lets you see them — they each give out light if you pass an electric current through them. Each noble gas gives out a particular colour of light.

	Group 6	Group 7	Group 0
			4 He Helium 2
	O	F	20 Ne Neon 10
	S	Cl	40 Ar Argon 18
	Se	Br	84 Kr Krypton 36
	Te	I	131 Xe Xenon 54
	Po	At	222 Rn Radon 86

The Noble Gases have Many Everyday Uses...

Neon is used in Electrical Discharge Tubes

Neon lights are used in tacky shop signs — the kind you'd expect to see if you visited Las Vegas. They don't use much current so they're cheap to run, and they give out a bright red light.

Noble Gases are used in Lasers too

There's the famous red helium-neon laser and the more powerful argon laser.

He-Ne laser Uh - oh Argon laser

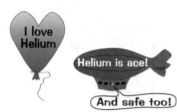

I love Helium

Helium is ace!

And safe too!

Helium is used in Airships and Party Balloons

Helium has a lower density than air — so it makes balloons float. And it's a lot safer to use than hydrogen (the famous airship Hindenburg was filled with hydrogen and caught fire).

Argon is used in Filament Lamps (Light Bulbs)

It provides an inert atmosphere which stops the very hot filament from burning away.

They don't react — that's Noble De use to us chemists...

Well, they don't react so there's a bit less to learn about the noble gases. Nevertheless, there's likely to be a question or two on them so make sure you learn everything on this page...

Properties of Metals

Metals are all similar but slightly different. They have some basic properties in common, but each has its own specific combination of properties, which means you use different ones for different purposes.

Metals are on the Left and Middle of the Periodic Table

Most of the elements are metals — so they cover most of the periodic table.

In fact, only the elements on the far right are non-metals.

The so-called transition metals are found in the centre block of the periodic table. Many of the metals in everyday use are transition metals — such as titanium, iron and nickel.

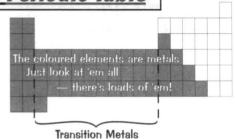

The coloured elements are metals
Just look at 'em all
— there's loads of 'em!

Transition Metals

Metals are Strong and Bendy, and They're Great Conductors

All metals have some fairly similar basic properties.

1) Metals are strong (hard to break), but they can be bent or hammered into different shapes.

2) They're great at conducting heat.

3) They conduct electricity well.

Metals (and especially transition metals) have loads of everyday uses because of these properties...

Transition metals have loads of everyday uses — partly because they're not crazily reactive like, say, potassium (which would catch fire if it got rained on).

• Their strength and 'bendability' makes them handy for making into things like bridges and car bodies.

• Metals are ideal if you want to make something that heat needs to travel through, like a saucepan base (see page 94).

• And their conductivity makes them great for making things like electrical wires.

It's the Structure of Metals That Gives Them Their Properties

1) All metals have the same basic properties. These are due to the special type of bonding in metals.

2) Metals consist of a giant structure of atoms held together with metallic bonds.

3) These special bonds allow the outer electron(s) of each atom to move freely.

4) This creates a "sea" of free electrons throughout the metal, which is what gives rise to many of the properties of metals.

5) This includes their conduction of heat and electricity (see p94).

Metal atoms

Free electrons

A Metal's Exact Properties Decide How It's Best Used

1) The properties above are typical properties of metals.
Not all metals are the same though — their exact properties determine how they're used.

2) If you wanted to make an aeroplane, you'd probably use metal as it's strong and can be bent into shape. But you'd also need it to be light — so aluminium would be a good choice.

3) And if you were making replacement hips, you'd pick a metal that won't corrode when it comes in contact with water — it'd also have to be light too, and not too bendy.
Titanium has all of these properties so it's used for this.

Metal fatigue? — yeah, I've had enough of this page too...

So, all metals conduct electricity and heat and can be bent into shape. But lots of them have special properties too. You have to decide what properties you need and use a metal with those properties.

Extraction of Metals

You don't tend to find big lumps of pure metal in the ground* — the metal atoms tend to be joined to other atoms in compounds. It can be a bit of a tricky, expensive process to separate the metal out. (*You only find underlined metals, e.g. gold, in their unreacted state. That makes sense if you think about it.)

Ores Contain Enough Metal to Make Extraction Worthwhile

1) Minerals are just solid elements and compounds.

2) Rocks are made of minerals.

3) A metal ore is a rock or mineral which contains enough metal to make it worthwhile extracting the metal from it. Ores are "finite resources" — there's only so much of them.

As technology improves, it becomes possible to extract more metal from a sample of rock than previously. So it might now be worth extracting metal that wasn't worth extracting in the past.

4) In many cases the ore is an oxide of the metal. Here are a few examples:

   a) A type of iron ore is called haematite. This is iron(III) oxide (Fe_2O_3).
   b) The main aluminium ore is called bauxite. This is aluminium oxide (Al_2O_3).
   c) A type of copper ore is called chalcopyrite. This is copper iron sulphide ($CuFeS_2$).

Chalcopyrite — a copper ore

Some Metals can be Extracted by Reduction with Carbon

1) Electrolysis (splitting with electricity — see next page) is one way of extracting a metal from its ore. The other common way is chemical reduction using carbon or carbon monoxide.

2) When an ore is reduced, oxygen is removed from it, e.g.

$$Fe_2O_3 \quad + \quad 3CO \quad \rightarrow \quad 2Fe \quad + \quad 3CO_2$$
iron(III) oxide + carbon monoxide $\rightarrow$ iron + carbon dioxide

3) The position of the metal in the reactivity series determines how it's extracted...

a) Metals higher than carbon in the reactivity series have to be extracted using electrolysis, which is expensive.

   Extracted using electrolysis

b) Metals below carbon in the reactivity series can be extracted by reduction using carbon.

   This is because carbon can only take the oxygen away from metals which are less reactive than carbon itself is.

   Extracted by reduction using carbon

The Reactivity Series		
Potassium	K	more
Sodium	Na	reactive
Calcium	Ca	
Magnesium	Mg	
Aluminium	Al	
CARBON	C	
Zinc	Zn	
Iron	Fe	
Tin	Sn	less
Copper	Cu	reactive

A More Reactive Metal Displaces a Less Reactive Metal

1) More reactive metals react more strongly than less reactive metals, so a metal can be extracted from its oxide by any more reactive metal. E.g. tin could be extracted from tin oxide by more reactive iron.

   tin oxide + iron → iron oxide + tin

2) And if you put a more reactive metal into the solution of a dissolved metal compound, the more reactive metal will replace the less reactive metal in the compound.

   tin sulphate + iron → iron sulphate + tin

3) But if a piece of copper metal is put into a solution of tin sulphate, nothing happens. The more reactive metal (tin) is already in the solution.

Learn how metals are extracted — ore else...

Extracting metals isn't cheap. You have to pay for special equipment, energy and labour. Then there's the cost of getting the ore to the extraction plant. If there's a choice of extraction methods, a company always picks the cheapest, unless there's a good reason not to — they're not extracting it for fun.

Extracting Pure Copper

In theory, the copper could be extracted by <u>reducing</u> it with carbon. The problem is that the copper produced by reduction <u>isn't pure enough</u> for use in <u>electrical conductors</u>.

Electrolysis is Used to Obtain Very Pure Copper

1) Electrolysis means "splitting up with electricity".
2) It needs a liquid (called the <u>electrolyte</u>) which will <u>conduct electricity</u>.
3) Electrolytes are usually <u>free ions dissolved in water</u>.

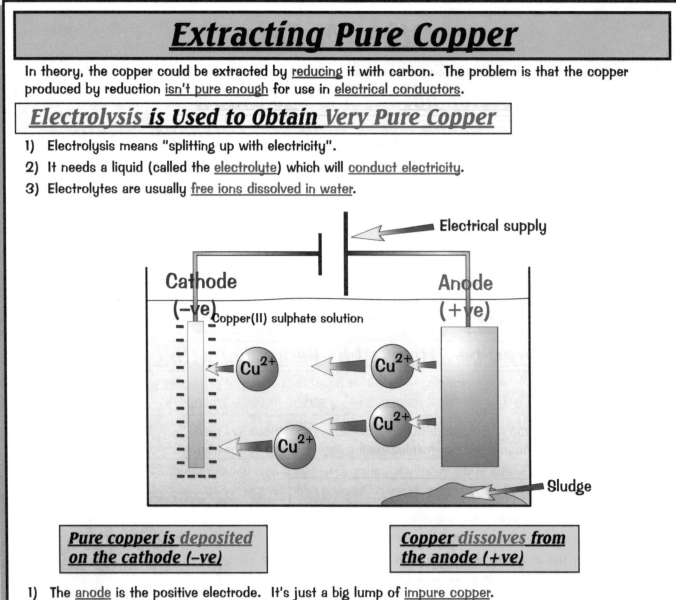

Pure copper is <u>deposited</u> on the cathode (–ve)

Copper <u>dissolves from</u> the anode (+ve)

1) The <u>anode</u> is the positive electrode. It's just a big lump of <u>impure copper</u>.
2) The <u>cathode</u> is the negative electrode. It starts as a <u>thin</u> piece of <u>pure copper</u> and more pure copper <u>adds</u> to it.
3) The <u>impurities</u> are dropped at the <u>anode</u> as a <u>sludge</u>, while <u>pure copper atoms</u> bond to the <u>cathode</u>.
4) The electrolysis can go on for <u>weeks</u> and the cathode is often <u>twenty times bigger</u> at the end of it.

Recycling Copper Saves Money and Resources

1) The supply of copper-rich ores is <u>limited</u>.
2) This means it's important to <u>recycle</u> as much copper as possible.
3) Recycling copper uses only 15% of the energy that'd be used to mine and extract the same amount. So recycling copper helps to conserve <u>fossil fuels</u> and reduce <u>carbon dioxide emissions</u>.
4) Scientists are looking into new ways of extracting copper from ores that only contain small amounts of copper, or from the <u>waste</u> that is currently produced when copper is extracted.
5) One way is to use <u>bacteria</u> to separate copper from copper sulphide. The bacteria get energy from the bond between copper and sulphur, separating out the <u>copper</u> from the ore in the process.

Revision and Electrolysis — they can both go on for weeks...

Electrolysis ain't cheap — it takes a lot of electricity, which costs money. It's the only way of getting pure enough copper for electrical wires though, so it's worth it. This isn't such a bad page to learn — try writing a mini-essay about it. Don't forget to have a go at drawing the diagram <u>from memory</u> too.

Other Metals

There are loads of metals. But if none of them have quite the properties you need, you could try an alloy.

Aluminium is Useful, but Expensive to Extract

1) Aluminium has a low density and is corrosion-resistant.
2) This makes aluminium a very useful structural material. It can be used for loads of things, from window frames to electricity cables and aircraft.
3) You can't extract aluminium from its oxide by the cheap method of reduction with carbon.
4) It has to be extracted by electrolysis. This requires lots of energy, which makes it an expensive process. This means aluminium is a fairly expensive metal.

Pure Iron Tends to be a Bit Too Bendy

1) 'Iron' straight from the blast furnace is only 96% iron. The other 4% is impurities.
2) This impure iron is brittle. It doesn't have many uses. So all the impurities are removed from most blast furnace iron.
3) This pure iron has a regular arrangement of identical atoms. The layers of atoms can slide over each other. This makes the iron soft and easily shaped — but far too bendy for most uses.
4) Most of the pure iron is changed into alloys called steels. Steels are made by adding small amounts of carbon (plus maybe other metals) to the iron.

Alloys are Harder Than Pure Metals

1) An alloy is a mixture of two or more metals, or a mixture of a metal and a non-metal.
2) The different-sized atoms in alloys upset the regular structure. This makes it more difficult for the atoms to slide over each other — so alloys are harder.
3) Many metals in use today are actually alloys. E.g.:

> BRONZE = COPPER + TIN   Bronze is harder than copper. It's good for making medals and statues from.
>
> GOLD ALLOYS ARE USED TO MAKE JEWELLERY   Pure gold is too soft. Metals such as zinc, copper, silver, palladium and nickel are used to harden the "gold".
>
> ALUMINIUM ALLOYS ARE USED TO MAKE AIRCRAFT   Aluminium has a low density, but it's alloyed with small amounts of other metals to make it stronger.

4) In the past, the development of alloys was by trial and error. But nowadays we understand much more about the properties of metals, so alloys can be designed for specific uses.

Smart Alloys Return to Their Original Shape

1) Nitinol is a "shape memory alloy" — it has a shape memory property.
2) If you bend a wire made of this smart alloy, it'll go back to its original shape when it's heated.
3) You can get specs with frames made from a smart alloy — you can sit on them and not destroy them.

bend → heat →

A brass band — harder than Iron Maiden...

The Eiffel Tower is made of iron — but the problem with iron is that it goes rusty if air and water get to it. So the Eiffel Tower has to be painted every seven years to make sure that it doesn't rust. This is quite a job and takes an entire year for a team of 25 painters. Too bad they didn't use stainless steel.

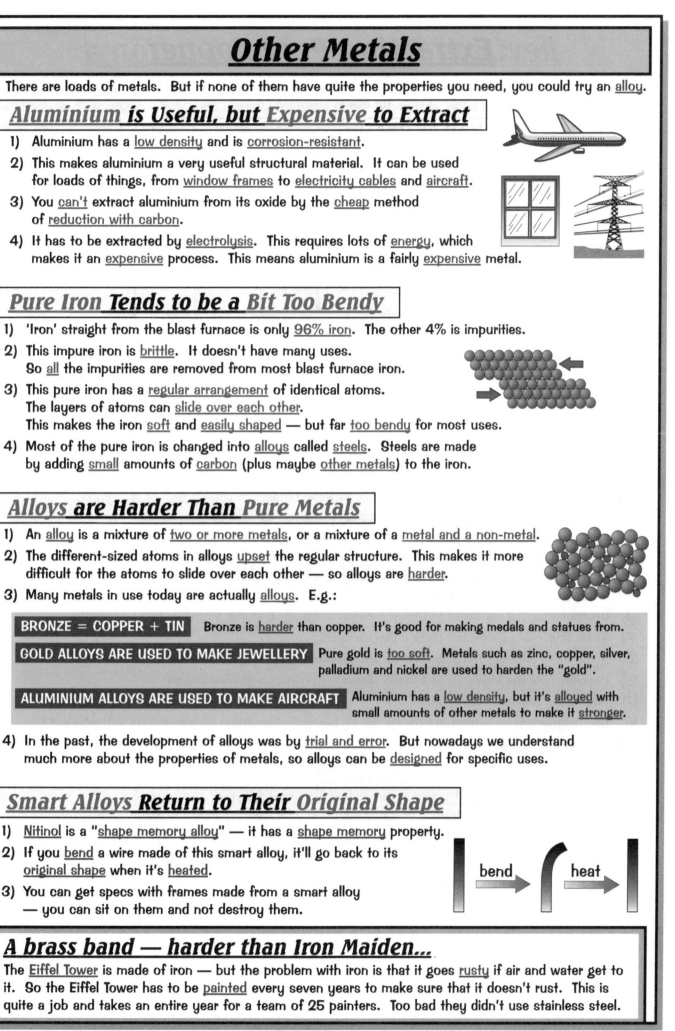

Revision Summary for Section 4

There wasn't anything too ghastly in this section, and a few bits were even quite interesting, I reckon. But you've got to make sure the facts are all firmly embedded in your brain and that you really understand them. These questions will let you see what you know and what you don't. If you get stuck on any, you need to look at that stuff again. Keep going till you can do them all without coming up for air.

1) Sketch an atom. Label the nucleus and the electrons.

2) Name the three types of particle in an atom. State the relative mass and charge of each particle.

3) What are the symbols for: a) calcium, b) carbon, c) sodium?
(Use the periodic table on the inside front cover.)

4) The element boron is written as $^{11}_{5}B$. How many neutrons do atoms of this element contain? How many electrons does a neutral boron atom have in its outer shell?

5) Describe the difference between a mixture and a compound.

6) Compounds and mixtures are both equally difficult to separate out — true or false?

7)* What atoms make up a molecule of Na_2CO_3?

8)* Say which of the diagrams on the right show:
    a) a mixture of compounds, b) a mixture of elements,
    c) an element, d) a compound

9)* Which element's properties are more similar to magnesium's: calcium or iron?

10)* Balance these equations: a) $CaCO_3 + HCl \rightarrow CaCl_2 + H_2O + CO_2$ b) $Ca + H_2O \rightarrow Ca(OH)_2 + H_2$

11) Write a balanced equation for the reaction between potassium and water.

12) Rubidium ($^{86}_{37}Rb$) is a Group 1 element. When placed in water, a lump of rubidium violently explodes.
    a) Name the gas that is produced by this reaction.
    b) Describe how the pH of the water changes during the experiment.
    c) The experiment is repeated with the same sized lump of sodium ($^{23}_{11}Na$).
       How would it be different?

13) Describe how the reactivity of Group 7 elements changes as the atomic number increases.

14) Name four noble gases and state a use for each.

15) Name three different transition metals and give an everyday use for each.

16) Describe how the structure of a metal allows it to carry an electric current.

17) What's the definition of an ore?

18) Can magnesium be extracted from its ore by heating with carbon monoxide? If not, why not?

19) What happens if you put:
    a) a piece of magnesium in a solution of zinc sulphate?
    b) a copper bracelet in a solution of iron chloride?

20) What method is used to purify copper once it's been extracted from its ore?
    Why is this method used?

21) What is the problem with using: a) iron straight from the blast furnace, b) very pure iron?

22) Why are alloys harder than pure metals? Give two examples of alloys and say what's in them.

23) What's so clever about smart alloys?

* Answers on page 140

Section 4 — Atoms, Elements and Compounds

Limestone

The Mendip Hills and the Yorkshire Dales are mainly made of a rock called limestone.

Limestone is Used as a Building Material

1) Limestone is a boring grey/white colour. It's formed from sea shells and, although the original shells are mostly crushed, there are still quite a few fossilised shells remaining.

2) It's quarried out of the ground. This causes some environmental problems though — see below.

3) Fine old buildings like cathedrals are often made purely from limestone blocks. It's also used for statues and fancy carved bits on nice buildings too.

4) Limestone's virtually insoluble in plain water. But acid rain reacts with the limestone and dissolves it away.

5) Limestone can also be crushed up into chippings and used in road surfacing.

St Paul's Cathedral is made from limestone.

Limestone is Mainly Calcium Carbonate

1) Limestone is mainly calcium carbonate — $CaCO_3$.

2) When it's heated it thermally decomposes (breaks down) to make calcium oxide (quicklime) and carbon dioxide.

$$\text{calcium carbonate} \rightarrow \text{calcium oxide} + \text{carbon dioxide}$$
$$CaCO_3(s) \rightarrow CaO(s) + CO_2(g)$$

When other carbonates are heated, they decompose in the same way: e.g. $Na_2CO_3 \rightarrow Na_2O + CO_2$.

3) When you add water to quicklime you get slaked lime (calcium hydroxide).

$$\text{quicklime} + \text{water} \longrightarrow \text{slaked lime}$$
$$CaO + H_2O \longrightarrow Ca(OH)_2$$

4) Slaked lime is an alkali which can be used to neutralise acid soils in fields.

Limestone is Used to Make Other Building Materials Too

1) Powdered limestone is heated in a kiln with powdered clay to make cement.

2) Cement can be mixed with sand and water to make mortar. Mortar is the stuff you stick bricks together with.

3) Or you can mix cement with sand, water and gravel to make concrete. And by including steel rods, you get reinforced concrete — a composite material with the hardness of concrete and the strength of steel.

4) And believe it or not — limestone is also used to make glass. You just heat it with sand and sodium carbonate until it melts.

Extracting Rocks Can Cause Environmental Damage

1) Quarrying uses up land and destroys habitats. And the waste materials from mines and quarries produce unsightly tips.

2) Transporting rock can cause noise and pollution.

3) The quarrying process itself produces dust and makes a lot of noise — they often use dynamite to blast the rock out of the ground.

4) Disused sites can be dangerous. Disused mines have been known to collapse. And quarries are sometimes turned into (very deep) lakes — people drown in them every year.

Limestone — a sea creature's cementery...

It sounds like you can achieve pretty much anything with limestone. Fred Flintstone even managed to make his car wheels and bowling balls out of rock (although I'm not 100% certain it was limestone).

Useful Products from Air and Salt

The Earth supplies us with pretty much everything we ever use. And until we learn to go into space and mine stuff from asteroids (or whatever), we're going to be absolutely reliant on it in the future as well.

Fractional Distillation of Air Produces Nitrogen and Oxygen

1) Air is made up mainly of two gases — nitrogen (about 78%) and oxygen (about 21%).

2) The other 1% is mainly argon. But there's also carbon dioxide, water vapour, and other gases.

3) Nitrogen and oxygen can be separated by fractional distillation. This uses the fact that the two gases boil at different temperatures (nitrogen at –196 °C, and oxygen at –187 °C).

4) Air is first cooled until it liquefies at about –200 °C.
As you 'warm up' the liquefied air, nitrogen boils off first. Easy.

Salt is Taken from the Sea — and from Underneath Cheshire

1) In hot countries they just pour sea water into big open tanks and let the Sun evaporate the water to leave salt. This is no good in cold countries (like Britain, as if you need reminding) — not enough sunshine.

2) In Britain, rock salt is extracted from underground deposits left millions of years ago when ancient seas evaporated. Rock salt is a mixture of mainly sand and salt.

3) Unrefined rock salt can be used in winter on roads to melt any ice and to give a bit more grip.

4) Or the sand can be filtered out of the mixture to leave refined salt.

5) Refined salt is added to most processed foods to enhance the flavour. (But it's now reckoned to be unhealthy to eat too much salt.)

I'm just waiting for the great day of reckoning when finally every single food has been declared either generally unhealthy or else downright dangerous. Perhaps we should all lay bets on what'll be the last food still considered safe to eat. My money's on dried locusts.

Salt is Used for Making Chemicals

1) Salt's important for the chemical industry.

2) Hydrogen, chlorine, sodium and sodium hydroxide can all be extracted from salt.

3) All these products can be collected, and then used in all sorts of industries.

Chlorine
1) Used in bleach, for sterilising water, for making hydrochloric acid and insecticides.
2) For making plastics (e.g. it's the C in PVC), pesticides, weedkillers, pharmaceuticals...

Hydrogen
1) Used to make ammonia.
2) Used to change oils into fats for making margarine ('hydrogenated vegetable oil').
3) Used as a fuel in fuel cells, and for welding and metal cutting.

Sodium Sodium's used to make detergents, and lots of other organic chemicals (among other things).

Sodium Hydroxide (Old name: caustic soda) Sodium hydroxide's a very strong alkali and is used widely in the chemical industry to make, e.g. soap, ceramics, organic chemicals, paper pulp, oven cleaner, 'drain unblocker', bleach...

Rock salt — think of the pollution as it runs into the sea...

Seawater can even be desalinated (have the salt removed) to provide fresh water — but the process needs energy. Eeeh... air, seawater, and rocks under the ground... they give us loads. Don't forget it.

Fractional Distillation of Crude Oil

Crude oil is formed from the buried remains of plants and animals — it's a fossil fuel. Over millions of years, with high temperature and pressure, the remains turn to crude oil, which can be drilled up.

Crude Oil Can be Split into Separate Hydrocarbons

1) Crude oil is a mixture of hydrocarbons — molecules which are made of just carbon and hydrogen.
2) Fractional distillation splits crude oil into fractions (groups of compounds with carbon chains of similar length).
3) Heated crude oil is piped in at the bottom of a fractionating column.
The various fractions are constantly tapped off at the different levels where they condense.

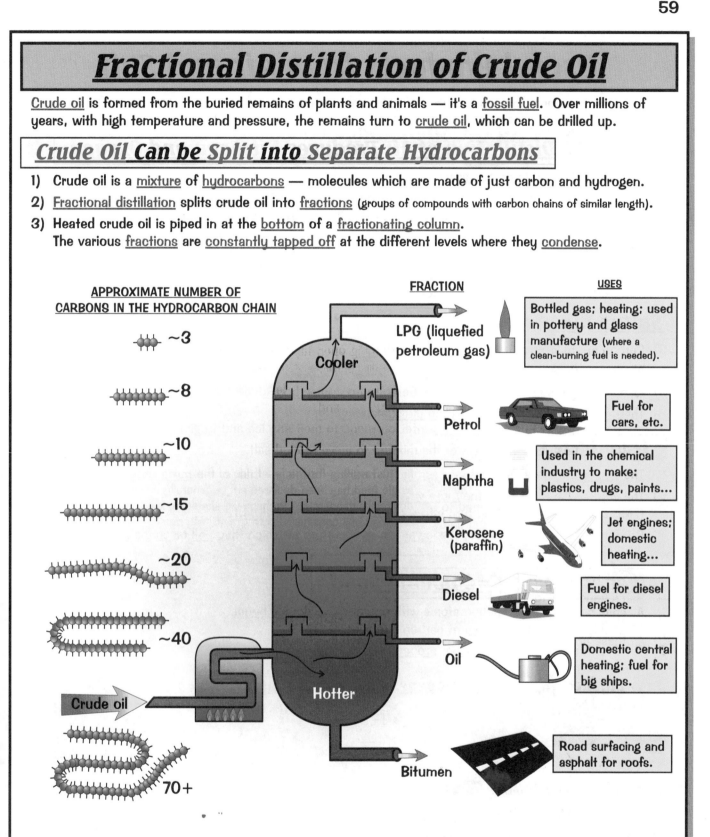

APPROXIMATE NUMBER OF CARBONS IN THE HYDROCARBON CHAIN

~3
~8
~10
~15
~20
~40
Crude oil
70+

Cooler
Hotter

FRACTION

LPG (liquefied petroleum gas)
Petrol
Naphtha
Kerosene (paraffin)
Diesel
Oil
Bitumen

USES

Bottled gas; heating; used in pottery and glass manufacture (where a clean-burning fuel is needed).

Fuel for cars, etc.

Used in the chemical industry to make: plastics, drugs, paints...

Jet engines; domestic heating...

Fuel for diesel engines.

Domestic central heating; fuel for big ships.

Road surfacing and asphalt for roofs.

1) The big hydrocarbon molecules are the first to condense, because they have higher boiling points.
2) As the molecules get smaller, they condense higher up the fractionating column.
3) Fractional distillation is an example of a physical process — there are no chemical reactions.

The diesel engine was named after its inventor — Rudolf Engine...

Crude oil is useful stuff, there's no doubt about it. But using it is not without its problems (see page 63 for more about fuels). For example, oil is shipped around the planet, which can lead to slicks if there's an accident. Also, burning oil is thought to cause climate change, acid rain and global dimming. And oil is going to start running out one day, which will lead to big difficulties.

Alkanes and Alkenes

Crude oil contains both alkanes and alkenes (although mostly alkanes).

Alkanes Have All C–C Single Bonds

1) <u>Alkanes</u> are made up of <u>chains</u> of carbon atoms joined together, and surrounded by <u>hydrogen atoms</u>.

2) Different alkanes have chains of different <u>lengths</u>.
   The first four alkanes are <u>methane</u> (natural gas), <u>ethane</u>, <u>propane</u> and <u>butane</u>.

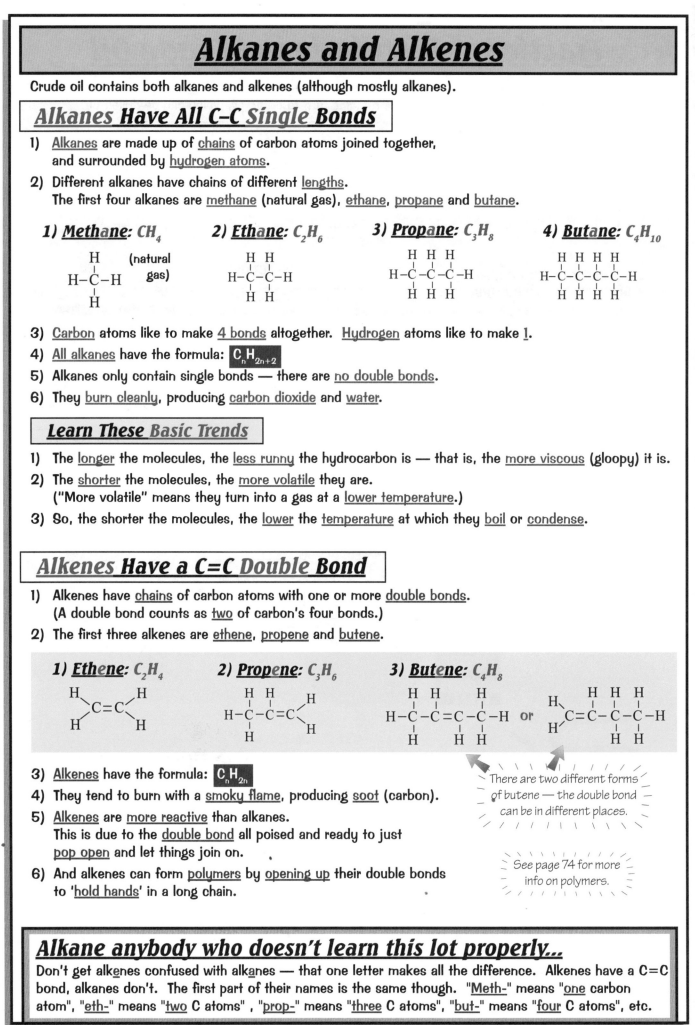

1) Methane: CH_4 **2) Ethane:** C_2H_6 **3) Propane:** C_3H_8 **4) Butane:** C_4H_{10}

3) <u>Carbon</u> atoms like to make <u>4 bonds</u> altogether. <u>Hydrogen</u> atoms like to make <u>1</u>.

4) <u>All alkanes</u> have the formula: C_nH_{2n+2}

5) Alkanes only contain single bonds — there are <u>no double bonds</u>.

6) They <u>burn cleanly</u>, producing <u>carbon dioxide</u> and <u>water</u>.

Learn These Basic Trends

1) The <u>longer</u> the molecules, the <u>less runny</u> the hydrocarbon is — that is, the <u>more viscous</u> (gloopy) it is.

2) The <u>shorter</u> the molecules, the <u>more volatile</u> they are.
   ("More volatile" means they turn into a gas at a <u>lower temperature</u>.)

3) So, the shorter the molecules, the <u>lower</u> the <u>temperature</u> at which they <u>boil</u> or <u>condense</u>.

Alkenes Have a C=C Double Bond

1) Alkenes have <u>chains</u> of carbon atoms with one or more <u>double bonds</u>.
   (A double bond counts as <u>two</u> of carbon's four bonds.)

2) The first three alkenes are <u>ethene</u>, <u>propene</u> and <u>butene</u>.

1) Ethene: C_2H_4 **2) Propene:** C_3H_6 **3) Butene:** C_4H_8

3) <u>Alkenes</u> have the formula: C_nH_{2n}

4) They tend to burn with a <u>smoky flame</u>, producing <u>soot</u> (carbon).

5) <u>Alkenes</u> are <u>more reactive</u> than alkanes.
   This is due to the <u>double bond</u> all poised and ready to just <u>pop open</u> and let things join on.

6) And alkenes can form <u>polymers</u> by <u>opening up</u> their double bonds to 'hold hands' in a long chain.

There are two different forms of butene — the double bond can be in different places.

See page 74 for more info on polymers.

Alkane anybody who doesn't learn this lot properly...

Don't get alkenes confused with alkanes — that one letter makes all the difference. Alkenes have a C=C bond, alkanes don't. The first part of their names is the same though. "<u>Meth-</u>" means "<u>one</u> carbon atom", "<u>eth-</u>" means "<u>two</u> C atoms", "<u>prop-</u>" means "<u>three</u> C atoms", "<u>but-</u>" means "<u>four</u> C atoms", etc.

Cracking Crude Oil

After the distillation of crude oil, you've still got both short and long hydrocarbons, just not all mixed together. But there's <u>more demand</u> for some products, like <u>petrol</u>, than for others.

Cracking Means Splitting Up Long-Chain Hydrocarbons...

1) <u>Long-chain hydrocarbons</u> form <u>thick gloopy liquids</u> like <u>tar</u> which aren't all that useful, so...

2) ... a lot of the longer molecules produced from <u>fractional distillation</u> are <u>turned into smaller ones</u> by a process called <u>cracking</u>.

3) Some of the products of cracking are useful as fuels, e.g. petrol for cars and paraffin for jet fuel.

4) Cracking also produces short alkenes like <u>ethene</u>, which are needed for <u>making plastics</u> (see p74).

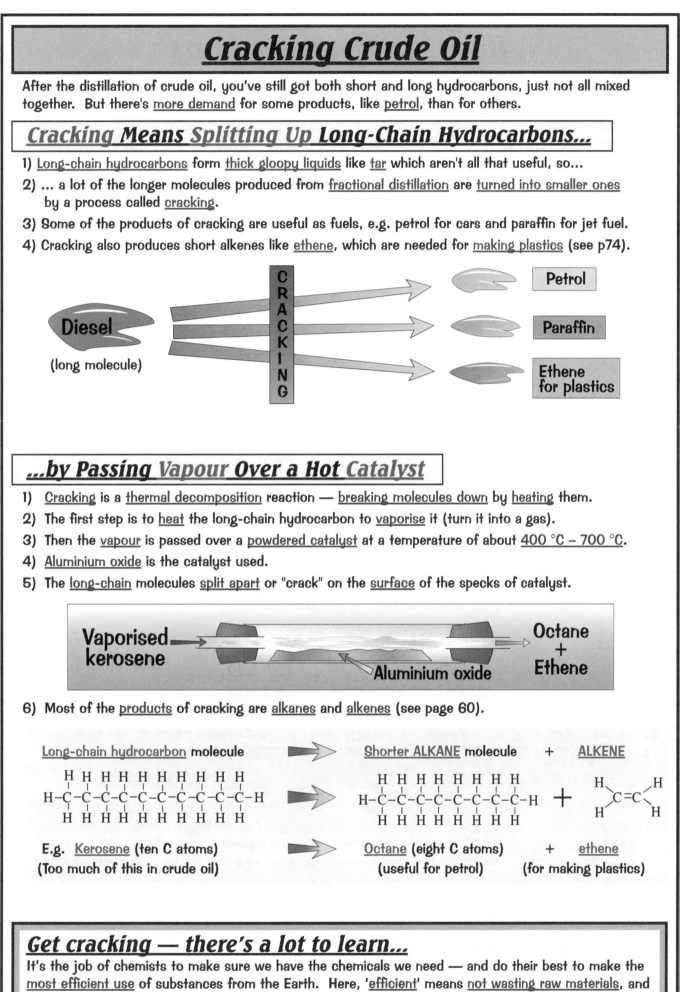

...by Passing Vapour Over a Hot Catalyst

1) <u>Cracking</u> is a <u>thermal decomposition</u> reaction — <u>breaking molecules down</u> by <u>heating</u> them.

2) The first step is to <u>heat</u> the long-chain hydrocarbon to <u>vaporise</u> it (turn it into a gas).

3) Then the <u>vapour</u> is passed over a <u>powdered catalyst</u> at a temperature of about <u>400 °C – 700 °C</u>.

4) <u>Aluminium oxide</u> is the catalyst used.

5) The <u>long-chain</u> molecules <u>split apart</u> or "crack" on the <u>surface</u> of the specks of catalyst.

6) Most of the <u>products</u> of cracking are <u>alkanes</u> and <u>alkenes</u> (see page 60).

Long-chain hydrocarbon molecule ➡ Shorter ALKANE molecule + ALKENE

E.g. <u>Kerosene</u> (ten C atoms)   ➡   <u>Octane</u> (eight C atoms) + <u>ethene</u>
(Too much of this in crude oil)   (useful for petrol)   (for making plastics)

Get cracking — there's a lot to learn...

It's the job of chemists to make sure we have the chemicals we need — and do their best to make the <u>most efficient use</u> of substances from the Earth. Here, 'efficient' means <u>not wasting raw materials</u>, and also <u>not making more waste than is necessary</u>. It's a tough job, but someone's probably got to do it.

Burning Hydrocarbons

A <u>fuel</u> is a substance that <u>reacts with oxygen</u> to <u>release useful energy</u>. Remember that.

Complete Combustion Happens When There's Plenty of Oxygen

The <u>complete combustion</u> of any hydrocarbon in oxygen will produce only <u>carbon dioxide</u> and <u>water</u> as waste products, which are both quite <u>clean</u> and <u>non-poisonous</u>.

hydrocarbon + oxygen ⟹ carbon dioxide + water (+ energy)

1) Many <u>gas heaters</u> release these <u>waste gases</u> into the room, which is perfectly OK. As long as the gas heater is <u>working properly</u> and the room is <u>well ventilated</u> there's no problem.

2) This reaction, when there's plenty of <u>oxygen</u>, is known as <u>complete combustion</u>. When there's <u>plenty of oxygen</u> and combustion is complete, the gas burns with a <u>clean blue flame</u>.

3) It releases <u>lots of energy</u> and only produces those two <u>harmless waste products</u>. (Lots of CO_2 isn't ideal, but the alternatives are worse — see below.)

4) You can show a fuel burns to give CO_2 and H_2O like this...

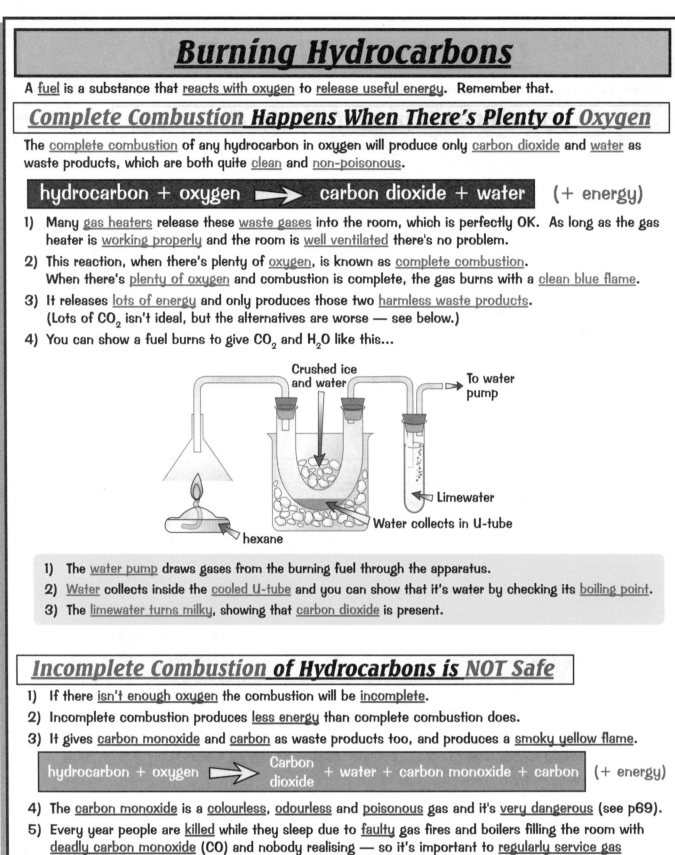

1) The <u>water pump</u> draws gases from the burning fuel through the apparatus.
2) <u>Water</u> collects inside the <u>cooled U-tube</u> and you can show that it's water by checking its <u>boiling point</u>.
3) The <u>limewater turns milky</u>, showing that <u>carbon dioxide</u> is present.

Incomplete Combustion of Hydrocarbons is NOT Safe

1) If there <u>isn't enough oxygen</u> the combustion will be <u>incomplete</u>.

2) Incomplete combustion produces <u>less energy</u> than complete combustion does.

3) It gives <u>carbon monoxide</u> and <u>carbon</u> as waste products too, and produces a <u>smoky yellow flame</u>.

hydrocarbon + oxygen ⟹ Carbon dioxide + water + carbon monoxide + carbon (+ energy)

4) The <u>carbon monoxide</u> is a <u>colourless</u>, <u>odourless</u> and <u>poisonous</u> gas and it's <u>very dangerous</u> (see p69).

5) Every year people are <u>killed</u> while they sleep due to <u>faulty</u> gas fires and boilers filling the room with <u>deadly carbon monoxide</u> (CO) and nobody realising — so it's important to <u>regularly service gas appliances</u>. The black carbon given off produces <u>sooty marks</u> — a <u>clue</u> the fuel's <u>not</u> burning fully.

5) So basically, you want <u>lots of oxygen</u> when you're burning fuel — you get <u>more energy</u> given out, and you don't get any <u>messy soot</u> or <u>poisonous gases</u>.

Blue flame good, orange flame bad...

This is why people should get their gas appliances serviced every year, and get <u>carbon monoxide detectors fitted</u>. Carbon monoxide really can kill people in their sleep — scary stuff. Don't let that scare you off learning everything that's on this page — any of it could come up in the exam.

Using Crude Oil as a Fuel

Nothing as amazingly useful as crude oil would be without its problems. No, that'd be too good to be true.

Crude Oil Provides an Important Fuel for Modern Life

1) Crude oil fractions make good <u>fuels</u>. Most modern transport is fuelled by a crude oil fraction, e.g. cars, boats, trains and planes. Parts of crude oil are also burned in <u>central heating systems</u> and in <u>power stations</u> to <u>generate electricity</u>.

2) There's a <u>massive industry</u> with scientists working to find oil reserves, take it out of the ground, and turn it into useful products. As well as fuels, crude oil also provides the raw materials for making various <u>chemicals</u>, including <u>plastics</u>. (There's more on this on page 74.)

3) Often, <u>alternatives</u> to using crude oil fractions as fuel are possible — e.g. electricity can be generated by <u>nuclear</u> or <u>wind</u> power, and <u>solar</u> energy can be used to heat water. See p70 for a bit more info.

4) But things tend to be <u>set up</u> for using oil fractions. For example, cars are designed for <u>petrol or diesel</u> and it's <u>readily available</u>. There are filling stations all over the country, with storage facilities and pumps specifically designed for these crude oil fractions. So crude oil fractions are often the <u>easiest and cheapest</u> thing to use.

5) Crude oil fractions are often <u>more reliable</u> too — e.g. solar and wind power won't work without the right weather conditions.

But it Might Run Out One Day... Eeek

1) Most scientists think that oil will <u>run out</u>. But no one knows exactly when.

2) There have been heaps of <u>different predictions</u> — e.g. about 40 years ago, some scientists predicted that it'd all be gone by the year 2000.

3) <u>New oil reserves</u> are discovered from time to time. No one knows <u>how much</u> oil will be discovered in the future though.

4) Also, <u>technology</u> is constantly improving, so it's now possible to extract oil that was once too <u>difficult</u> or <u>expensive</u> to extract.

5) In the <u>worst-case scenario</u>, oil may be pretty much gone in about 25 years — and that's not far off.

6) Some people think we should <u>immediately stop</u> using oil for things like transport, for which there are alternatives, and keep it for things that it's absolutely <u>essential</u> for, like some chemicals and medicines.

7) It will take time to <u>develop</u> alternative fuels that will satisfy all our energy needs (see page 70 for more info). It'll also take time to <u>adapt things</u> — e.g. we might need different kinds of car engines, or special storage tanks built.

8) So however long oil does last for, it's a good idea to start <u>conserving</u> it and finding <u>alternatives</u> now.

Crude Oil is NOT the Environment's Best Friend

1) <u>Oil spills</u> can happen as the oil is being transported by tanker — this spells <u>disaster</u> for the local environment. <u>Birds</u> get covered in the stuff and are <u>poisoned</u> as they try to clean themselves. Other creatures, like <u>sea otters</u> and <u>whales</u>, are poisoned too.

2) You have to <u>burn oil</u> to release the energy from it. But burning oil is thought to be a major cause of <u>global warming</u> (p68), <u>acid rain</u> (p69) and <u>global dimming</u> (p72).

If oil alternatives aren't developed, we might get caught short...

Crude oil is <u>really important</u> to our lives. Take <u>petrol</u> for instance — at the first whisper of a shortage, there's mayhem. Loads of people dash to the petrol station and start filling up their tanks. This causes a queue, which starts everyone else panicking. I don't know what they'll do when it runs out totally.

The Earth's Structure

It's tricky to study the structure of the Earth — you can't just dig down to the Earth's centre. But after studying the evidence, this is what scientists think is down there...

Crust, Mantle, Outer and Inner Core

1) The crust is Earth's thin outer layer of solid rock.
2) There are two types of crust — continental crust (forming the land), and oceanic crust (under oceans).
3) The mantle extends from the crust almost halfway to the centre of the Earth.
4) The lithosphere includes the crust and the top part of the mantle.
5) At the centre is the Earth's core.
6) Radioactive decay creates a lot of the heat inside the Earth.
7) This heat causes convection currents, which cause the plates of the lithosphere to move (which is bad news for some people — see below).

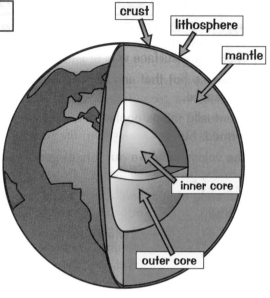

The Earth's Surface is Made Up of Tectonic Plates

1) The lithosphere is cracked into a number of large pieces called tectonic plates. These plates are a bit like big rafts that 'float' on the mantle.
2) The plates don't stay in one place though. The convection currents in the mantle cause the plates to drift.
3) The map shows the edges of the plates and the directions they're moving in (red arrows).
4) Most plates move at speeds of a few centimetres per year.
5) Occasionally, the plates move very suddenly, causing an earthquake.
6) Volcanoes often form at the boundaries between two tectonic plates too.

Scientists Can't Predict Earthquakes and Volcanic Eruptions

1) Tectonic plates can stay more or less put for a while and then suddenly lurch forwards.
2) Scientists are trying to find out if there are any clues that an earthquake might happen soon.
3) But it's impossible to predict exactly when they'll move.

Plate Tectonics — it's a smashing theory...

There's a mixture of plain facts and scientific thinking here. Learn the details of the Earth's structure, and make sure you can explain how tectonic plates move and what happens at plate boundaries. It's important to remember that earthquakes are unpredictable even with the best equipment.

The Evolution of the Atmosphere

For 200 million years or so, the atmosphere has been about how it is now: 78% nitrogen, 21% oxygen, and small amounts of other gases, mainly CO_2 and noble gases. There can be a lot of water vapour too. But it wasn't always like this. Here's how the past 4.5 billion years may have gone:

Phase 1 — Volcanoes Gave Out Gases

1) The Earth's surface was originally molten.
2) It was so hot that any atmosphere just 'boiled away' into space.
3) Eventually things cooled down a bit and a thin crust formed, but volcanoes kept erupting.
4) The volcanoes gave out lots of gas — including carbon dioxide, water vapour and nitrogen.
5) The early atmosphere was probably mostly CO_2, with virtually no oxygen.
6) The oceans formed when the water vapour condensed.

The First Two Billion Years

Steam CO_2 CO_2 N_2 N_2

Holiday report: Not a nice place to be. Take strong walking boots and a good coat.

Phase 2 — Green Plants Evolved and Produced Oxygen

The Next Two Billion Years

O_2 O_2 O_2 O_2 O_2 O_2 O_2 O_2 O_2 O_2

Holiday report: A bit slimy underfoot. Take wellies and a lot of suncream.

1) Green plants evolved over most of the Earth. They were quite happy in the CO_2 atmosphere.
2) A lot of the early CO_2 dissolved into the oceans.
3) The green plants also removed CO_2 from the air and produced O_2 by photosynthesis.
4) When some plants died, they were buried under layers of sediment.
5) The carbon they had removed from the air (as CO_2) then became 'locked up' in sedimentary rocks as fossil fuels.
6) When we burn fossil fuels today, this 'locked-up' carbon is released and the concentration of CO_2 in the atmosphere rises.

Phase 3 — Ozone Layer Allows Evolution of Complex Animals

1) The build-up of oxygen in the atmosphere killed off some early organisms that couldn't tolerate it.
2) But it allowed other, more complex organisms to evolve and flourish.
3) The oxygen also created the ozone layer (O_3) which blocked harmful rays from the Sun. This enabled even more complex organisms to evolve — us, eventually.
4) There is virtually no CO_2 left now.

The Last Billion Years or so

Nice safe OZONE, O_3

Holiday report: A nice place to be. Visit before the crowds ruin it.

The atmosphere's evolving — shut the window will you...

We've learned a lot about the past atmosphere from Antarctic ice cores. Each year, a layer of ice forms and bubbles of air get trapped inside it, then it's buried by the next layer. So the deeper the ice, the older the air — and if you examine the bubbles in different layers, you can see how the air has changed.

Changes in the Atmosphere

We have evidence for how the atmosphere evolved from rocks and other sources. But no one was there to record the changes as they happened. So we can't be 100% sure about our theories.

There are Competing Theories About Atmospheric Change

There are different theories about how the Earth's atmosphere changed millions of years ago. All these theories have to be judged on the evidence.

For example, one theory says that the water on Earth came mainly from comets rather than volcanoes. Space science research soon found that lots of small icy comets really are hitting the Earth every day. So far so good.

But studies of comets found that the water in comets isn't the same as the water on Earth.

So current thinking is that most of Earth's water probably didn't come from comets.

The Atmosphere Changes All the Time

1) This is a graph of CO_2 and global temperature data. It shows CO_2 levels and temperature rising rapidly over the last few thousand years.

2) But the graph also shows that there have been huge changes in the climate before. (These changes are small beer compared with the changes described on page 65, when the entire composition of the atmosphere was changing... but they're still pretty big.)

3) For instance, there have been several ice ages over the last few million years — when large areas of the Earth's surface were covered with ice.

4) So changes in the Earth's temperature happen all the time.

5) However, we've found the planet might be warming up faster than we'd expect... (see page 68).

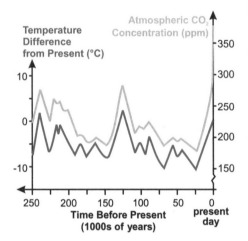

The Atmosphere is Still Changing

Levels of CO_2 in the atmosphere have increased by about 25% since 1750...

1) Burning fossil fuels releases CO_2 — and as the world has become more industrialised, more fossil fuels have been burnt in power stations and in car engines.

2) Carbon dioxide is a greenhouse gas — it traps heat from the Sun. You'd expect that more carbon dioxide would mean a hotter planet. (See page 68 for more info.)

3) However, a few scientists say that the concentration of CO_2 naturally goes up and down. They argue that a little increase now might be just a blip.

Over the last 50 years, the amount of ozone in the ozone layer has decreased...

1) Currently, holes in the Earth's ozone layer form over Antarctica and the Arctic each year.

2) Ozone is broken down by man-made gases called CFCs. These used to be used in aerosols and fridges, but were phased out in the 1990s.

3) The ozone layer protects us from the harmful UV radiation which can cause skin cancer.

4) It's difficult to test whether changes in the ozone layer are to blame for increases in skin cancer, though. People sunbathe more now and have more beach holidays abroad, so they expose themselves to more UV radiation anyway.

Show me the evidence, then I'll believe you...

Whether people believe scientific theories or not depends on the evidence that people produce to support them. Without evidence, a theory goes nowhere. Quite right too, I say.

Human Impact on the Environment

We have an <u>impact</u> on the world around us — and the <u>more humans</u> there are, the bigger the impact.

There are Six Billion People in the World...

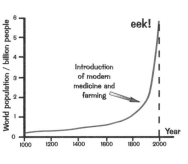

1) The <u>population</u> of the world is currently <u>rising</u> very quickly, and it's not slowing down — look at the graph...

2) This is mostly due to modern <u>medicine</u> and <u>farming</u> methods, which have <u>reduced</u> the number of <u>people dying</u> from <u>disease</u> and <u>hunger</u>.

3) This is great for all of us <u>humans</u>.

4) But it means we're having a <u>bigger effect</u> on the <u>environment</u>...

...With Increasing Demands on the Environment

When the <u>Earth's population</u> was much smaller, the effects of <u>human activity</u> were usually <u>small</u> and <u>local</u>. Nowadays though, our actions can have a far more <u>widespread</u> effect.

1) The increasing <u>population</u> puts pressure on the <u>environment</u>, as we take more and more resources.

2) But people around the world are also demanding a higher <u>standard of living</u> (and so want luxuries to make life more comfortable — cars, computers, etc.).

   So we use more <u>raw materials</u> (e.g. oil to make plastics), and we also use more <u>energy</u> for the manufacturing processes.

3) Unfortunately, many raw materials are being used up quicker than they're being replaced.
   So if we carry on like we are, one day we're going to <u>run out</u>.

We're Also Producing More Waste

As we make more and more things we produce more and more <u>waste</u>.
This can easily lead to more <u>harmful pollution</u>. This affects water, land and air.

Water   <u>Sewage</u> and <u>toxic chemicals</u> can pollute lakes, rivers and oceans, affecting the plants and animals that rely on them for survival. The chemicals used on land (e.g. fertilisers) can be washed into water.

Land   We use <u>toxic chemicals</u> for farming (e.g. pesticides and herbicides). We also bury <u>nuclear waste</u> underground, and we dump a lot of <u>household waste</u> in landfill sites.

Air   <u>Smoke</u> and <u>gases</u> released into the atmosphere can pollute the air (see pages 68, 69 and 72 for more info). For example, <u>sulphur dioxide</u> can cause <u>acid rain</u>.

More People Means Less Land for Plants and Other Animals

Humans also <u>reduce</u> the amount of <u>land and resources</u> available to other <u>animals</u> and <u>plants</u>.
The <u>four main human activities</u> that do this are:

1) <u>Building</u>

2) <u>Farming</u>

3) <u>Dumping Waste</u>

4) <u>Quarrying</u>

More people, more mess, less space, less resources...

In the exam you might be given some data about <u>environmental impact</u>, so make sure you understand what's going on. Just keep your head and work out exactly what the data's saying. Job's a good 'un.

Global Warming and the Carbon Cycle

Most environmentalists and scientists now believe that <u>human activities</u> are <u>changing</u> the proportion of <u>carbon dioxide</u> in the <u>atmosphere</u> — and that that's going to have <u>massive effects</u> on life on Planet Earth.

Carbon Dioxide <u>and</u> Methane Trap Heat <u>from the Sun</u>

1) The <u>temperature</u> of the Earth is a <u>balance</u> between the heat it gets from the Sun and the heat it radiates back out into space.

2) Gases in the <u>atmosphere</u> absorb heat, and radiate some of it back towards Earth. (If this didn't happen, then at night we'd get <u>very cold</u>. But recently we've started to worry this effect is getting a bit out of hand...)

3) There are several different gases in the atmosphere which help keep the <u>heat in</u>. They're called "<u>greenhouse gases</u>" (oddly enough) and the <u>main ones</u> we worry about are <u>carbon dioxide</u> and <u>methane</u> — because the levels of these two gases are rising quite sharply.

4) <u>Humans</u> release <u>carbon dioxide</u> into the atmosphere as part of our <u>everyday lives</u> — e.g. as we <u>burn fossil fuels</u> in power stations or cars.

5) This could be a big problem, but it's hard to be 100% sure (since Earth's climate is so complicated).

6) For example, the Earth's temperature <u>varies</u> over the years anyway (see p66) — so even if Earth is warming up, it <u>might</u> be nothing to do with humans and fossil fuels.

7) But nowadays, <u>most</u> scientists think that:

> (i) Earth <u>is</u> gradually warming, and (ii) fossil fuel use <u>has</u> got something to do with it.

Carbon <u>is Constantly Being Recycled</u>

Carbon is the key to the greenhouse effect — it exists in the atmosphere as <u>carbon dioxide gas</u>, and is also present in many other <u>greenhouse gases</u> such as methane.

1) The carbon on Earth moves in a big cycle.

2) <u>Respiration</u> (see p14), <u>combustion</u> (see p62) and <u>decay</u> of plants and animals add carbon dioxide to the air and remove oxygen.

3) <u>Photosynthesis</u> (see p36) does the <u>opposite</u> — it removes carbon dioxide and adds oxygen.

4) These processes should <u>balance out</u>. However, it looks like <u>humans</u> have upset the natural carbon cycle.

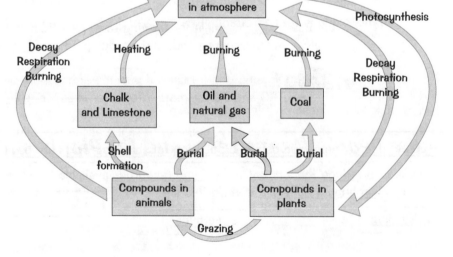

Eeeek — the carbon cycle's got a puncture...

Releasing masses of CO_2 due to <u>fossil fuel use</u> is the worst problem here. But <u>deforestation</u> (cutting down large areas of forest) is also bad for the carbon cycle, in <u>three</u> ways. First off, <u>carbon dioxide</u> is <u>released</u> when trees are <u>burnt</u> to clear land. Secondly, <u>microorganisms</u> feeding on the dead wood <u>release CO_2</u> due to respiration. And thirdly, fewer trees means there's <u>less photosynthesis</u> going on.

Air Pollution and Acid Rain

Carbon dioxide isn't the only gas released when fossil fuels burn — you also get other nasties like oxides of nitrogen, sulphur dioxide and carbon monoxide.

Acid Rain is Caused by Sulphur Dioxide and Oxides of Nitrogen

1) When fossil fuels are burned they release mostly CO_2.
   But they also release other harmful gases — e.g. sulphur dioxide and various nitrogen oxides.

2) The sulphur dioxide (SO_2) comes from sulphur impurities in the fossil fuels.

3) The nitrogen oxides form from a reaction between the nitrogen and oxygen in the air.
   This is caused by the heat of the burning.

4) When these gases mix with clouds they form sulphuric acid and nitric acid, which fall as acid rain.

5) Power stations and internal combustion engines in cars are the main causes of acid rain.

Acid Rain Kills Fish, Trees and Statues

1) Acid rain causes lakes to become acidic.
   Many plants and animals die as a result.

2) Acid rain kills trees and damages stone buildings and statues.
   It also makes metal corrode. It's shocking.

Oxides of Nitrogen Also Cause Photochemical Smog

1) Photochemical smog is a type of air pollution caused by sunlight acting on oxides of nitrogen.

2) These combine with oxygen to produce ozone (O_3), which can cause breathing difficulties, headaches and tiredness.

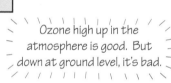

Ozone high up in the atmosphere is good. But down at ground level, it's bad.

Carbon Monoxide is a Poisonous Gas

1) Carbon monoxide (CO) can stop your blood doing its proper job of carrying oxygen around the body.

2) A lack of oxygen in the blood can lead to fainting, a coma or even death.

3) Carbon monoxide is formed during incomplete combustion (see p62 for more details).

It's Important That Atmospheric Pollution is Controlled

1) The build-up of these pollutants can make life unhealthy and miserable for humans, animals and plants.

2) Cases of respiratory illnesses (e.g. asthma) have increased recently — especially among young people. Many people blame atmospheric pollution for this, so efforts are being made to improve things.

3) Catalytic converters on motor vehicles reduce the amount of carbon monoxide and nitrogen oxides getting into the atmosphere.

4) They convert carbon monoxide into carbon dioxide, which is less dangerous (though more CO_2 isn't ideal).

5) And Flue Gas Desulphurisation (FGD) technology in some fossil-fuel power stations removes sulphur dioxide from the exhaust gases.

Revision and pollution — the two bugbears of modern life...

Eeee.... cars and fossil fuels — they're nowt but trouble. But at least this topic is kind of interesting, what with its relevance to everyday life and all. Just think... you could see this kind of stuff on TV.

The Atmosphere in the Future

What to do... what to do... How can we look after the atmosphere...

Computer Models are Used to Make Predictions

1) Computer models are used to predict the temperature of the Earth's atmosphere in the future.
2) They use data collected by thousands of monitoring stations all over the world.
3) The data is fed into the models, then millions of calculations are carried out.
4) However, computer models are only as good as the data you put into them, and the assumptions made when working out the calculations.
5) If the assumptions are wrong, this could lead to false results. And one small error in an early calculation could be magnified if it's used to predict further into the future. (Having said that, early comparisons of computer predictions and observed events look pretty good.)

Alternative Fuels are Being Developed

Some alternatives to fossil fuels already exist, and there are others in the pipeline (so to speak).
They should reduce the amount of fossil fuels burnt.

> BIOGAS is a mixture of methane and carbon dioxide.
>
> 1) It's produced when microorganisms digest waste material (e.g. waste plant matter).
> 2) It can be produced on a large scale, or on a small scale where each family has its own generator.
> 3) Biogas is burned and the energy can be used for cooking, heating or lighting.
>
> PROS: Waste material is readily available and cheap.
> It's 'carbon neutral' — the carbon it releases when it's burnt was absorbed by the plants used to make it as they were growing.
> CONS: Biogas production is slow in cool weather.

And see page 83 about using ethanol as a fuel.

> HYDROGEN GAS can also be used to power vehicles.
>
> 1) You get the hydrogen from the electrolysis of water.
> 2) There's plenty of water about but it takes electrical energy to split it up.
> 3) However, this energy can come from a renewable source, e.g. solar.
>
> PROS: Hydrogen combines with oxygen in the air to form just water — so it's very clean.
> CONS: You need a special, expensive engine and hydrogen isn't widely available.
> You still need to use energy from another source to make it.
> Hydrogen's hard to store — it's very explosive.

There's Lots to Consider When Choosing a Fuel

When you're choosing a fuel, there are lots of things you might need to think about...

1) Energy value (i.e. amount of energy) — oddly, this isn't always as important as it may seem.
2) Availability — there's not much point in choosing a fuel you can't get hold of easily.
3) Storage — some fuels take up a lot of space, and some produce flammable gases.
4) Cost — some fuels are expensive, but still good value in terms of energy content etc.
5) Toxicity — poisonous fumes are a problem.
6) Pollution — e.g. will you add to acid rain and the greenhouse effect? Or cause lots of smoke?

I produce a kind of biogas already...

As it's mostly fossil fuel use that gives the atmosphere such a hard time, alternative fuels are a good thing to start looking for. And getting people to use less energy is also a pretty sensible idea too.

Sustainable Development

It's not all doom and gloom... if we do things sustainably, we'll be okay. (To be honest, some of the stuff on this page is a bit more Biology-ish than Chemistry-esque. But it's all to do with the Earth, so it's here...)

Sustainable Development Needs Careful Planning

1) Some of the environmental damage we do can't easily be <u>repaired</u> (e.g. destruction of rainforests).

2) We're also placing <u>greater pressure</u> on our planet's <u>limited resources</u> (e.g. oil will eventually run out).

3) This means that we need to <u>plan carefully</u> to make sure that our activities today don't mess things up for <u>future generations</u> — this is the idea behind <u>sustainable development</u>...

> <u>SUSTAINABLE DEVELOPMENT</u> meets the needs of <u>today's</u> population <u>without</u> harming the ability of <u>future</u> generations to meet their own needs.

4) This isn't easy. It needs detailed thought at every level to make it happen —
e.g. <u>governments</u>, the people in charge at a <u>regional</u> level, etc.

Reduction in Biodiversity Could Be a Big Problem

1) Biodiversity is the <u>variety of different species</u> present in an area.

2) Ecosystems (especially tropical <u>rainforests</u>) can contain a <u>huge number</u> of different species, so when a habitat is destroyed there's a danger of <u>many species becoming extinct</u>.

3) This causes a number of problems:

> There are probably loads of <u>useful products</u> that we will <u>never know about</u> because the organisms that produced them have become extinct. <u>Plants</u> and <u>animals</u> are a great source of <u>new foods</u>, new fibres for <u>clothing</u> and <u>new medicines</u>.

> • Loss of one or more species from an ecosystem <u>unbalances it</u>, e.g. the extinct animal's predators may die out or be reduced.
> • Loss of biodiversity can have a '<u>snowball effect</u>' which prevents the ecosystem providing things we need, such as rich soil, clean water, and the oxygen we breathe.

Human Impact can be Measured Using Indicator Species

Getting an accurate picture of the human impact on the environment is hard.
One technique that's used involves <u>indicator species</u>.

1) Some <u>organisms</u> are very <u>sensitive to changes</u> in their environment. By studying these <u>indicator species</u>, scientists can see the effect of human activities.

2) For example, <u>air pollution</u> can be monitored by looking at types of <u>lichen</u>.
These give a good idea about the level of pollution because they're very sensitive to levels of pollutants such as <u>sulphur dioxide</u>.
The number and type of lichen at a particular location will indicate <u>how clean</u> the air is (e.g. the air is clean if there are <u>lots of lichen</u>).

3) Similarly, animals like <u>mayfly larvae</u> are <u>good indicators</u> for water pollution. If you find mayfly larvae in a river, it <u>indicates</u> that the <u>water is clean</u>.

Teenagers are an indicator species — not found in clean rooms...

In the exam, make sure you remember the details about the <u>environmental problems</u> that development can cause. If you get an essay-type question, stick 'em in to show off your '<u>scientific knowledge</u>'.

Recycling Materials

Many governments now accept a <u>balance</u> is needed between <u>economic development</u> (and therefore standards of living) and the <u>environment</u>. And recycling materials is usually much more environmentally friendly and cheaper than starting from scratch. So this is important stuff...

It's Important to Recycle

There are various reasons why...

① **Use less resources** — There's a <u>finite amount</u> of materials (e.g. metals, oil for plastics) in the Earth. Recycling <u>conserves</u> these resources.

② **Use less energy** — Mining, extracting and making materials need lots of <u>energy</u>, which mostly comes from burning <u>fossil fuels</u>.
Fossil fuels will <u>run out</u> one day, and they also cause <u>pollution</u>.
Recycling things like <u>copper</u>, <u>aluminium</u> and <u>glass</u> takes a <u>fraction</u> of the energy.

③ **Use less money** — Energy doesn't come cheap, so recycling <u>saves money</u> too.

④ **Make less rubbish** — Recycling also cuts down on the amount of rubbish we produce.

Global Dimming — Caused by Burning Fossil Fuels (maybe)

Over the last few years, some scientists have measured how much <u>sunlight</u> is reaching Earth.

They've found that in some areas nearly <u>25% less sunlight</u> has been reaching the surface compared to 50 years ago.
They've called this <u>global dimming</u>.

They think it's caused by <u>particles</u> of soot and ash that are produced when <u>fossil fuels</u> are burnt.

(There are many scientists who don't believe that the change is real though, and blame it on inaccurate recording equipment.)

London by night. (And by day too if global dimming gets really bad.)

There May be Economic and Environmental Benefits

1) Working out the <u>cost benefits</u> of recycling can get a bit <u>tricky</u>.

2) Recycling isn't free. There are <u>costs</u> involved in <u>collecting</u> waste material, <u>transporting</u> it, <u>sorting</u> it, and then <u>processing</u> it.

3) But if you didn't recycle, say, <u>aluminium</u>, you'd have to <u>mine</u> more aluminium ore.
But mining makes a mess of the <u>landscape</u> (and these mines are often in <u>rainforests</u>).
The ore then needs to be <u>transported</u>, and the aluminium <u>extracted</u> (which uses <u>loads</u> of electricity).
And don't forget the cost of sending your <u>used</u> aluminium to <u>landfill</u>.

4) But for every 1 kg of aluminium cans you recycle, you <u>save</u>:

- <u>95%</u> or so of the <u>energy</u> needed to mine and extract 'fresh' aluminium,
- <u>4 kg</u> of aluminium ore,
- a <u>lot</u> of waste.

In fact, aluminium's about the most cost-effective metal to recycle.

5) But even if all these differences were very <u>small</u>, maybe it's still worth recycling — you're getting people <u>involved</u> in doing their bit for the environment. Can't be a bad thing.

Hard work never killed anyone, but why take a chance...*

You can calculate the <u>financial</u> benefits of recycling any material, but remember there are the 'resources', 'energy' and 'rubbish' benefits too. With <u>paper</u>, <u>sustainable forests</u> are good (where for every tree you cut down, you plant another one), but that doesn't reduce the amount of <u>landfill</u>.

* This is presented here in aid of Recycle an Elderly Joke Week

Revision Summary for Section 5

The structure and atmosphere of the Earth, limestone, alkanes, alternative fuels — can they really belong in the same section, I almost hear you ask. Whether you find the topics easy or hard, interesting or dull, you need to learn it all before the exam. Try these questions... see how much you know:

1) How is glass made? Cement? Concrete?

2) List three environmental impacts of extracting rocks from the Earth.

3) Explain briefly the principle of fractional distillation.

4) Explain why rock salt is sometimes spread over roads in the winter.

5) Name four substances obtained from seawater or rock salt, and give a use for each.

6) What does crude oil consist of? Draw the full diagram of the fractional distillation of crude oil.

7) What are hydrocarbons?

8) What's the general formula for an alkane? What's the formula for a 5-carbon alkane?

9) What kind of carbon-carbon bond do alkenes have?

10) Draw the chemical structure of ethene.

11) What is "cracking"? Why is it done? What two conditions are needed for cracking to happen?

12) Give a typical example of a substance that is cracked, and the products that you get from cracking it.

13) Describe what you get from complete and incomplete combustion of hydrocarbons.

14) Explain how incomplete combustion can be harmful to humans.

15) Describe two ways in which oil slicks affect wildlife.

16) What is the lithosphere?

17) How does tectonic plate movement cause earthquakes?
What causes the Earth's tectonic plates to move?

18) For a long time, the Earth's early atmosphere was mostly CO_2. Where did this CO_2 come from?

19) Name the two main gases that make up the Earth's atmosphere today.

20) Describe two ways in which the atmosphere is changing today.

21) Suggest three ways in which a rising population affects the environment.

22) Name two "greenhouse gases". How do they affect the temperature of the Earth?

23) Sketch and label a diagram of the carbon cycle.

24) Which gases cause "acid rain"? How do they get into the air?
Describe two ways of reducing acid rain.

25) Describe what is meant by "photochemical smog".

26) Name a poisonous gas that catalytic converters help to remove from car exhausts.

27) Explain the benefits and difficulties of using hydrogen to power vehicles. Do the same for biogas.

28) Define sustainable development.

29) What are indicator species? Explain how lichen can be used as an indicator of air pollution.

30) Give four reasons why recycling is a good idea.

Polymers

Plastics are made up of lots of molecules joined together. They're like long chains.

Plastics are Long-Chain Molecules Called Polymers

1) Plastics are formed when lots of small molecules called monomers join together to give a polymer.

2) They're usually carbon based, and the monomers are very often alkenes — see p60.

Addition Polymers are Made Under High Pressure

1) The monomers that make up addition polymers have a double bond.

2) Under high pressure and with a catalyst (see p90), lots of these small molecules open up those double bonds and "join hands" (polymerise) to form long saturated chains called polymers.

Ethene becoming polyethene or "polythene", is the easiest example:

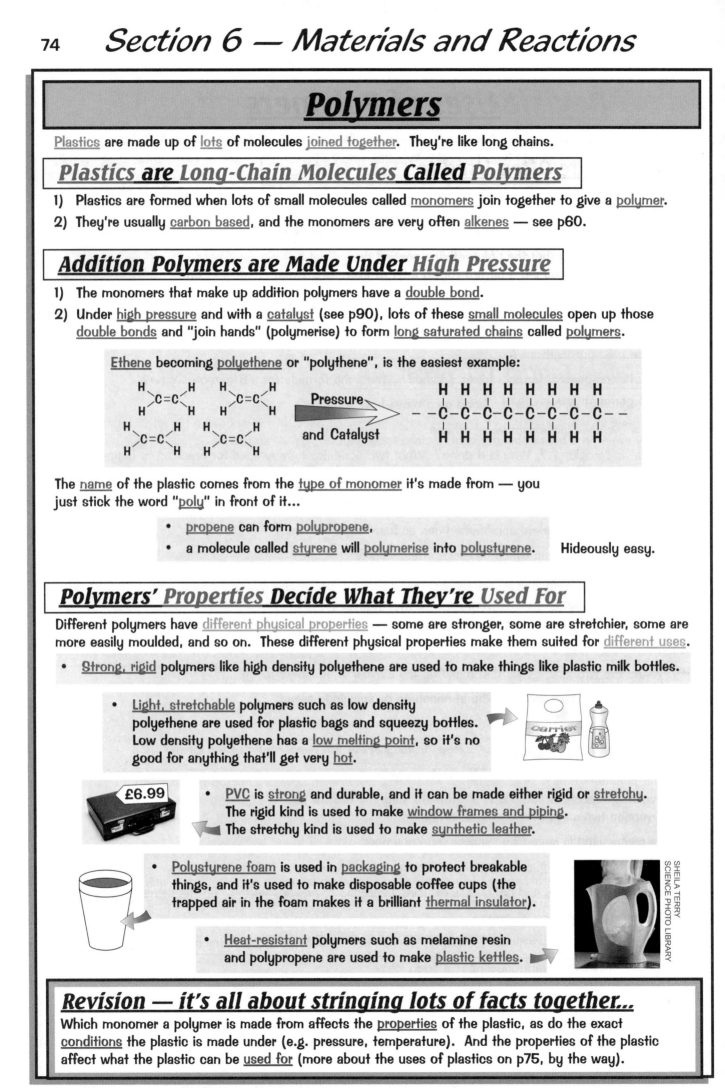

The name of the plastic comes from the type of monomer it's made from — you just stick the word "poly" in front of it...

- propene can form polypropene,
- a molecule called styrene will polymerise into polystyrene.   Hideously easy.

Polymers' Properties Decide What They're Used For

Different polymers have different physical properties — some are stronger, some are stretchier, some are more easily moulded, and so on. These different physical properties make them suited for different uses.

- Strong, rigid polymers like high density polyethene are used to make things like plastic milk bottles.

- Light, stretchable polymers such as low density polyethene are used for plastic bags and squeezy bottles. Low density polyethene has a low melting point, so it's no good for anything that'll get very hot.

- PVC is strong and durable, and it can be made either rigid or stretchy. The rigid kind is used to make window frames and piping. The stretchy kind is used to make synthetic leather.

- Polystyrene foam is used in packaging to protect breakable things, and it's used to make disposable coffee cups (the trapped air in the foam makes it a brilliant thermal insulator).

- Heat-resistant polymers such as melamine resin and polypropene are used to make plastic kettles.

SHEILA TERRY
SCIENCE PHOTO LIBRARY

Revision — it's all about stringing lots of facts together...

Which monomer a polymer is made from affects the properties of the plastic, as do the exact conditions the plastic is made under (e.g. pressure, temperature). And the properties of the plastic affect what the plastic can be used for (more about the uses of plastics on p75, by the way).

Uses of Polymers

Plastics are fantastically useful. You can make novelty football pencil sharpeners and all sorts.

Polymers are Often Used to Make Clothes

1) Nylon is a synthetic polymer often used to make clothes.

2) Fabrics made from nylon are not waterproof on their own, but can be coated with polyurethane to make tough, hard-wearing and waterproof outdoor clothing.

3) One big problem is that the polyurethane coating doesn't let water vapour pass through it. So if you get a bit hot (or do a bit of exercise), sweat condenses on the inside.

4) This makes skin and clothes get wet and uncomfortable — the material isn't breathable.

Breathable Fabrics Let Sweat Out

1) Some garments are made of breathable fabrics.

2) They have all the useful properties of nylon/polyurethane ones, but they have a big advantage... If you sweat in a breathable material, water vapour can escape — so there's no condensation.

> 1) Some breathable fabrics are made by combining a thin film of a plastic called expanded PTFE with a layer of another fabric, such as nylon. (PTFE on its own is too fragile.)
>
> 2) The PTFE film has tiny holes which let water vapour pass through — so it's breathable.
>
> water molecules pass through the tiny holes
>
> nylon
>
> 3) But it's waterproof, since the holes aren't big enough to let big water droplets through. Also the PTFE repels liquid water.
>
> PTFE film
>
> sweat evaporating from skin (as water vapour)
>
> raindrop too big to get through holes
>
> 4) This material is great for outdoorsy types — they can hike without getting rained on or soaked in sweat.

Non-biodegradable Plastics Cause Disposal Problems

1) Most polymers aren't "biodegradable" — they're not broken down by microorganisms, so they don't rot. This property is actually kind of useful until it's time to get rid of your plastic.

2) It's difficult to get rid of plastics — if you bury them in a landfill site, they'll still be there years later.

3) This means landfill sites fill up quickly and you need more of them, which is a waste of land. And a waste of plastic.

4) When plastics are burnt, some of them release gases such as acidic sulphur dioxide and poisonous hydrogen chloride and hydrogen cyanide. So burning's out, really. Plus it's a waste of plastic.

5) The best thing is to reuse plastics as many times as possible and then recycle them if you can. Sorting out lots of different plastics for recycling is difficult and expensive, though.

6) Chemists are working on a variety of ideas to produce biodegradable polymers.

Polymers — great until you don't need them any more...

If you're making a product, you need to pick your plastic carefully. It's no good trying to make a kettle out of a plastic that melts at 50 °C — you'll end up with a messy kitchen, a burnt hand and no cuppa. You'd also have a bit of difficulty trying to wear clothes made of brittle, unbendy plastic.

Paints and Pigments

Different minerals in the Earth are different colours, and these minerals have been used as pigments for thousands of years. Nowadays of course, you get those fancy paint mixing machines in DIY warehouses.

Pigments **Give Paints Their** Colours

1) Paint usually contains the following bits: solvent, binding medium and pigment.

2) The pigment gives the paint its colour.

3) The binding medium is a liquid that carries the pigment bits and holds them together.
   When the binding medium turns to solid, it sticks the pigments to the surface you've painted.

4) The solvent is the stuff that keeps the binding medium and pigment runny —
   as a liquid when it's in the tin or as a paste when it's still in the tube.

Paints are Colloids

1) A colloid consists of really tiny particles of one kind of stuff dispersed in (mixed in with) another kind of stuff. They're mixed in, but not dissolved.

2) The particles can be bits of solid, droplets of liquid or bubbles of gas.

3) In an oil paint, the pigment is in really tiny bits dispersed in the oil.
   And then the solvent (if there is one — there isn't always) dissolves the oil to keep it all runny.

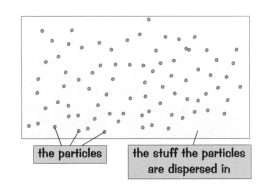

the particles | the stuff the particles are dispersed in

Some Paints are Water-based **and Some are** Oil-based

1) Emulsion paints are water-based.
   The solvent in the paint is water, and the binding medium is usually a polymer such as polyurethane, acrylic or latex.

2) Traditional gloss paint and artists' oil paints are oil-based.
   This time, the binding material is oil, and the solvent in the paint is an organic compound that'll dissolve oil.
   Turpentine is used as a solvent for artists' oil paints.
   Some solvents in oil-based paints produce fumes which can be harmful — it's best to make sure there's plenty of ventilation when using oil-based gloss.

Some modern gloss paints are water-based.

3) Whether you're creating a masterpiece in oils or painting your bedroom wall, you normally brush on the paint as a thin layer.
   The paint dries as the solvent evaporates.
   (A thin layer dries a heck of a lot quicker than a thick layer.)

4) With a water-based emulsion, the solvent evaporates, leaving behind the binder and pigment as a thin solid film. A thin layer of emulsion paint dries quite quickly.

The world was black and white before the 1950s — I saw it on TV...

There's heaps of different types of paint — and some are more suitable for certain jobs than others. Like if you're repainting your car, watercolours are definitely not the way to go. And likewise if you painted your little sister's face with gloss paint, your mum would probably ground you for a year.

Perfumes

Some things smell nice, some don't... it's all down to the chemicals a substance contains.

Perfumes **Can be** Natural **or** Artificial

1) Chemicals that smell nice are used as perfumes and air fresheners.

2) Esters are often used as perfumes as they usually smell quite pleasant.

3) Esters are pretty common in nature. Loads of common food smells (plus those in products like perfumes) contain natural esters.

4) Esters are also manufactured synthetically to enhance food flavours or aromas.

5) For example, there are esters (or combinations of esters) that smell of rum, apple, orange, pineapple, and so on. And esters are responsible for the distinctive smell of pear drops.

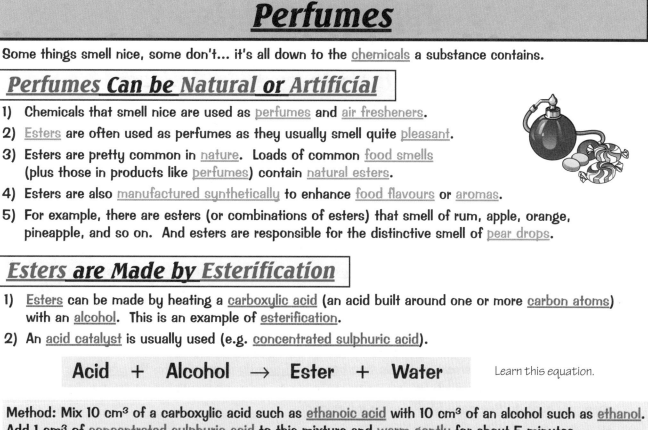

Esters **are Made by** Esterification

1) Esters can be made by heating a carboxylic acid (an acid built around one or more carbon atoms) with an alcohol. This is an example of esterification.

2) An acid catalyst is usually used (e.g. concentrated sulphuric acid).

| **Acid** + **Alcohol** → **Ester** + **Water** | *Learn this equation.* |

Method: Mix 10 cm³ of a carboxylic acid such as ethanoic acid with 10 cm³ of an alcohol such as ethanol. Add 1 cm³ of concentrated sulphuric acid to this mixture and warm gently for about 5 minutes. Tip the mixture into 150 cm³ of sodium carbonate solution (to neutralise the acids) and smell carefully (by wafting the smell towards your nose). The fruity-smelling product is the ester.

Perfumes **Need** Certain Properties

You can't use any old chemical with a smell as a perfume. You need a substance with certain properties:

1) Easily evaporates — or else the perfume particles won't reach your nose and you won't be able to smell it... bit useless really.

2) Non-toxic — it mustn't seep through your skin and poison you.

3) Doesn't react with water — or else it would react with the water in sweat.

4) Doesn't irritate the skin — or else you couldn't apply it directly to your neck or wrists. If you splash on any old substance you risk burning your skin.

5) Insoluble in water — if it was soluble in water it would wash off every time you got wet.

New **Perfumes and** Cosmetics **Have to be** Tested

1) Before new cosmetics are put on sale, they need to be tested thoroughly to make sure they're safe.

2) They should be non-toxic and shouldn't irritate the eyes or skin. Pretty obvious, I'm sure you'll agree. But some tests are carried out using animals, which is a bit more controversial.

Advantages of testing on animals	Disadvantages of testing on animals
We get an idea of whether they're likely to irritate the skin or be toxic before humans use them (though the results of an animal test won't necessarily apply to humans).	The tests could cause pain to the animals. And animals can't choose whether or not to take part in the tests. Using human volunteers instead could be a possibility in certain circumstances.

My dog's got no nose — how does he smell? *(Answer below)*

Perfume needs to smell nice, but not everyone agrees on what smells nice. Perfume also needs to be safe, but not everyone agrees on the best way to test for this. That's life for you.

Like I said, he's got no nose so he can't smell.

Fancy Materials

New materials are continually being developed. Their properties determine what they can be used for.

New Materials are Sometimes Invented by Accident

1) Teflon® is what the non-stick coating on non-stick saucepans is made from. It was discovered by accident. Scientists were trying to make a new refrigerant and came up with Teflon® instead.

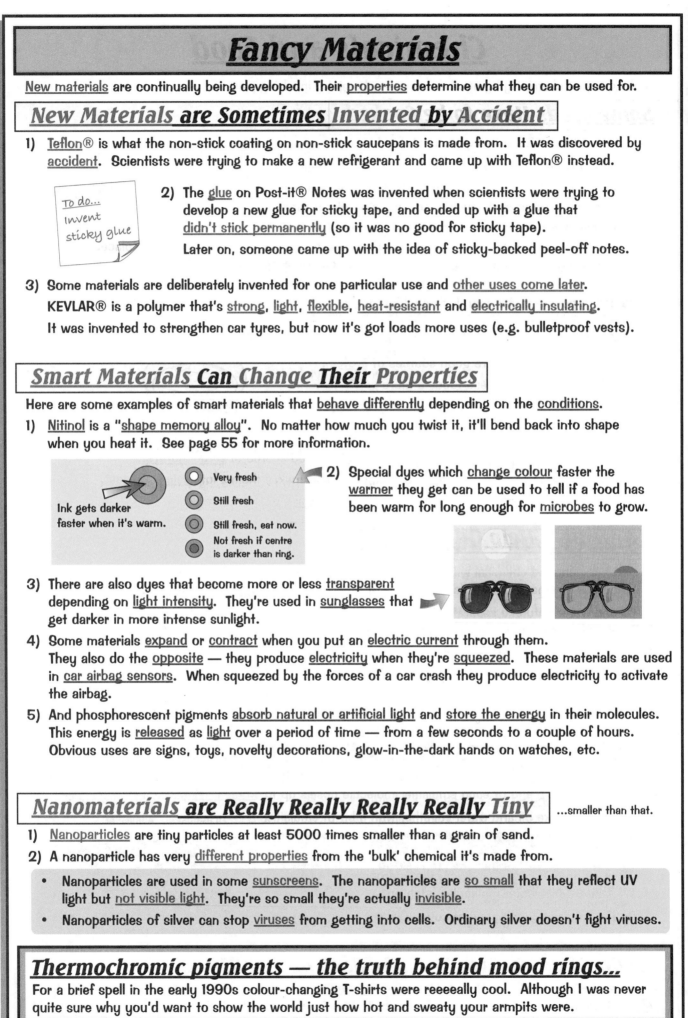

To do...
Invent
sticky glue

2) The glue on Post-it® Notes was invented when scientists were trying to develop a new glue for sticky tape, and ended up with a glue that didn't stick permanently (so it was no good for sticky tape).

Later on, someone came up with the idea of sticky-backed peel-off notes.

3) Some materials are deliberately invented for one particular use and other uses come later. KEVLAR® is a polymer that's strong, light, flexible, heat-resistant and electrically insulating. It was invented to strengthen car tyres, but now it's got loads more uses (e.g. bulletproof vests).

Smart Materials Can Change Their Properties

Here are some examples of smart materials that behave differently depending on the conditions.

1) Nitinol is a "shape memory alloy". No matter how much you twist it, it'll bend back into shape when you heat it. See page 55 for more information.

Ink gets darker faster when it's warm.

Very fresh
Still fresh
Still fresh, eat now.
Not fresh if centre is darker than ring.

2) Special dyes which change colour faster the warmer they get can be used to tell if a food has been warm for long enough for microbes to grow.

3) There are also dyes that become more or less transparent depending on light intensity. They're used in sunglasses that get darker in more intense sunlight.

4) Some materials expand or contract when you put an electric current through them. They also do the opposite — they produce electricity when they're squeezed. These materials are used in car airbag sensors. When squeezed by the forces of a car crash they produce electricity to activate the airbag.

5) And phosphorescent pigments absorb natural or artificial light and store the energy in their molecules. This energy is released as light over a period of time — from a few seconds to a couple of hours. Obvious uses are signs, toys, novelty decorations, glow-in-the-dark hands on watches, etc.

Nanomaterials are Really Really Really Really Tiny   ...smaller than that.

1) Nanoparticles are tiny particles at least 5000 times smaller than a grain of sand.

2) A nanoparticle has very different properties from the 'bulk' chemical it's made from.

- Nanoparticles are used in some sunscreens. The nanoparticles are so small that they reflect UV light but not visible light. They're so small they're actually invisible.

- Nanoparticles of silver can stop viruses from getting into cells. Ordinary silver doesn't fight viruses.

Thermochromic pigments — the truth behind mood rings...

For a brief spell in the early 1990s colour-changing T-shirts were reeeeally cool. Although I was never quite sure why you'd want to show the world just how hot and sweaty your armpits were.

Chemicals and Food

Cooking is just chemistry by another name — chemistry involving pies.

Some Foods Have to be Cooked

There are loads of different ways to cook food — e.g. boiling, steaming, grilling, frying...

1) Many foods have a better taste and texture when cooked.

2) Some foods are easier to digest once they're cooked (e.g. potatoes, flour).

3) The high temperatures involved in cooking also kill off those nasty little microbes that cause disease (see p23) — this is very important with meat.

4) Cooking food produces new substances. That means chemical changes have taken place. Once cooked, you can't change it back. The cooking process is irreversible.

5) Some foods are poisonous when raw, and must be cooked to make 'em edible — e.g. red kidney beans contain a poison that's only destroyed by at least 10 minutes boiling (and 2 hours cooking in total).

Example: Eggs and meat

- Eggs and meat are good sources of protein.
- Cooking gives these foods a more edible texture.

Example: Potatoes

- Potatoes are a good source of carbohydrates.
- Cooking potatoes makes them a lot easier to digest.

Emulsifiers Help Oil and Water Mix

1) You can mix an oil with water to make an emulsion.

   Emulsions are made up of lots of droplets of one liquid suspended in another liquid.

2) Oil and water naturally separate into two layers with the oil floating on top of the water — they don't "want" to mix. Emulsifiers help to stop the two liquids in an emulsion from separating out.

3) Mayonnaise, low-fat spread and ice cream are foods which contain emulsifiers.

4) Emulsifiers are molecules with one part that's attracted to water and another part that's attracted to oil or fat. The bit that's attracted to water is called hydrophilic, and the bit that's attracted to oil is called hydrophobic.

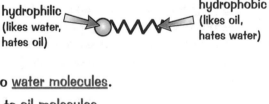

emulsifier molecule

hydrophilic (likes water, hates oil)

hydrophobic (likes oil, hates water)

5) The hydrophilic end of each emulsifier molecule latches onto water molecules.

6) The hydrophobic end of each emulsifier molecule cosies up to oil molecules.

7) When you shake oil and water together with a bit of emulsifier, the oil forms droplets, surrounded by a coating of emulsifier... with the hydrophilic bit facing outwards.

   Other oil droplets are repelled by the hydrophilic bit of the emulsifier, while water molecules latch on.

   So the emulsion won't separate out. Clever.

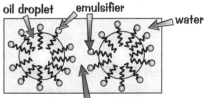

oil droplet emulsifier water

oil droplets can't join together

You'll need to learn this page for your eggsam...

When you cook something, you're bringing about chemical change. The changes are irreversible, as you'll know if you've ever tried to unscramble an egg.

Food Additives

Humans have been adding stuff to food for years. Before fridges were invented, we added salt to meat to stop it going off. Now we use additives not just to preserve food, but to make it look or taste different.

Processed Foods Often Contain Additives

1) Food manufacturers add various chemical compounds to food to improve its appearance, taste, texture and shelf life. These additives must be listed in the ingredients list on the back of the packet.

2) Most additives used in the UK have E-numbers.
   Additives with E-numbers have passed safety tests and can be used in Europe.

   • Preservatives help food stay fresh. Without them, more food would go off and need throwing away.
   • Some foods 'go off' after reacting with oxygen — e.g. butter goes rancid.
     Antioxidants are added to foods that contain fat or oil to stop them reacting so quickly with oxygen.
   • Colourings and flavourings make food look and taste better.
   • Emulsifiers and stabilisers stop emulsions like mayonnaise (see page 79) from separating out.
   • Sweeteners can replace sugar in some processed foods — helpful to diabetics and dieters.

There Are Natural and Synthetic Additives

1) Some food additives are of natural origin, e.g. lecithin from soya beans.
   Some synthetic additives are identical to natural substances.
   Others are completely new synthetic substances.

2) Some people think that some synthetic food colourings make children hyperactive.
   But many scientific studies haven't found any connection between additives and hyperactivity at all.

3) A small number of people are allergic to some additives, for example the food dye tartrazine.

4) Some additives aren't suitable for vegetarians. For example, the food colouring cochineal comes from crushed insects. And gelatin from animal bones is used to thicken and set some foods.

Artificial Colours Can Be Detected by Chromatography

To identify different colourings in a food sample, you can use chromatography.

Paper chromatography uses the fact that different dyes wash through wet filter paper at different rates.

Here's how you'd analyse food colourings...

1) Extract the colour from each food sample by placing it in a small cup with a few drops of solvent (e.g. water, ethanol, salt water etc). Use a different cup for each different food sample.

2) Put spots of each coloured solution on a pencil baseline on filter paper. (Label them in pencil — don't use pen because it might dissolve in the solvent and confuse everything.)

3) Roll up the sheet and put it in a beaker with some solvent — but keep the baseline above the level of the solvent.

4) The solvent seeps up the paper, taking the food dyes with it. Different dyes form spots in different places.

5) Watch out though — a chromatogram with four spots means at least four dyes, not exactly four dyes. There could be five dyes, with two of them making a spot in the same place.

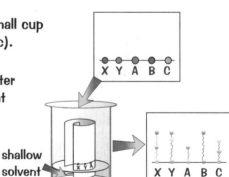

shallow solvent

Long shelf life — sounds very cramped...

Chromatography can separate even complex mixtures if you choose the right equipment and conditions. On a different note, there's a lot about food additives in the media. Some reports are based on facts, but not all of them. Without evidence to support a claim, it's not worth a bean.

Plant Oils in Food

Plant oils come from plants. I know it's tricky, but just do your best to remember.

We Can Extract Oils from Plants

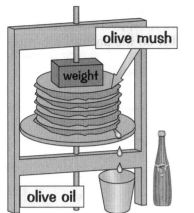

olive mush

weight

olive oil

1) Some fruits and seeds contain a lot of oil.
   For example, avocados and olives are oily fruits.
2) These oils can be extracted and used for food or for fuel.
3) To get the oil out, the plant material is crushed.
   The next step is to press the crushed plant material between metal plates and squash the oil out.
4) Oil can be separated from crushed plant material by a centrifuge — rather like using a spin-dryer to get water out of wet clothes.
   Or solvents can be used to get the oil from the plant material.
5) Distillation is used to refine the oil, and it also removes water, solvents and impurities.

Vegetable Oils Are Used in Food

1) Vegetable oils provide a lot of energy.
2) There are other nutrients in vegetable oils too.
   For example, vegetable oils contain essential fatty acids. And oils from seeds contain vitamin E.
3) Vegetable oils tend to be unsaturated, while animal fats tend to be saturated.
4) In general, saturated fats are less healthy than unsaturated fats.
5) Saturated fats increase the amount of cholesterol in the blood, which can block up the arteries and increase the risk of heart disease.

- Oils and fats contain long-chains of carbon atoms. They can be either unsaturated (with C=C double bonds) or saturated (without double bonds).
- C=C double bonds can be detected using bromine or iodine.
  An unsaturated oil will decolourise bromine water or iodine water (as the bromine or iodine opens up the double bond and joins on).

bromine water decolourises

Unsaturated Oils Can Be Hydrogenated

1) Unsaturated vegetable oils are liquid at room temperature.
2) They can be hardened by reacting them with hydrogen in the presence of a nickel catalyst at about 60 °C.

   This is called hydrogenation. The hydrogen reacts with the double-bonded carbons and opens out the double bonds.

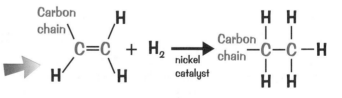

3) Hydrogenated oils have higher melting points than unsaturated oils, so they're more solid at room temperature. This makes them useful in spreads and for baking cakes.
4) Margarine is usually made from partially hydrogenated vegetable oil — turning all the double bonds in vegetable oil to single bonds would make margarine too hard and difficult to spread. Hydrogenating most of them gives margarine a nice, buttery, spreadable consistency.

Double bonds — licensed to saturate...

In a nutshell... there's saturated and unsaturated fats, which are generally bad and good for you (in that order). And too much of the wrong types of fats can lead to heart disease. Got that...

Plant Oils as Fuel

Fuel from vegetable oil is possible too — but as always, you have to weigh up the pros and cons.

Vegetable Oils Can Be Used to Produce Fuels

1) Vegetable oils such as rapeseed oil and soybean oil can be processed and turned into fuels.

2) Vegetable oil provides a lot of energy — that's why it's suitable for use as a fuel.

3) A particularly useful fuel made from vegetable oils is called biodiesel. Biodiesel has similar properties to ordinary diesel fuel — it burns in the same way, so you can use it to fuel a diesel engine.

4) Most diesel engines can burn 100% biodiesel, but usually biodiesel is mixed with ordinary diesel.

5) Engines burning biodiesel produce 90% as much power as engines burning ordinary diesel.

Biodiesel is a Renewable Fuel

1) Biodiesel comes from plant crops, which can be planted and harvested every year. You can always keep making biodiesel.

2) Compare this to ordinary diesel, which is made by distilling crude oil. Crude oil was formed millions of years ago and it'll take millions of years to make more — once it runs low that's it.

Biodiesel Releases Less Pollution than Ordinary Diesel

1) Engines burning biodiesel produce much less sulphur dioxide pollution than engines burning diesel or petrol.

2) Burning biodiesel doesn't release as many "particulates" as burning diesel or petrol.

> Particulates are little pieces of solid crud that you get in smoke and car exhausts.

3) Biodiesel is also biodegradable and it's less toxic than regular diesel.

4) Biodiesel engines do release the same amount of carbon dioxide (CO_2) as ordinary diesel engines. BUT biodiesel comes from recently grown plants. The plants took in carbon dioxide from the air when they were alive, and it's this same carbon which is released again when the biodiesel is burned. So net increase in carbon dioxide in the atmosphere: nil.

5) Regular diesel, on the other hand, comes from crude oil, which has been under the ground for millions of years. The carbon in crude oil was taken out of the atmosphere millions of years ago. Burning regular diesel does create a net increase in carbon dioxide in the atmosphere.

Biodiesel is Expensive and It's Difficult to Make Enough

1) We can't make enough biodiesel to replace regular diesel — there aren't enough veg oil crops. Biodiesel can be made from used vegetable oil, but there isn't enough of that either.

2) Because of this, biodiesel is expensive. Most people won't want to use it until it's cheaper.

3) Biodiesel has fewer drawbacks than some other "green" car fuels like biogas or electricity, though. Car engines need modification to run on gas — most diesel cars run on biodiesel without any tinkering. And biodiesel could use the same filling stations and pumps as diesel. (Compare this with electric cars, which would need a new network of recharging stations.)

Plant oils — but don't be too upset if they won't grow...

In Science, you need to be able to use scientific evidence to weigh up the pros and cons of an idea. And you can't stop there — you have to take into account the social, economic and ethical issues too.

Ethanol

There are different kinds of alcohol, but the one that's in beer, wine and so on is ethanol.

Ethanol Can be Made by Fermentation

1) Fermentation is the process of using yeast to convert sugars into ethanol. Carbon dioxide is also produced. Which my Dad discovered when his homebrew exploded one year.

This is the formula for glucose — a common sugar.

The products are ethanol and carbon dioxide.

$$C_6H_{12}O_6 \xrightarrow{\text{yeast}} 2C_2H_5OH + 2CO_2$$

2) The yeast cells contain an enzyme (a naturally occurring catalyst.)

3) Fermentation happens fastest at a temperature of about 30 °C. At lower temperatures, the reaction slows down. If it's too hot the enzyme in the yeast is destroyed.

4) It's important to prevent oxygen getting to the fermentation process. If oxygen is present, a different reaction happens and you don't get ethanol.

5) When the concentration of alcohol reaches about 10 to 20%, the fermentation reaction stops, because the yeast gets killed off by the alcohol.

6) Different types of alcoholic drinks are made using sugars from different sources — usually from grains, fruits or vegetables, e.g. barley is used to make beer and grapes are used for making wine.

7) The fermented mixture can be distilled to produce more concentrated alcohol. Brandy is distilled from wine, whisky is distilled from fermented grain and vodka's distilled from fermented grain or potatoes.

8) The ethanol produced this way can also be used as quite a cheap fuel in countries which don't have oil reserves for making petrol (see below).

Ethene Can be Reacted with Steam to Produce Ethanol

1) Ethene (C_2H_4) will react with steam (H_2O) to make ethanol.

2) The reaction needs a temperature of 300 °C and a pressure of 70 atmospheres.

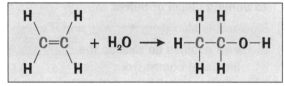

3) Phosphoric acid is used as a catalyst.

4) At the moment this is a cheap process, because ethene's fairly cheap and not much of it is wasted.

5) The trouble is that ethene's produced from crude oil, which is a non-renewable resource and which will start running out fairly soon. This means using ethene to make ethanol will become very expensive.

Alcohol Can be Used as a Fuel

1) Ethanol can be used as fuel. It burns to give just CO_2 and water.

2) Cars can be adapted to run on a mixture of about 10% ethanol and 90% petrol — 'gasohol'.

3) Some countries (e.g. Brazil) make extensive use of gasohol. It's best used in areas where there's plenty of fertile land for growing the crops needed, and good crop-growing weather.

4) Using gasohol instead of pure petrol means that less crude oil is being used. Another advantage is the crops needed for ethanol production absorb CO_2 from the atmosphere in photosynthesis while growing. This goes some way towards balancing out the release of CO_2 when the gasohol is burnt.

5) But distilling the ethanol after fermentation needs a lot of energy, so it's not a perfect solution.

Excessive ethanol drinking — when a tipple becomes a topple...

People have been making alcohol for thousands of years. It could explain why there are so many ancient ruins all over the place — the Romans were always too drunk to finish the job properly...

Hydration and Thermal Decomposition

There are different kinds of chemical reaction you need to get your head round —
including hydration, dehydration and thermal decomposition.

Hydration Reactions have Water as a Reactant

Hydration reactions are ones where water reacts with another substance to form a new product.

Example 1: Calcium oxide (quicklime) reacts with water to produce calcium hydroxide (slaked lime).

| Calcium oxide + water → calcium hydroxide | $CaO + H_2O → Ca(OH)_2$ |

Example 2: Ethene (C_2H_4) will react with steam (H_2O) to make ethanol.

| ethene + steam → ethanol | $C_2H_4 + H_2O → C_2H_5OH$ |

Dehydration Reactions have Water as a Product

Dehydration reactions are where water is removed from one or more substances, forming new products.

Example 1: Dehydration reactions separate carbohydrates into carbon and water.
Concentrated sulphuric acid is a strong dehydrating agent, and it'll grab water from
sucrose (sugar) to turn it into water and a spongy lump of black carbon.

$$sucrose \xrightarrow[\text{sulphuric acid}]{\text{Catalyst of conc.}} carbon + water$$

Your teacher might demonstrate this in the fume cupboard.

Reactions which join small molecules together to make a bigger molecule
sometimes produce a molecule of water as well. These are usually called
condensation reactions, but they're a kind of dehydration reaction too.

Example 2: Alcohol reacts with organic acids to form an ester and water.

| ethanol + ethanoic acid → ethyl ethanoate + water |

Carbonates and Hydrogencarbonates Release CO_2 when Heated

1) Carbonates and hydrogencarbonates release carbon dioxide gas (CO_2) when they're heated.

2) It's an example of thermal decomposition, which is when a substance
breaks down into simpler substances when heated.

3) Learn the word equations for the thermal decomposition of carbonates and hydrogencarbonates:

E.g.
| calcium carbonate → calcium oxide + carbon dioxide |

| sodium hydrogencarbonate → sodium carbonate + carbon dioxide + water |

4) You can check it really is carbon dioxide that's released by testing it with
limewater — CO_2 turns limewater cloudy when it's bubbled through.

5) Baking powder contains sodium hydrogencarbonate. Baking
powder is added to cake mixture — the carbon dioxide
produced when it's heated in the oven makes the cake rise.

CO₂ gas

Limewater

Thermal decomposition — when your vest unravels...

Dehydration reactions take away hydrogen and oxygen from a molecule and produce new products —
dehydrating sugar doesn't give you dry sugar, it gives you carbon.

Neutralisation and Oxidation

Have a look at this stuff on acids and bases.

Substances can be Acids, Bases or Neutral

There's a sliding scale from very strong acid to very strong base, with neutral water in the middle.

These are the colours you get when you add universal indicator to an acid or an alkali.

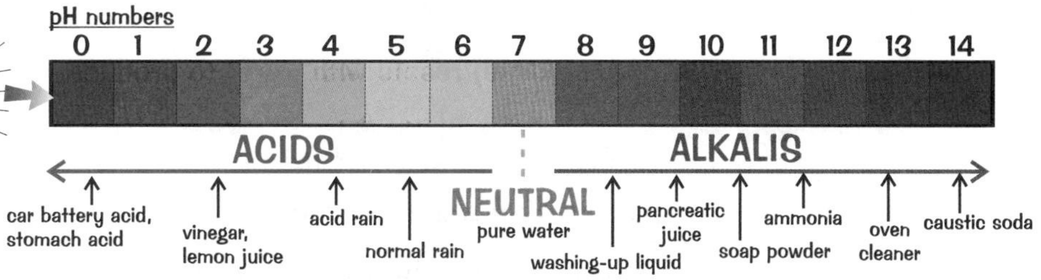

An alkali is a soluble base.

pH numbers
0 1 2 3 4 5 6 7 8 9 10 11 12 13 14

ACIDS   NEUTRAL   ALKALIS

car battery acid, stomach acid — vinegar, lemon juice — acid rain — normal rain — NEUTRAL pure water — pancreatic juice — washing-up liquid — ammonia — soap powder — oven cleaner — caustic soda

Metal Oxides and Metal Hydroxides are Often Bases

1) An acid and a base react together to form a salt and water.

   The products of the reaction aren't strongly acidic or alkaline — they're neutral.
   So it's called a neutralisation reaction.
   This is the equation for any neutralisation reaction:

   Acid + base → salt + water

2) Metal oxides and metal hydroxides are generally bases.
   This means they'll react with acids to form
   a salt and water.

   Acid + Metal Oxide → Salt + Water
   Acid + Metal Hydroxide → Salt + Water

The Combination of Metal and Acid Decides the Salt

Here are a couple of examples — an acid with: (i) a metal oxide, and (ii) a metal hydroxide...

| Hydrochloric acid | + | Copper oxide | → | Copper chloride | + | water |
| $2HCl$ | + | CuO | → | $CuCl_2$ | + | H_2O |

| Sulphuric acid | + | Calcium hydroxide | → | Calcium sulphate | + | water |
| H_2SO_4 | + | $Ca(OH)_2$ | → | $CaSO_4$ | + | $2H_2O$ |

Rust is an Example of a Metal Oxide

The word "rust" is only used for the corrosion of iron, not other metals.

Iron corrodes easily. In other words, it rusts.

1) When iron rusts, it's combining with oxygen (and also water).
   The iron gains oxygen to form iron(III) oxide. Water then becomes loosely bonded
   to the iron(III) oxide and the result is hydrated iron(III) oxide — which we call rust.

2) Unfortunately, rust is a soft crumbly solid that soon flakes off to leave more iron available to rust.
   And if the water's salty or acidic, rusting will take place a lot quicker.

   Cars in coastal places rust a lot because they get covered in salty sea spray.
   Cars in dry deserty places hardly rust at all.

3) Aluminium is used to make some cars, as it doesn't corrode. The metal on the surface oxidises to
   form aluminium oxide, but the aluminium oxide forms a tough protective coating — very unlike rust.
   But the downside is that aluminium is more expensive than steel.

If you've learned all this, then you probably deserve a good rest...

In everyday life, 'salt' means table salt. But there are loads of different kinds of salts. Some are used
in fertilisers (e.g. ammonium nitrate, ammonium phosphate), others are in fireworks (they're often
used to supply the colour of the explosion — e.g. calcium chloride gives an orange flash, copper
chloride gives a bluey-green one). Aye... they're dead useful, and need learning about. So get to it...

Chemical Tests

If you have a mystery substance, there are various chemical tests you can do to find out what it is.

Flame Tests — Spot the Colour

1) Some metals give a characteristic <u>colour</u> when heated, as you see every November 5th when a <u>firework explodes</u>. So, remember, remember...

> (i) <u>Sodium</u>, Na, burns with a yellow/orange flame.
> (ii) <u>Potassium</u>, K, burns with a lilac flame.
> (iii) <u>Calcium</u>, Ca, burns with a brick-red flame.
> (iv) <u>Copper</u>, Cu, burns with a blue-green flame.

2) So if you stick a bit of <u>copper wire</u> in a Bunsen flame, you'll see a <u>blue-green flame</u>.

3) But flame tests don't just work when you've got a sample of a <u>pure element</u> — they also work with a <u>compound</u> that contains that element. So if you stick a sample of, say, <u>copper sulphate</u> in a Bunsen flame, you'll also see a <u>blue-green flame</u>. Marvellous.

4) So, for example, a <u>forensic scientist</u> might examine a sample of <u>white crystals</u> found at a <u>crime scene</u>. The scientist could perform a <u>flame test</u> on the crystals and see that they burn with a <u>lilac coloured flame</u>. This test would show that the crystals must contain <u>potassium</u>.

To flame-test a compound, dip a <u>clean wire loop</u> into a sample of the compound, and put the wire loop in the clear blue part of the Bunsen flame (the hottest bit).

Add Sodium Hydroxide and Look for a Coloured Precipitate

1) You can sometimes find out what metal an <u>unknown substance</u> (e.g. a salt) contains by adding it (in solution) to <u>sodium hydroxide solution</u>.

2) When you do this a <u>chemical reaction</u> occurs and a <u>solid substance</u> containing the metal is formed (this solid substance is called a <u>precipitate</u>).

3) The precipitate has a <u>characteristic colour</u> which depends on the <u>metal</u> it contains.

4) Here are some typical precipitate colours...

sodium hydroxide (NaOH) solution → chemical reaction forms precipitate

mystery compound in solution → precipitate containing metal

Metal	Colour of precipitate
Copper	Blue
Iron	Sludgy red or sludgy green
Zinc	White

There are Tests for 5 Common Gases

1) Chlorine Chlorine <u>bleaches</u> damp <u>litmus paper</u>, turning it white. (It may turn <u>red</u> for a moment first though — that's because a solution of chlorine is <u>acidic</u>.)

Damp litmus paper

Glowing splint

2) Oxygen Oxygen <u>relights</u> a <u>glowing splint</u>.

3) Carbon Dioxide Carbon dioxide <u>turns limewater cloudy</u> — just bubble the gas through a test tube of limewater and watch what happens.

CO_2 gas

Limewater

Squeaky Pop!

4) Hydrogen Hydrogen makes a "<u>squeaky pop</u>" with a <u>lighted splint</u>. (as the hydrogen burns, forming water).

5) Ammonia Ammonia <u>turns</u> damp <u>red litmus paper blue</u> (and has a very strong <u>smell</u>).

ammonia

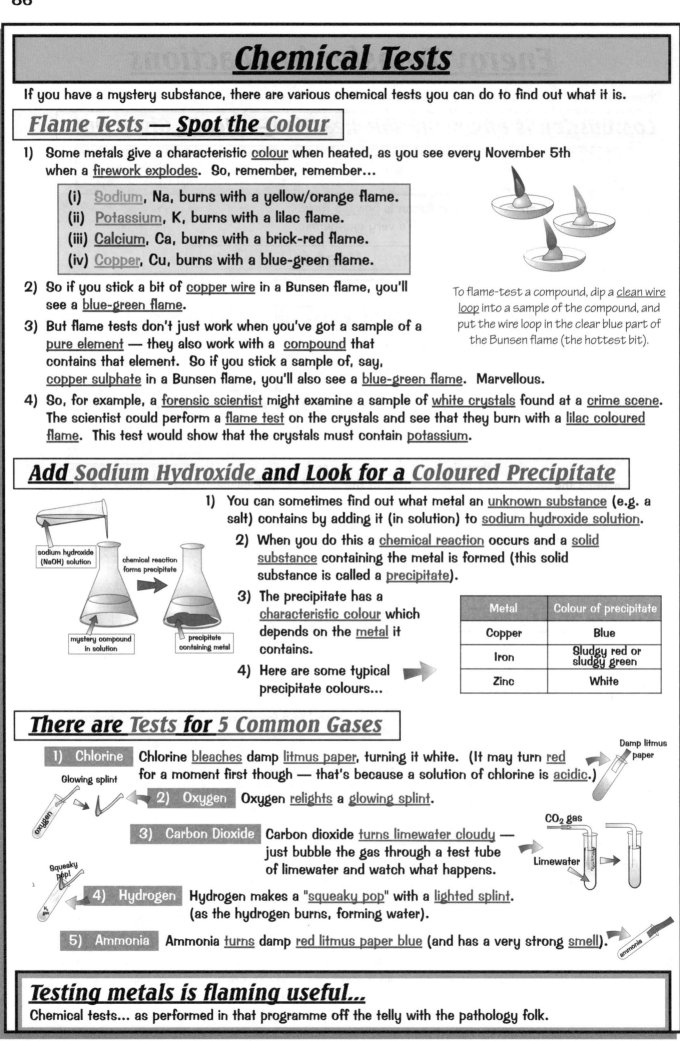

Testing metals is flaming useful...

Chemical tests... as performed in that programme off the telly with the pathology folk.

Energy Transfer in Reactions

Chemical reactions can either _release_ heat energy, or _take in_ heat energy.

Combustion is an Exothermic Reaction — Heat's Given Out

An **EXOTHERMIC REACTION** is one which **GIVES OUT ENERGY** to the surroundings, usually in the form of **HEAT**, which is shown by a **RISE IN TEMPERATURE**.

The best example of an exothermic reaction is burning fuels.
This obviously gives out a lot of heat — it's very exothermic.

In an Endothermic Reaction, Heat is Taken In

An **ENDOTHERMIC REACTION** is one which **TAKES IN ENERGY** from the surroundings, usually in the form of **HEAT**, which is shown by a **FALL IN TEMPERATURE**.

Endothermic reactions are less common and less easy to spot. One example is thermal decomposition.
Heat must be supplied to cause the compound to decompose (see page 84, or cracking on p61).

Temperature Changes Help Decide If a Reaction's Exo or Endo

1) You can measure the amount of energy produced by a chemical reaction (in solution) by taking the temperature of the reactants, mixing them in a polystyrene cup and measuring the temperature of the solution at the end of the reaction. Easy.

2) Adding an acid to an alkali is an exothermic reaction. Measure the temperature of the alkali before you add the acid, then measure the temperature again after adding the acid and mixing — you'll see an increase in temperature.

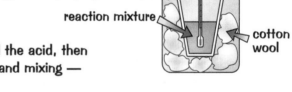

thermometer
lid
polystyrene cup
reaction mixture
cotton wool

Energy Must Always be Supplied to Break Bonds... ...and Energy is Always Released When Bonds Form

1) During a chemical reaction, old bonds are broken and new bonds are formed.

2) Energy must be supplied to break existing bonds — so bond breaking is an endothermic process.

3) Energy is released when new bonds are formed — so bond formation is an exothermic process.

BOND BREAKING - ENDOTHERMIC

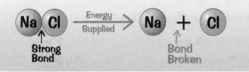

BOND FORMING - EXOTHERMIC

4) In an exothermic reaction, the energy released in bond formation is greater than the energy used in breaking old bonds.

5) In an endothermic reaction, the energy required to break old bonds is greater than the energy released when new bonds are formed.

Chemistry in "real-world application" shocker...

When you see Stevie Gerrard hobble off the pitch and press a bag to his leg, he's using an endothermic reaction. The cold pack contains an inner bag full of water and an outer one full of ammonium nitrate. When he presses the pack the inner bag breaks and they mix together. The ammonium nitrate dissolves in the water and, as this is an endothermic reaction, it draws in heat from Stevie's injured leg.

Forces Between Particles

You can explain a lot of things (including <u>perfumes</u>) if you get your head round this lot.

States of Matter — Depend on the Forces Between Particles

All stuff is made of <u>particles</u> (molecules, ions or atoms) that are <u>constantly moving</u>, and the <u>forces</u> between these particles can be weak or strong, depending on whether it's a <u>solid</u>, <u>liquid</u> or a <u>gas</u>.

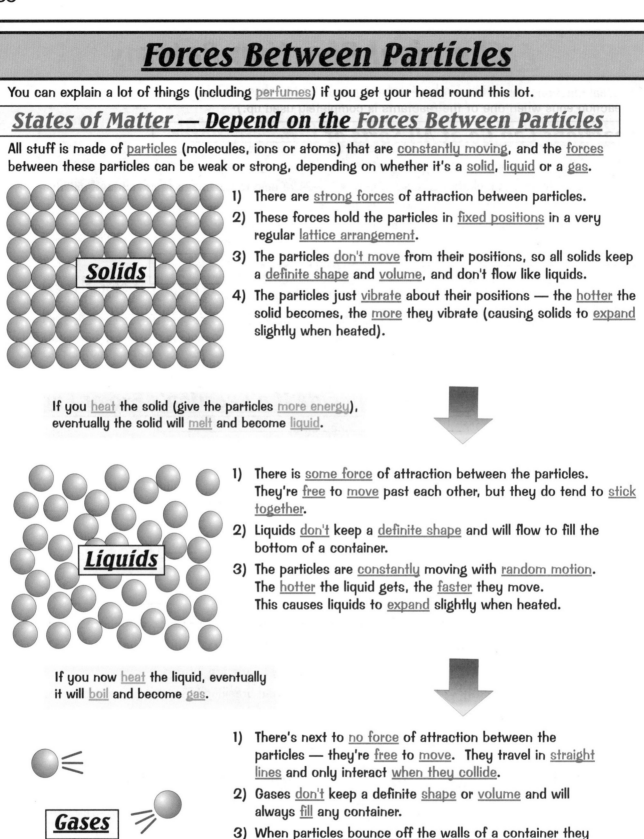

Solids

1) There are <u>strong forces</u> of attraction between particles.
2) These forces hold the particles in <u>fixed positions</u> in a very regular <u>lattice arrangement</u>.
3) The particles <u>don't move</u> from their positions, so all solids keep a <u>definite shape</u> and <u>volume</u>, and don't flow like liquids.
4) The particles just <u>vibrate</u> about their positions — the <u>hotter</u> the solid becomes, the <u>more</u> they vibrate (causing solids to <u>expand</u> slightly when heated).

If you <u>heat</u> the solid (give the particles <u>more energy</u>), eventually the solid will <u>melt</u> and become <u>liquid</u>.

Liquids

1) There is <u>some force</u> of attraction between the particles. They're <u>free</u> to <u>move</u> past each other, but they do tend to <u>stick together</u>.
2) Liquids <u>don't</u> keep a <u>definite shape</u> and will flow to fill the bottom of a container.
3) The particles are <u>constantly</u> moving with <u>random motion</u>. The <u>hotter</u> the liquid gets, the <u>faster</u> they move. This causes liquids to <u>expand</u> slightly when heated.

If you now <u>heat</u> the liquid, eventually it will <u>boil</u> and become <u>gas</u>.

Gases

1) There's next to <u>no force</u> of attraction between the particles — they're <u>free</u> to <u>move</u>. They travel in <u>straight lines</u> and only interact <u>when they collide</u>.
2) Gases <u>don't</u> keep a definite <u>shape</u> or <u>volume</u> and will always <u>fill</u> any container.
3) When particles bounce off the walls of a container they exert a <u>pressure</u> on the walls.
4) The particles move <u>constantly</u> with <u>random motion</u>. The <u>hotter</u> the gas gets, the <u>faster</u> they move. Gases either <u>expand</u> when heated, or their <u>pressure increases</u>.

Don't get yourself in a state about all this — just learn it...

Right then... a nice easy page for you. <u>But it still needs learning</u>. So close the book and draw the three diagrams. Then write a description of what's going on in each one. If you miss any points out, then do it again. And again, if you have to, until you get it spot on. You'll be glad you did it one day.

Chemical Reaction Rates

The rate of a chemical reaction is how fast the reactants are changed into products.
(A reaction ends when one of the reactants is completely used up.)

Reactions Can Go at All Sorts of Different Rates

1) One of the slowest is the rusting of iron (it's not slow enough though — what about my little MGB).

2) Other slow reactions include chemical weathering — like acid rain damage to limestone buildings.

3) Burning is a fast reaction, but an explosion is really fast and releases
   a lot of gas. Explosive reactions are all over in a fraction of a second.

You Can Do an Experiment to Follow a Reaction

The rate of a reaction that produces a gas can be observed by measuring how quickly the gas is produced.
There are two ways of doing this:

MEASURE THE CHANGE IN MASS

If you carry out the reaction on a balance, the mass will fall as the gas is
released. You need to take readings of the mass at regular time intervals.

MEASURE THE VOLUME OF GAS GIVEN OFF

This method is pretty similar, except you use a gas syringe to
measure the volume of gas given off after regular time intervals.

Whichever of these methods you use, you can plot your results on a graph...

The Rate of a Reaction Depends on Four Things:

① TEMPERATURE   ③ SIZE OF PARTICLES — (or SURFACE AREA)
② CONCENTRATION — (or PRESSURE for gases)   ④ CATALYSTS (see p90 for more info)

The plot below shows how the speed of a particular reaction varies under different conditions.
The quickest reaction is shown by the steepest line — this will be the one that becomes flat fastest.

1) Graph 1 represents the original fairly slow reaction.

2) Graphs 2 and 3 represent the reaction taking place quicker
   but with the same initial amounts. (Notice that the slope
   of the graphs is steeper than for the original reaction.)

3) The increased rate could be due to any of these:

   > a) increase in temperature
   > b) increase in concentration (or pressure)
   > c) catalyst added
   > d) solid reactant crushed up into smaller bits.

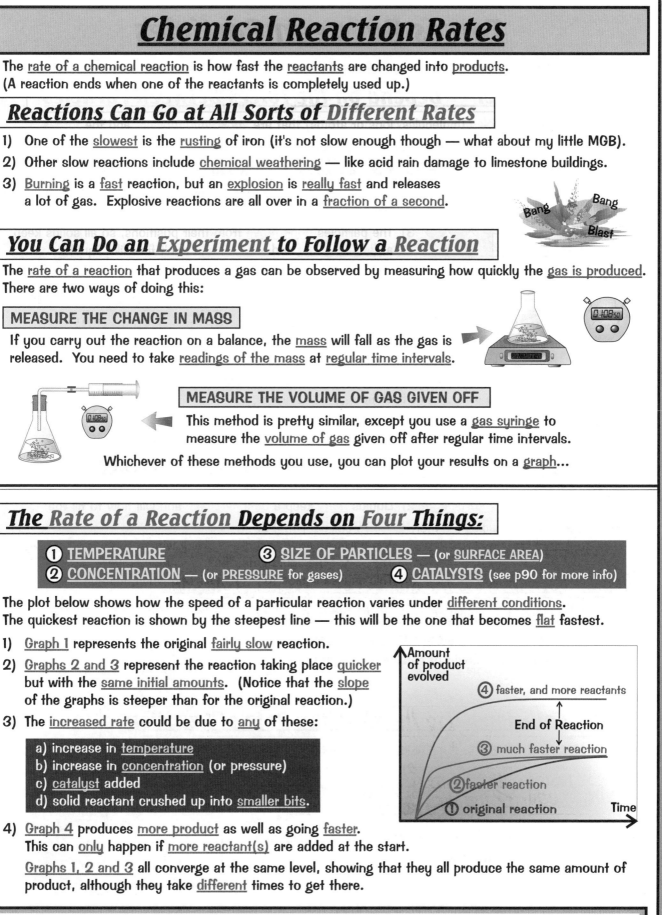

4) Graph 4 produces more product as well as going faster.
   This can only happen if more reactant(s) are added at the start.

   Graphs 1, 2 and 3 all converge at the same level, showing that they all produce the same amount of
   product, although they take different times to get there.

Get a fast, furious reaction — tickle your teacher...

First off... remember that the amount of product you get depends on the amount of reactants you start
with. So all this stuff about the rate of a reaction is only talking about how quickly your products form
— not how much of them you get. It's an important difference — so get your head round it asap.

Collision Theory

Reaction rates are explained perfectly by Collision Theory. It's really simple.

It just says that the rate of a reaction simply depends on how often and how hard the reacting particles collide with each other. The basic idea is that particles have to collide in order to react, and they have to collide hard enough as well.

More Collisions Increases the Rate of Reaction

All four methods of increasing the rate of reactions can be explained in terms of increasing the number of successful collisions between the reacting particles:

1) TEMPERATURE Increases the Number of Collisions

When the temperature is increased the particles all move quicker. If they're moving quicker, they're going to have more collisions.

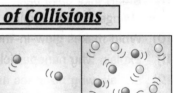

2) CONCENTRATION (or PRESSURE) Increases the Number of Collisions

If a solution is made more concentrated it means there are more particles of reactant knocking about between the water molecules, which makes collisions between the important particles more likely.

In a gas, increasing the pressure means the molecules are more squashed up together so there are going to be more collisions.

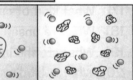

3) SIZE OF SOLID PARTICLES (or SURFACE AREA) Increases Collisions

If one of the reactants is a solid then breaking it up into smaller pieces will increase its surface area.

This means other particles are more likely to collide with it so there'll be more useful collisions.

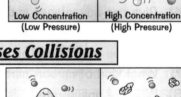

4) CATALYSTS Increase the Number of Successful Collisions

A catalyst is a substance that increases the rate of a reaction without being used up.

Catalysts increase the number of successful collisions too.

(Usually only a small amount of catalyst is required.)

Faster Collisions Also Increase the Rate of Reaction

Higher temperature increases the energy of the collisions, because it makes all the particles move faster.

Faster collisions are ONLY caused by increasing the temperature

Reactions only happen if the particles collide with enough energy.
At a higher temperature there will be more particles colliding with enough energy to make the reaction happen.

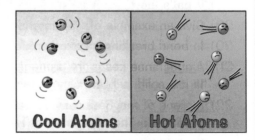

Collision Theory — it's always the other driver...

This is quite easy I think. Isn't it all kind of obvious — at least once you've been told it, anyway. The more often particles collide and the harder they hit, the greater the reaction rate. There's a few extra picky details of course (isn't there always...), but you've only got to LEARN them...

Revision Summary for Section 6

The only way that you can tell if you've learned this module is to test yourself. Try these questions, and if there's something you don't know, it means you need to go back and learn it. Even if it is all that tricky business about rates of reaction. And don't miss any questions out — you don't get a choice about what comes up on the exam so you need to be sure that you've learnt it all.

1) What are polymers?
2) Explain how fabrics can be made both breathable and waterproof.
3) Give one disadvantage of burning plastics and one disadvantage of burying plastics to get rid of them.
4) What is the name for the substance that gives a paint its colour?
5) Paint is a colloid — what is a colloid?
6) Give three properties that a substance must have in order to make a good perfume.
7) Give two examples of new materials which were discovered by accident.
8) What kind of metal are "memory" glasses which remember their shape made from?
9) Smart inks have been developed which get darker with time. The warmer they get, the faster they change colour. Explain why this is a useful property for a freshness indicator in food packaging.
10) What makes glow-in-the-dark watches glow in the dark?
11) Explain why nanoparticles are used in some sunscreens.
12) Explain why potatoes are cooked before they're eaten. What about eggs and meat?
13) Explain what is meant by "emulsion". List three foods which contain emulsions.
14) Give two advantages and two disadvantages of using food additives.
15) Describe how chromatography can be used to separate the different colours in a sweet.
16) Describe how oil can be extracted from some plants.
17) What kind of carbon-carbon bond do unsaturated oils contain?
18) Why are unsaturated oils hardened by reacting them with hydrogen?
19) What are the industrial conditions for the hydrogenation of unsaturated vegetable oil?
20) What is biodiesel made from?
21) State one advantage and one disadvantage of biodiesel compared to ordinary diesel.
22) Describe two ways in which ethanol can be made.
23) When concentrated sulphuric acid is added to sugar, the sugar turns into a spongy black mess. What kind of reaction is this?
24) What products are formed by the thermal decomposition of calcium carbonate?
25) Where on the pH scale do acids and bases fall? What do you get if an acid reacts with a base?
26) How does rust form? Is that an example of oxidation or reduction?
27) A forensic scientist carries out a flame test to identify a metal. The metal burns with a blue-green flame. a) Which metal does this result indicate? b) Describe a different test that the scientist could have used to identify the metal sample.
28) What's the test for each of the following: chlorine, hydrogen, oxygen, carbon dioxide, ammonia?
29) Give an example of: a) an endothermic reaction, b) an exothermic reaction.
30) Is bond breaking an exothermic or an endothermic process?
31) A substance keeps the same volume, but changes its shape according to the container it's held in. Is it a solid, a liquid or a gas? How strong are the forces of attraction between its particles?
32)*A piece of magnesium is added to a dilute solution of hydrochloric acid, and hydrogen gas is produced. The experiment is repeated with a more concentrated hydrochloric acid. How can you tell from the experiment which concentration of acid produces a faster rate of reaction?
33) What four things affect the rate of a reaction?
34) Why do gases react faster when they're under higher pressure?

* Answer on page 140

Section 6 — Materials and Reactions

Moving and Storing Heat

When it starts to get a bit nippy, on goes the heating to warm things up a bit. Heating is all about the transfer of energy. Here are a few useful definitions to begin with.

Heat *is a Measure of* Energy

1) When a substance is heated, its particles gain energy.

2) This energy makes the particles in a gas or a liquid move around faster. In a solid, the particles vibrate more rapidly.

3) The unit of heat energy is the joule (J).

Temperature *is a Measure of* Hotness

1) The hotter something is, the higher its temperature.

2) Temperature is usually measured in °C (degrees Celsius), but there are other temperature scales, like °F (degrees Fahrenheit).

3) Energy tends to flow from hot objects to cooler ones — e.g. warm radiators heat the cold air in your room.

4) And the bigger the temperature difference, the faster heat is transferred. Kinda makes sense.

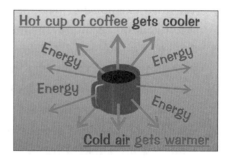

Hot cup of coffee gets cooler

Energy   Energy
Energy
Energy

Cold air gets warmer

> If there's a **DIFFERENCE IN TEMPERATURE** between two places, then **ENERGY WILL FLOW** between them.

Specific Heat Capacity *Tells You How Much Energy Stuff Can Store*

1) It takes more heat energy to increase the temperature of some materials than others.

2) For example, you need 4200 J to warm 1 kg of water by 1 °C, but only 139 J to warm 1 kg of mercury by 1 °C.

3) Materials which need to gain lots of energy to warm up also release loads of energy when they cool down again. They can 'store' a lot of heat.

4) The measure of how much energy a substance can store is called its specific heat capacity.

5) Specific heat capacity is the amount of energy needed to raise the temperature of 1 kg of a substance by 1 °C. Water has a specific heat capacity of 4200 J/kg/°C.

6) The specific heat capacity of water is high. Once water's heated, it stores a lot of energy, which makes it good for central heating systems.

7) Also, water's a liquid so it can easily be pumped around a building.

8) This makes water good for cooling systems too. Water can absorb a lot of energy and carry it away. Water-based cooling systems are used in car engines and some computers.

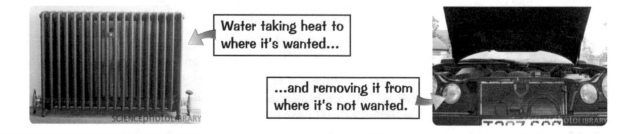

Water taking heat to where it's wanted...

...and removing it from where it's not wanted.

I wish I had a high specific fact capacity...

So there are two reasons why water's used in central heating systems — it's a liquid and it has a high specific heat capacity. You know the drill by now... cover the page and write down what you know.

Melting and Boiling

If you heat up a pan of water on the stove, the water never gets any hotter than 100 °C. You can carry on heating it up, but the temperature won't rise. How come, you say? It's all to do with latent heat...

You Need to Put In Energy to Break Intermolecular Bonds...

1) When you heat a solid that's below its melting point, the heat energy causes a rise in temperature.

2) But when the solid reaches its melting point, something slightly different happens.

3) Now when you heat the solid, the heat energy is used to change the solid to a liquid.

4) While this is happening, the temperature stays the same.

5) This is why there's a flat spot on the heating graph at the melting point.

6) What's happening is that the heat energy is being used to overcome the forces holding the particles together until eventually the particles start to move around — this is melting.

7) It's the same when you heat a liquid.
Below the boiling the point, the heat causes an increase in temperature.
But when the liquid reaches its boiling point, the energy is used to change the liquid into a gas instead, so there's another flat spot on the graph.

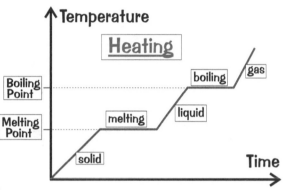

...And Energy is Released When Intermolecular Bonds Form

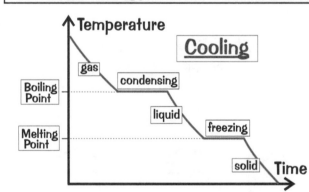

1) You see a similar kind of thing on the cooling graph. Away from the condensing and freezing points, the heat loss is seen as a fall in temperature.

2) But when a substance is condensing or freezing, bonds are forming between particles, which releases energy.
This means the temperature doesn't go down until all the substance has turned into a liquid (condensing) or a solid (freezing).

Specific Latent Heat is the Energy Needed to Change State

1) The specific latent heat of melting is the amount of energy needed to melt 1 kg of material without changing its temperature (i.e. the material's got to be at its melting temperature already).

2) The specific latent heat of boiling is the energy needed to boil 1 kg of material without changing its temperature (i.e. the material's got to be at its boiling temperature already).

3) Specific latent heat is different for different materials, and it's different for boiling and melting.

4) You don't have to remember what all the numbers are, though. Phew.

Breaking Bonds — Blofeld never quite manages it...

Melting a solid or boiling a liquid means you've got to break bonds between particles. That takes energy. Specific latent heat is just the amount of energy you need per kilogram of stuff. Incidentally, this is how sweating cools you down — your body heat's used to change liquid sweat into gas. Nice.

Conduction and Convection

If you build a house, there are regulations about doing it properly, mainly so that it doesn't fall down, but also so that it keeps the heat in. Easier said than done — there are several ways that heat is 'lost'.

Conduction Is Most Important in Solids

Houses lose heat through their windows even when they're shut. One reason for this is conduction.

1) When a substance is heated, some particles get extra energy — this makes them vibrate faster.

2) These particles then pass on their extra movement energy (kinetic energy) to neighbouring particles, which makes them vibrate faster as well.

3) This process continues throughout the solid and gradually the extra kinetic energy (or heat) is spread all the way through the solid. This causes a rise in temperature at the other side.

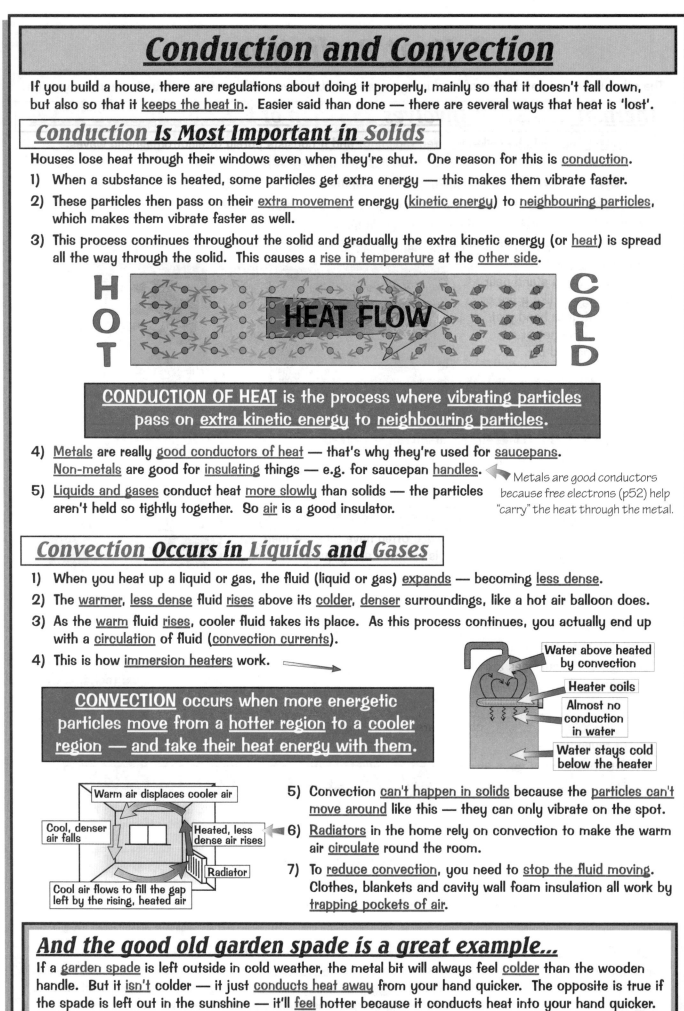

HOT **HEAT FLOW** **COLD**

> **CONDUCTION OF HEAT** is the process where vibrating particles pass on extra kinetic energy to neighbouring particles.

4) Metals are really good conductors of heat — that's why they're used for saucepans. Non-metals are good for insulating things — e.g. for saucepan handles.

Metals are good conductors because free electrons (p52) help "carry" the heat through the metal.

5) Liquids and gases conduct heat more slowly than solids — the particles aren't held so tightly together. So air is a good insulator.

Convection Occurs in Liquids and Gases

1) When you heat up a liquid or gas, the fluid (liquid or gas) expands — becoming less dense.

2) The warmer, less dense fluid rises above its colder, denser surroundings, like a hot air balloon does.

3) As the warm fluid rises, cooler fluid takes its place. As this process continues, you actually end up with a circulation of fluid (convection currents).

4) This is how immersion heaters work.

Water above heated by convection

Heater coils

Almost no conduction in water

Water stays cold below the heater

> **CONVECTION** occurs when more energetic particles move from a hotter region to a cooler region — and take their heat energy with them.

Warm air displaces cooler air

Cool, denser air falls

Heated, less dense air rises

Radiator

Cool air flows to fill the gap left by the rising, heated air

5) Convection can't happen in solids because the particles can't move around like this — they can only vibrate on the spot.

6) Radiators in the home rely on convection to make the warm air circulate round the room.

7) To reduce convection, you need to stop the fluid moving. Clothes, blankets and cavity wall foam insulation all work by trapping pockets of air.

And the good old garden spade is a great example...

If a garden spade is left outside in cold weather, the metal bit will always feel colder than the wooden handle. But it isn't colder — it just conducts heat away from your hand quicker. The opposite is true if the spade is left out in the sunshine — it'll feel hotter because it conducts heat into your hand quicker.

Heat Radiation

The other way heat can be transferred is by <u>radiation</u>. This is very different to conduction and convection.

Thermal Radiation Involves Emission of Electromagnetic Waves

<u>Heat radiation</u> can also be called <u>infrared radiation</u>, and it consists purely of electromagnetic waves. It's next to visible light in the <u>electromagnetic spectrum</u> (see p112).

1) <u>All</u> objects continually <u>emit and absorb</u> heat radiation.

2) An object that's <u>hotter</u> than its surroundings <u>emits more radiation</u> than it <u>absorbs</u> — it <u>cools</u> down. And an object that's <u>cooler</u> than its surroundings <u>absorbs more radiation</u> than it <u>emits</u> — it <u>warms</u> up.

3) And the <u>hotter</u> an object gets, the <u>more</u> heat radiation it <u>emits</u>.

4) You can <u>feel</u> this <u>heat radiation</u> if you stand near something <u>hot</u> like a fire or if you put your hand just above the bonnet of a recently parked car.

(recently parked car)

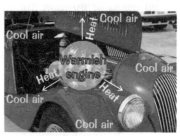
(after an hour or so)

The Amount of Heat Radiated and Emitted Depends on...

1) Surface Area

1) <u>Heat</u> is <u>radiated</u> from the <u>surface</u> of an object.

2) The <u>bigger</u> the <u>surface area</u>, the <u>quicker heat</u> can be <u>emitted</u>.

3) This is why <u>car and motorbike engines</u> often have '<u>fins</u>' — they <u>increase</u> the <u>surface area</u> so heat is radiated away quicker.

4) It's the same with <u>heating</u> something up — the bigger the surface area exposed to the heat radiation, the <u>quicker it'll heat up</u>.

2) Colour and Texture

1) <u>Matt black</u> surfaces are very <u>good absorbers and emitters</u> of radiation.

2) Painting a wood-burning stove <u>matt black</u> means it'll <u>radiate</u> as much <u>heat</u> as possible.

3) <u>Light-coloured, smooth</u> objects are very <u>poor absorbers and emitters</u> of radiation.

4) But they're very good at <u>reflecting</u> heat radiation.

5) This is why some people put shiny foil behind their radiators — to reflect radiation back into the room rather than heat up the walls.

6) Another good example is <u>survival blankets</u> for people rescued from snowy mountains.

Their shiny, smooth surface <u>reflects</u> the body heat back inside the blanket, and also <u>minimises</u> heat radiation being <u>emitted</u> by the blanket.

Radiate happiness — stand by the fire and smile...

The most confusing thing about radiation is that those white things on your walls called 'radiators' actually transfer <u>most</u> of their heat by <u>convection</u>, as rising warm air. They do radiate some heat too, of course, but whoever chose the name 'radiator' obviously hadn't swotted up their physics first.

Saving Energy

It'd be daft to keep buying hamsters and letting them all escape. It's also daft to keep paying for energy to heat your home only to let the heat escape straight out again.

Insulating Your Home Saves Energy and Money

1) To save energy, you need to insulate your home. It costs money to buy and install the insulation, but it also saves you money, because your heating bills are lower.

2) Eventually, the money you've saved on heating bills will equal the initial cost of installing the insulation. The time this takes is called the payback time.

3) Cheaper methods of insulation are usually less effective — they tend to save you less money per year, but they often have shorter payback times.

4) If you look at it over, say, a five-year period then a cheap and cheerful hot water tank jacket wins over expensive double glazing.

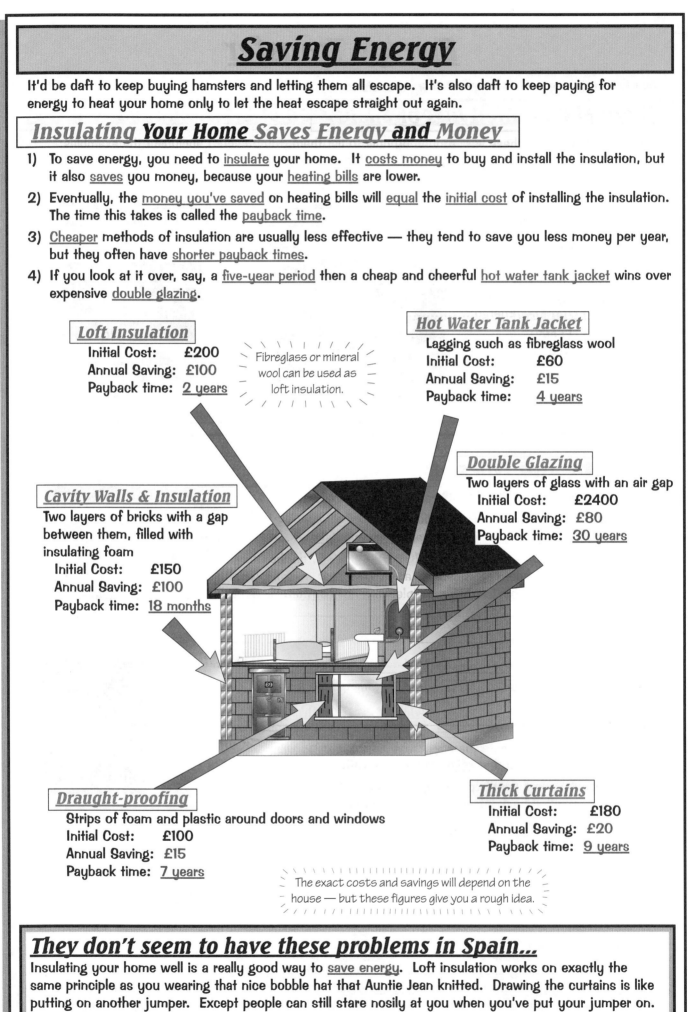

Loft Insulation
Initial Cost: £200
Annual Saving: £100
Payback time: 2 years

Fibreglass or mineral wool can be used as loft insulation.

Hot Water Tank Jacket
Lagging such as fibreglass wool
Initial Cost: £60
Annual Saving: £15
Payback time: 4 years

Double Glazing
Two layers of glass with an air gap
Initial Cost: £2400
Annual Saving: £80
Payback time: 30 years

Cavity Walls & Insulation
Two layers of bricks with a gap between them, filled with insulating foam
Initial Cost: £150
Annual Saving: £100
Payback time: 18 months

Draught-proofing
Strips of foam and plastic around doors and windows
Initial Cost: £100
Annual Saving: £15
Payback time: 7 years

Thick Curtains
Initial Cost: £180
Annual Saving: £20
Payback time: 9 years

The exact costs and savings will depend on the house — but these figures give you a rough idea.

They don't seem to have these problems in Spain...

Insulating your home well is a really good way to save energy. Loft insulation works on exactly the same principle as you wearing that nice bobble hat that Auntie Jean knitted. Drawing the curtains is like putting on another jumper. Except people can still stare nosily at you when you've put your jumper on.

Energy Transfer

Heat is just one type of energy, but there are lots more as well:

Learn These Nine Types of Energy

You should know all of these well enough by now to list them from memory, including the examples:

1) ELECTRICAL Energy......................................— whenever a current flows.
2) LIGHT Energy.. — from the Sun, light bulbs, etc.
3) SOUND Energy... — from loudspeakers or anything noisy.
4) KINETIC Energy, or MOVEMENT Energy.........— anything that's moving has it.
5) NUCLEAR Energy.. — released only from nuclear reactions.
6) THERMAL Energy or HEAT Energy................. — flows from hot objects to colder ones.
7) GRAVITATIONAL POTENTIAL Energy...............— possessed by anything which can fall.
8) ELASTIC POTENTIAL Energy........................ — possessed by springs, elastic, rubber bands, etc.
9) CHEMICAL Energy..— possessed by foods, fuels, batteries etc.

Potential- and Chemical- Are Forms of Stored Energy

The last three above are forms of stored energy because the energy is not obviously doing anything, it's kind of waiting to happen, i.e. waiting to be turned into one of the other forms.

There Are Two Types of "Energy Conservation"

Try and get your head round the difference between these two:

1) "ENERGY CONSERVATION" is all about using fewer resources because of the damage they do and because they might run out. That's all environmental stuff.

2) The "PRINCIPLE OF THE CONSERVATION OF ENERGY", on the other hand, is one of the major cornerstones of modern physics. It's an all-pervading principle which governs the workings of the entire physical Universe. If this principle were not so, then life as we know it would simply cease to be.

Got it now? Good. Well don't forget.

The Principle of the Conservation of Energy Can Be Stated Thus:

ENERGY CAN NEVER BE CREATED NOR DESTROYED
— IT'S ONLY EVER CONVERTED FROM ONE FORM TO ANOTHER.

Solar hot water panel
Light → Heat

falling object
Gravitational Potential → Kinetic

Another important principle which you need to learn is this one:

Energy is only useful when it can be converted from one form to another.

Potential energy — I COULD go jogging, if I got off the sofa...

Make sure you can work out the energy transformations involved in other processes too. For example... electrical devices convert electrical energy into sound, light, heat, etc. Batteries convert chemical energy to electrical energy. Electricity generation always involves converting other forms of energy into electrical energy. But you always get a little bit of wasted heat too — see the next page for more.

Efficiency

An open fire looks cosy, but a lot of its heat energy goes straight up the chimney, by convection, instead of heating up your living room. All this energy is 'wasted', so open fires aren't very efficient.

Machines _Always_ Waste _Some_ Energy

1) Useful machines are only useful because they convert energy from one form to another.

2) Take cars for instance — you put in chemical energy (petrol or diesel) and the engine converts it into kinetic (movement) energy.

3) The total energy output is always the same as the energy input, but only some of the output energy is useful.

4) This is because some of the input energy is always lost or wasted, often as heat.

5) In the car example, the rest of the chemical energy is converted (mostly) into heat and sound energy. This is wasted energy — although you could always stick your dinner under the bonnet and warm it up on the drive home.

6) The less energy that is wasted, the more efficient the device is said to be.

More Efficient Machines Waste Less Energy

The efficiency of a machine is defined as:

$$\text{Efficiency} = \frac{\text{USEFUL Energy OUTPUT}}{\text{TOTAL Energy OUTPUT}}$$

1) To work out the efficiency of a machine, first find out the Total Energy output. (This is the same as the energy supplied to the machine — the energy input.)

2) Then find how much useful energy the machine delivers — the USEFUL Energy output. (The question might tell you this directly, or it might tell you how much energy is wasted as heat/sound.)

3) Then just divide the smaller number by the bigger one to get a value for efficiency somewhere between 0 and 1. Easy. (If your number is bigger than 1, you've done the division upside down.)

4) You can convert the efficiency to a percentage, by multiplying it by 100. E.g. 0.6 = 60%.

Electric kettle — 180 000 J of electrical energy supplied — 9000 J of heat given out to the room. Think about it!

$$\text{Efficiency} = \frac{\text{Useful En. Out}}{\text{Total En. Out}} = \frac{171\,000}{180\,000} = 0.95$$

EXAMPLE: 20 000 J of energy is supplied to a light bulb. 1000 J of light energy is given out. What is the bulb's efficiency?

ANSWER: Useful energy output = 1000 J.
Total energy input = 20 000 J.
So efficiency $= \dfrac{1000}{20\,000} = \underline{0.05} = \underline{5\%}$

Shockingly inefficient, those ordinary light bulbs. Low-energy light bulbs are roughly 4 times more efficient, and last about 8 times as long. They're more expensive though.

Efficiency = pages learned ÷ cups of tea made...

Some new appliances (like washing machines and fridges) come with a sticker with a letter from A to H on, to show how energy-efficient they are. A really well-insulated fridge might have an 'A' rating. But if you put it right next to the oven, or never defrost it, it will run much less efficiently than it should.

Energy Sources

Different <u>energy resources</u> fit into <u>two broad types</u>: <u>renewable</u> and <u>non-renewable</u>.

Non-Renewable Energy Resources <u>Will</u> Run Out <u>One Day</u>

The <u>non-renewables</u> are the <u>three FOSSIL FUELS</u> and <u>NUCLEAR</u>:

1) <u>Coal</u>
2) <u>Oil</u>
3) <u>Natural gas</u>
4) <u>Nuclear fuels</u> (<u>uranium</u> and <u>plutonium</u>)

> a) They will <u>all 'run out'</u> one day.
> b) They all do <u>damage</u> to the environment.
> c) But they provide <u>most of our energy</u>.

<u>There are</u> Environmental Problems <u>with the Use of</u> Non-Renewables

1) All three <u>fossil fuels</u> (coal, oil and gas) release CO_2.
   All this CO_2 adds to the <u>greenhouse effect</u>, and contributes to <u>climate change</u>.
   We could stop some of it entering the atmosphere — by 'capturing' it and <u>burying</u> it underground, for instance — but the technology is too <u>expensive</u> to be widely used yet.

2) Burning coal and oil releases <u>sulphur dioxide</u>, which causes <u>acid rain</u> (see page 69).

3) <u>Coal mining</u> makes a <u>mess</u> of the <u>landscape</u>, especially "<u>open-cast mining</u>".

4) <u>Oil spillages</u> cause <u>serious environmental problems</u>.

5) <u>Nuclear power</u> is <u>clean</u> but the <u>nuclear waste</u> is very <u>dangerous</u> and difficult to <u>dispose of</u> (see page 100).

6) But non-renewable fuels are generally <u>concentrated</u> energy resources, <u>reliable</u>, and <u>easy</u> to use.

Renewable Energy Resources <u>Will</u> Never Run Out

The <u>renewables</u> are:

1) <u>Geothermal</u>   5) <u>Waves</u>
2) <u>Wind</u>   6) <u>Tides</u>
3) <u>Solar</u>   7) <u>Hydroelectric</u>
4) <u>Biomass</u>

> a) These will <u>never run out</u>.
> b) Most of them do <u>damage the environment</u>, but in <u>less nasty</u> ways than non-renewables.
> c) The trouble is they <u>don't provide much energy</u> and some of them are <u>unreliable</u> because they depend on the <u>weather</u>.

The Sun <u>is the</u> Ultimate Source <u>of Loads of</u> Energy

1) A lot of these energy sources can be traced back to the Sun.
2) <u>Fossil fuels</u> (coal, oil and gas) are basically stores of the Sun's energy.
3) And when we use wind power, we're also using the Sun's energy — the Sun heats the <u>air</u>, the <u>hot air rises</u>, cold air whooshes in to take its place (wind), and so on.

Fossil fuels are the remains of plants and animals that lived long ago.

<u>Nuclear, Geothermal</u> and <u>Tidal</u> Energy Do <u>Not</u> Originate in the Sun

1) <u>Nuclear power</u> comes from the energy locked up in the <u>nuclei of atoms</u>.
2) Nuclear decay also creates heat inside the Earth for <u>geothermal energy</u>, though this happens much <u>slower</u> than in a nuclear reactor.
3) <u>Tides</u> are caused by the <u>gravitational attraction</u> of the Moon and Sun.

<u>Stop fuelling around and learn this stuff properly...</u>

There's lots more info about the various power sources over the next few pages. But the point is that <u>none</u> of them are <u>ideal</u> — they all have pros <u>and</u> cons, and the aim is to choose the least bad option overall. Unless we want to go without heating, light, transport, electricity... and so on. (I don't.)

Nuclear and Geothermal Energy

Well, who'd have thought... there's energy lurking about deep underground. And inside atoms.

Nuclear Power Uses Uranium as Fuel

1) A nuclear power station uses uranium to produce heat.

2) Nuclear power stations are expensive to build and maintain. And they take a long time to set up.

3) Once running, there's always a risk of leaks of radioactive material, or even a major catastrophe like at Chernobyl.

4) A big problem with nuclear power is the radioactive waste that you always get (see below).

5) But nuclear power doesn't produce any of the greenhouse gases which contribute to global warming. And there's still plenty of uranium left in the ground.

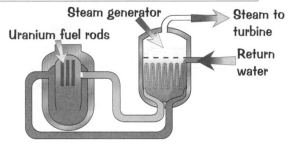

A nuclear reactor is just a fancy boiler

Steam generator — Steam to turbine
Uranium fuel rods
Return water

Radioactive Waste is Difficult to Dispose of Safely

1) Most waste from nuclear power stations and hospitals is 'low-level' (only slightly radioactive). This kind of waste can be disposed of by burying it in secure landfill sites.

2) High-level waste is the really dangerous stuff, and has to be treated very carefully. It's often sealed into glass blocks, which are then buried deep underground.

3) Not all radioactive waste has to be chucked out though — some of it is reprocessed. After reprocessing, you're left with more uranium (for reuse in power stations) and a bit of plutonium (which can be used to make nuclear weapons).

Geothermal Energy — Heat from Underground

1) This is only possible in certain places where hot rocks lie quite near to the surface.

2) The source of much of the heat is the slow decay of various radioactive elements including uranium deep inside the Earth.

3) Water is pumped in pipes down to hot rocks and returns as steam to drive a generator.

4) This is actually brilliant free energy with no real environmental problems. The main drawback is the cost of drilling down several km.

5) Unfortunately there are very few places where this seems to be an economic option (for now).

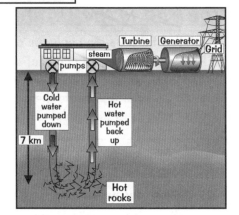

Turbine Generator Grid
steam
pumps
Cold water pumped down
Hot water pumped back up
7 km
Hot rocks

Radioactive sources — don't put them on your chips...

Most of the UK's nuclear power stations are quite old, and will have to be shut down soon. There's a debate going on over whether we should build new ones. Some people say no — if we can't deal safely with the radioactive waste we've got now, we certainly shouldn't make lots more. Others say that nuclear power is the only way to meet all our energy needs without causing catastrophic climate change.

Solar Energy

Solar energy is renewable — it'll never run out.

You Can Capture the Sun's Energy Using Solar Cells

1) <u>Solar cells</u> (<u>photocells</u>) generate <u>electricity directly</u> from sunlight.

2) They generate <u>direct current</u> (DC) — the same as a <u>battery</u> (not like the <u>mains electricity</u> in your home, which is AC — alternating current).

3) Solar cells are very <u>expensive initially</u>, but after that the energy is <u>free</u> and <u>running costs</u> are almost <u>nil</u>.

4) And there's <u>no pollution</u> (although they use a fair bit of energy to manufacture in the first place).

5) Solar cells can only <u>generate</u> enough <u>electricity</u> to be useful if they have <u>enough sunlight</u> — which can be a problem at <u>night</u> (and in <u>winter</u> in some places).

6) But the cells can be linked to <u>rechargeable batteries</u> to create a system that can <u>store energy</u> during the day for use at <u>night</u>.

7) Solar cells are often the best way to power <u>calculators</u> or <u>watches</u> that don't use much energy.

8) They're also used in <u>remote places</u> where there's not much choice (e.g. deserts) and in satellites.

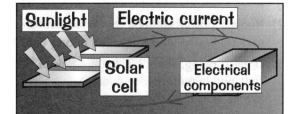

Passive Solar Heating — No Complex Mechanical Stuff

SOLAR PANELS

1) Solar panels are much less sophisticated than photocells — basically just <u>black water pipes</u> inside a <u>glass</u> box.

2) The <u>glass</u> lets <u>heat</u> and <u>light</u> from the Sun in, which is then <u>absorbed</u> by the black pipes and heats up the water.

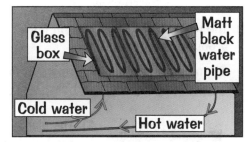

COOKING WITH SOLAR POWER

If you get a <u>curved mirror</u>, then you can <u>focus</u> the Sun's light and heat. This is what happens in a solar oven.

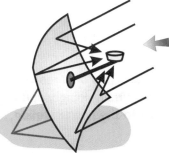

All the radiation that lands on the curved mirror is focused right on your pan.

CAREFULLY DESIGNED BUILDINGS CAN USE ENERGY MORE EFFICIENTLY

You can reduce the energy needed to <u>heat</u> a building if you build it sensibly in the first place — e.g. it can make a big difference which way the <u>windows</u> face.

MARTIN BOND / SCIENCE PHOTO LIBRARY

Learn about wind power — it can blow your mind...

The more directly a solar panel faces the Sun, the more energy it'll absorb. So to improve the efficiency of a solar panel, you can make it <u>track</u> the position of the <u>Sun</u> in the sky. Clever.

Biomass and Wind Energy

Biomass sounds pretty dull, but it's actually quite exciting. Well, kind of.

Wind Farms — Lots of Little Wind Turbines

1) Wind power involves putting lots of wind turbines up in <u>exposed</u> <u>places</u> — like on <u>moors</u>, around the <u>coast</u> or <u>out at sea</u>.

2) Wind turbines convert the kinetic energy of moving air into electricity. The <u>wind</u> turns the <u>blades</u>, which turn a <u>generator</u>.

3) Wind turbines are quite cheap to run — they're very <u>tough</u> and reliable, and the wind is <u>free</u>.

4) Even better, wind power doesn't produce any <u>polluting waste</u> and it's <u>renewable</u> — the wind's never going to run out.

5) But there are <u>disadvantages</u>. You need about 5000 wind turbines to replace one coal-fired power station.
Some people think that 'wind farms' spoil the view and the spinning blades cause noise pollution.

6) Another problem is that sometimes the wind isn't <u>strong enough</u> to generate any power. It's also impossible to increase supply when there's extra demand (e.g. when Coronation Street starts).

7) And although the wind is free, it's <u>expensive</u> to <u>set up</u> a wind farm, especially <u>out at sea</u>.

Biomass Is Waste That Can Be Burnt — Plant Waste and Animal Poo

1) <u>Biomass</u> is the general term for <u>organic 'stuff'</u> that can be burnt to produce electricity (e.g. <u>farm waste</u>, <u>animal droppings</u>, <u>landfill</u> <u>rubbish</u>, <u>specially grown forests</u>...).

2) The waste material is <u>burnt</u> in power stations to <u>drive turbines</u> and produce <u>electricity</u>.

3) Or sometimes it can be <u>fermented</u> to produce other fuels such as 'biogas' (mostly <u>methane</u>) or <u>ethanol</u>.

Plant material...

...rubbish...

4) The <u>plants</u> that grew to <u>produce the waste</u> (or to <u>feed the animals</u> that produced the dung) would have <u>absorbed carbon dioxide</u> from the atmosphere as they were growing. When the waste is burnt, this CO_2 is <u>re-released</u> into the <u>atmosphere</u>.

5) So it has a <u>neutral effect</u> on <u>atmospheric CO_2 levels</u>. (This only really works if you keep growing plants at the same rate you're burning things, and if you ignore any fossil fuels used in transporting the fuel to the power station, etc.)

6) <u>Set-up</u> and <u>fuel costs</u> are generally <u>low</u>, since the <u>fuel</u> is usually <u>waste</u>, and the fuels can often be burnt in <u>converted coal-fired power stations</u>.

7) This process can make use of <u>waste products</u>, which could be <u>great news</u> for our already <u>overflowing landfill sites</u>.

8) But the downside of using <u>unsorted landfill</u> rubbish, rather than just plant and animal waste, is that burning it can release <u>nasty gases</u> like <u>sulphur dioxide</u> and <u>nitrogen oxide</u> into the atmosphere.

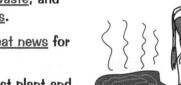

...and poo.

Where there's muck there's gas...

Britain's first <u>dung-fired power station</u> opened in 2002, using <u>animal manure</u> from nearby farms to produce <u>methane</u>. The methane was <u>burnt</u> to produce <u>electricity</u>, and the process also provided <u>hot</u> <u>water</u> for the surrounding area and <u>organic fertiliser</u> to be sold back to the farms. All clever stuff.

Hydroelectric and Pumped Storage

Here's another couple of renewables — learn the advantages and disadvantages.

Hydroelectricity and Pumped Storage Systems

1) Hydroelectric power often requires the flooding of a valley by building a big dam.
2) Rainwater is caught and allowed out through turbines. There is no pollution (as such).
3) But there is a big impact on the environment due to the flooding of the valley, and maybe loss of habitat for some species (sometimes even the loss of whole villages).

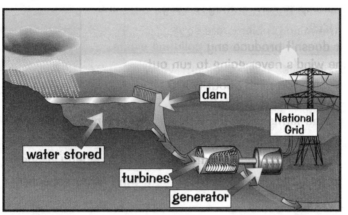

4) The reservoirs can also look very unsightly when they dry up. Location in remote valleys tends to avoid some of these problems.
5) A big advantage is immediate response to increased demand, and there's no problem with reliability except in times of drought.
6) Initial costs are high, but there's no fuel and minimal running costs.

Pumped Storage Gives Extra Supply Just When It's Needed

1) Most large power stations have huge boilers which have to be kept running all night even though demand is very low. This means there's a surplus of electricity at night.
2) It's surprisingly difficult to find a way of storing this spare energy for later use.
3) Pumped storage is one of the best solutions.
4) In pumped storage, 'spare' night-time electricity is used to pump water up to a higher reservoir.
5) This can then be released quickly during periods of peak demand such as at teatime each evening, to supplement the steady delivery from the big power stations.
6) Remember, pumped storage uses the same idea as hydroelectric power but it isn't a way of generating power — but simply a way of storing energy which has already been generated.

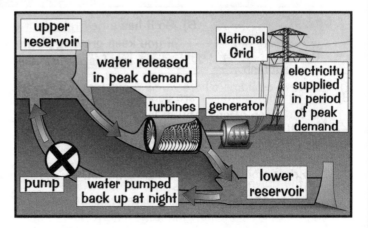

The hydroelectric power you're supplying — it's electrifying...

In Britain only a pretty small percentage of our electricity comes from hydroelectric power at the moment, but in some other parts of the world they rely much more heavily on it. For example, in the last few years, 99% of Norway's energy came from hydroelectric power. 99% — that's huge!

Wave and Tidal Power

Another couple of gems for you to learn all about... Enjoy.

Wave Power — Lots of Little Wave Converters

Don't confuse <u>wave power</u> with <u>tidal power</u> — they're <u>completely different</u>.

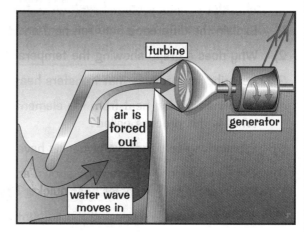

1) For wave power, you need lots of small <u>wave converters</u> located <u>around the coast</u>. As waves come in to the shore they provide an <u>up and down motion</u> which can be used to drive a <u>generator</u>.

2) There's <u>no pollution</u>. The main problems are <u>spoiling the view</u> and being a <u>hazard to boats</u>.

3) It's <u>fairly unreliable</u>, since waves tend to die out when the <u>wind drops</u>.

4) <u>Initial costs are high</u> but there are <u>no fuel costs</u> and <u>minimal running costs</u>. Wave power is unlikely to provide energy on a <u>large scale</u> but it can be <u>very useful</u> on <u>small islands</u>.

Tidal Barrages — Using the Sun and Moon's Gravity

1) <u>Tidal barrages</u> are <u>big dams</u> built across <u>river estuaries</u>, with <u>turbines</u> in them.

2) As the <u>tide comes in</u> it fills up the estuary to a height of <u>several metres</u>. This water can then be allowed out <u>through turbines</u> at a controlled speed. It also drives the turbines on the way in.

3) There's <u>no pollution</u>. The main problems are <u>preventing free access by boats</u>, <u>spoiling the view</u> and <u>altering the habitat</u> of the wildlife.

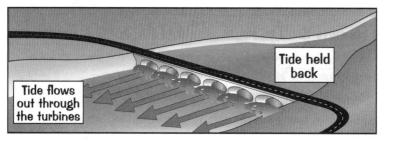

4) Tides are <u>pretty reliable</u>, but the <u>height</u> of the tide is <u>variable</u> so lower tides will provide <u>less energy</u> than higher ones.

5) <u>Initial costs are moderately high</u>, but there's <u>no fuel costs</u> and <u>minimal running costs</u>.

Setting Up a Power Station

1) Because coal and oil are running out fast, many old <u>coal- and oil-fired power stations</u> are being <u>taken out of use</u>.

2) Mostly they're being <u>replaced</u> by <u>gas-fired power stations</u>. But gas is <u>not</u> the <u>only option</u>.

3) When looking at the options for a <u>new power station</u>, there are <u>several factors</u> to consider:

- How much it <u>costs</u> to set up and run,
- <u>How long</u> it takes to <u>build</u>,
- <u>How much power</u> it can generate, etc.,
- <u>Damage to the environment</u>,
- <u>Impact on local communities</u>.

Learn about wave power — and bid your cares goodbye...

I do hope you appreciate the <u>big big differences</u> between <u>tidal power</u> and <u>wave power</u>. They both involve salty sea water, sure — but there the similarities end. Smile and enjoy. And <u>learn</u>.

Revision Summary for Section 7

Phew... what a relief, you've made it to the end of yet another nice long section. This one's been fairly straightforward though — after all, about half of it just covered the pros and cons of different renewable energy resources. But don't kid yourself — there are definitely a shedload of facts to remember here and you need to know the lot of them. The best way to check that you know it all is to work your way through these revision questions — and make sure you go back and revise anything you get wrong.

1) Explain the difference between heat and temperature. What units are they each measured in?

2) Why does a graph showing the temperature of a substance as it's heated have two flat bits?

3) Describe the process that transfers heat energy through a metal rod. What is this process called?

4) Describe how the heat from the element is transferred throughout the water in a kettle. What is this process called?

5) Explain why solar hot water panels have a matt black surface.

6) The two designs of car engine shown are made from the same material. Which engine will transfer heat quicker? Explain why.

7) Name five ways of reducing the amount of heat lost from a house.

Engine A   Engine B

8)* The table on the right gives some information about two different energy-saving light bulbs. What is the payback time for light bulbs A and B?

	Price of bulb	Annual saving
Light bulb A	£2.50	£1.25
Light bulb B	£3.00	£2.00

9) Name nine types of energy and give an example of each.

10) State the principle of the conservation of energy.

11) List the energy transformations that occur in a battery-powered toy car.

12) What is the useful type of energy delivered by a motor? In what form is energy wasted?

13) Write down the formula for calculating efficiency.

14)* What is the efficiency of a motor that converts 100 J of electrical energy into 70 J of useful kinetic energy?

15) What is meant by a non-renewable energy resource? Name four different non-renewable energy resources.

16) State two advantages and two disadvantages of using fossil fuels to generate electricity.

17) Outline two arguments for and two arguments against increasing the use, in the UK, of nuclear power.

18) Give two advantages and one disadvantage of using solar cells to generate electricity.

19) How do solar ovens focus the Sun's rays?

20) Describe how the following renewable resources are used to generate electricity. State one advantage and one disadvantage for each resource.
    a) wind   b) biomass   c) geothermal energy
    d) waves   e) the tide

* Answers on page 140

Section 7 — Heat and Energy

Electric Current

Isn't electricity great — generally, I mean. You can power all sorts of toys and gadgets with electricity. Mind you, it'll be a pain come exam time if you don't know the basics — like current, voltage and so on.

Electric Current is a Flow of Electrons Round a Circuit

1) <u>CURRENT</u> is the <u>flow of electrons</u> round a circuit. (Electrons are <u>negatively charged</u> particles — see p45.)

2) <u>VOLTAGE</u> is the <u>driving force</u> that pushes the current round. Kind of like "<u>electrical pressure</u>".

3) <u>RESISTANCE</u> is anything in the circuit which <u>slows the flow down</u>.

4) There's a <u>BALANCE</u>: the <u>voltage</u> is trying to <u>push</u> the current round the circuit, and the <u>resistance</u> is <u>opposing</u> it — the <u>relative sizes</u> of the voltage and resistance decide <u>how big</u> the current will be:

> If you <u>increase the VOLTAGE</u> — then <u>MORE CURRENT</u> will flow.
> If you <u>increase the RESISTANCE</u> — then <u>LESS CURRENT</u> will flow.

It's Just Like the Flow of Water Around a Set of Pipes

1) The <u>current</u> is simply like the <u>flow of water</u>.

2) <u>Voltage</u> is like the <u>pressure</u> provided by a <u>pump</u> which pushes the stuff round.

3) <u>Resistance</u> is any sort of <u>constriction</u> in the flow, which is what the pressure has to <u>work against</u>.

4) If you <u>turn up the pump</u> and provide more <u>pressure</u> (or "<u>voltage</u>"), the flow will <u>increase</u>.

5) If you put in more <u>constrictions</u> ("<u>resistance</u>"), the flow (current) will <u>decrease</u>.

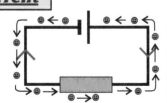

Electrons Flow the Opposite Way to Conventional Current

We <u>normally</u> say that current in a circuit flows from <u>positive to negative</u>. Alas, electrons were discovered long after that was decided and they turned out to be <u>negatively charged</u> — <u>unlucky</u>. This means they <u>actually flow</u> from −ve to +ve, <u>opposite</u> to the flow of "<u>conventional current</u>".

AC Keeps Changing Direction but DC Does Not

1) The <u>mains electricity</u> supply in your home is <u>alternating current</u> — <u>AC</u>. It keeps <u>reversing its direction</u> back and forth.

2) A cathode ray oscilloscope (CRO) trace for AC would be a <u>wave</u>. The <u>frequency</u> of the supply is <u>how many</u> of these <u>waves</u> you get <u>per second</u>.

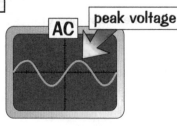

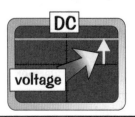

3) <u>Direct current</u> (<u>DC</u>) is <u>different</u>. It <u>always flows</u> in the <u>same direction</u>.

4) The <u>CRO trace</u> is a <u>horizontal line</u>. The <u>voltage doesn't vary</u> — so the <u>current</u> has a <u>constant</u> value too.

5) You get <u>DC current</u> from <u>batteries</u> and <u>solar cells</u> (see p101).

AC = wiggly   DC = straight

Remember — the two types of electric current are AC and DC. Learn all the differences between them. The other really important thing is this — the amount of <u>current</u> you get depends on the <u>voltage</u> of the power supply and the <u>resistance</u> of the appliance you're running.

Current, Voltage and Resistance

Resistance, current and voltage are all closely linked. And if you don't believe me, you can easily check.

Investigating How Current Varies with Voltage

1) This circuit can be used to investigate how current varies with voltage for any component.
2) The ammeter is always connected in series with the component.
3) The voltmeter is always connected in parallel with the component.
4) The supply voltage from the cell doesn't change.

   You adjust a variable resistor to pick different values for the current, and for each value measure the voltage across the component.

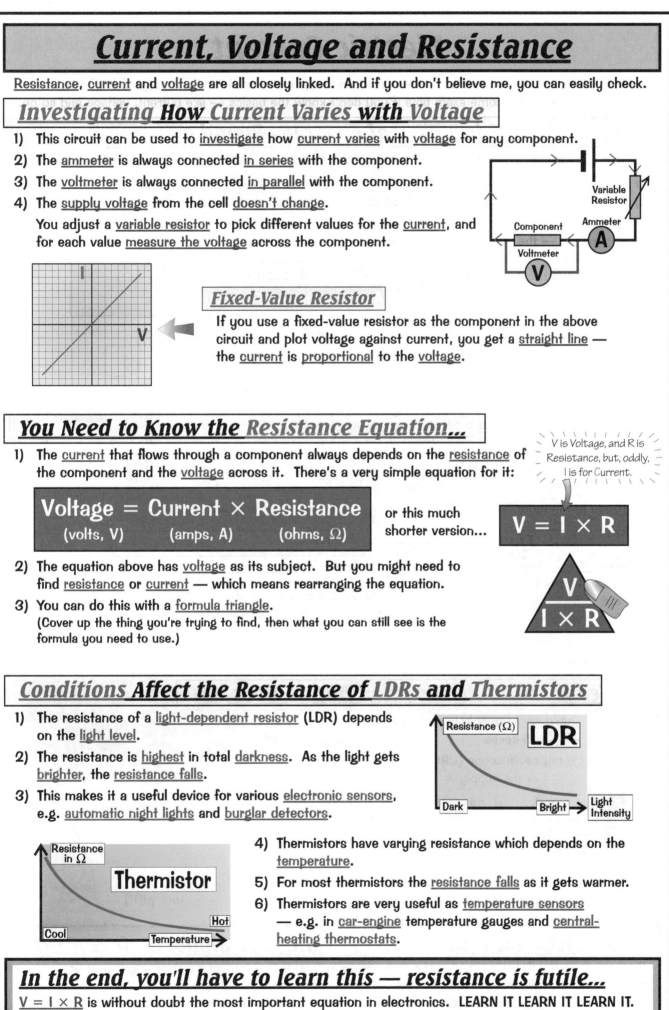

Fixed-Value Resistor

If you use a fixed-value resistor as the component in the above circuit and plot voltage against current, you get a straight line — the current is proportional to the voltage.

You Need to Know the Resistance Equation...

1) The current that flows through a component always depends on the resistance of the component and the voltage across it. There's a very simple equation for it:

V is Voltage, and R is Resistance, but, oddly, I is for Current.

$$\text{Voltage} = \text{Current} \times \text{Resistance}$$
(volts, V)   (amps, A)   (ohms, Ω)

or this much shorter version...

$$V = I \times R$$

$$\frac{V}{I \times R}$$

2) The equation above has voltage as its subject. But you might need to find resistance or current — which means rearranging the equation.
3) You can do this with a formula triangle.
   (Cover up the thing you're trying to find, then what you can still see is the formula you need to use.)

Conditions Affect the Resistance of LDRs and Thermistors

1) The resistance of a light-dependent resistor (LDR) depends on the light level.
2) The resistance is highest in total darkness. As the light gets brighter, the resistance falls.
3) This makes it a useful device for various electronic sensors, e.g. automatic night lights and burglar detectors.

4) Thermistors have varying resistance which depends on the temperature.
5) For most thermistors the resistance falls as it gets warmer.
6) Thermistors are very useful as temperature sensors — e.g. in car-engine temperature gauges and central-heating thermostats.

In the end, you'll have to learn this — resistance is futile...

$V = I \times R$ is without doubt the most important equation in electronics. **LEARN IT LEARN IT LEARN IT.**

The Dynamo Effect

Generators use a pretty cool piece of physics to make electricity from the movement of a turbine.
It's called electromagnetic (EM) induction — which basically means making electricity using a magnet.

ELECTROMAGNETIC INDUCTION: The creation of a VOLTAGE (and maybe current) in a wire which is experiencing a CHANGE IN MAGNETIC FIELD.

The Dynamo Effect — Move the Wire or the Magnet

1) Using electromagnetic induction to transform kinetic energy (energy of moving things) into electrical energy is called the dynamo effect.

2) There are two different situations where you get EM induction:
   a) An electrical conductor (a coil of wire is often used) moves through a magnetic field.
   b) The magnetic field through an electrical conductor changes (gets bigger or smaller or reverses).

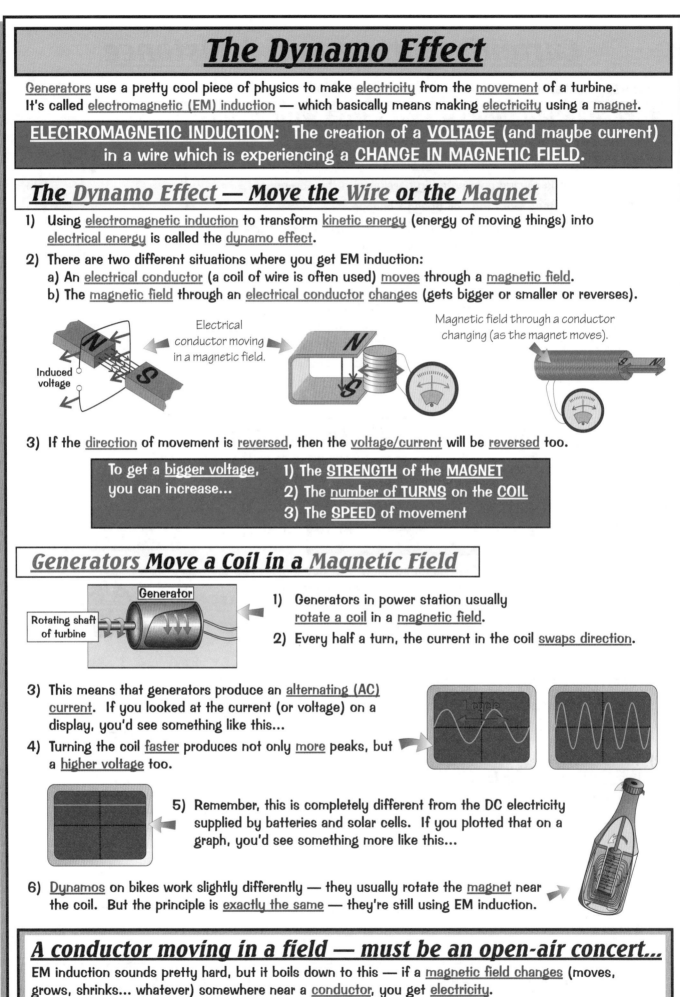

Electrical conductor moving in a magnetic field.

Induced voltage

Magnetic field through a conductor changing (as the magnet moves).

3) If the direction of movement is reversed, then the voltage/current will be reversed too.

To get a bigger voltage, you can increase...	1) The STRENGTH of the MAGNET
	2) The number of TURNS on the COIL
	3) The SPEED of movement

Generators Move a Coil in a Magnetic Field

Generator

Rotating shaft of turbine

1) Generators in power station usually rotate a coil in a magnetic field.

2) Every half a turn, the current in the coil swaps direction.

3) This means that generators produce an alternating (AC) current. If you looked at the current (or voltage) on a display, you'd see something like this...

4) Turning the coil faster produces not only more peaks, but a higher voltage too.

5) Remember, this is completely different from the DC electricity supplied by batteries and solar cells. If you plotted that on a graph, you'd see something more like this...

6) Dynamos on bikes work slightly differently — they usually rotate the magnet near the coil. But the principle is exactly the same — they're still using EM induction.

A conductor moving in a field — must be an open-air concert...

EM induction sounds pretty hard, but it boils down to this — if a magnetic field changes (moves, grows, shrinks... whatever) somewhere near a conductor, you get electricity.
It's a weird old thing, but important — this is how all our mains electricity is generated.

Power Stations and the National Grid

Most of the electricity you use arrives via the national grid.

The National Grid Connects Power Stations to Consumers

1) The <u>national grid</u> is the <u>network</u> of pylons and cables which covers <u>the whole country</u>.
2) It takes electricity from <u>power stations</u> to just where it's needed in <u>homes</u> and <u>industry</u>.
3) It enables power to be <u>generated</u> in a power station anywhere on the grid, and then <u>supplied</u> anywhere else on the grid.

All Power Stations are Pretty Much the Same...

1) The aim of a <u>power station</u> is to <u>convert</u> one kind of energy into <u>electricity</u>.
2) Usually this is done in <u>three stages</u>...

① The first stage is to use the <u>fuel</u> to generate <u>steam</u> — this is the job of the <u>boiler</u>.

② The moving steam drives the blades of a <u>turbine</u>...

③ ...and this rotating movement is converted to <u>electricity</u> by the <u>generator</u> (by <u>EM induction</u> — see previous page).

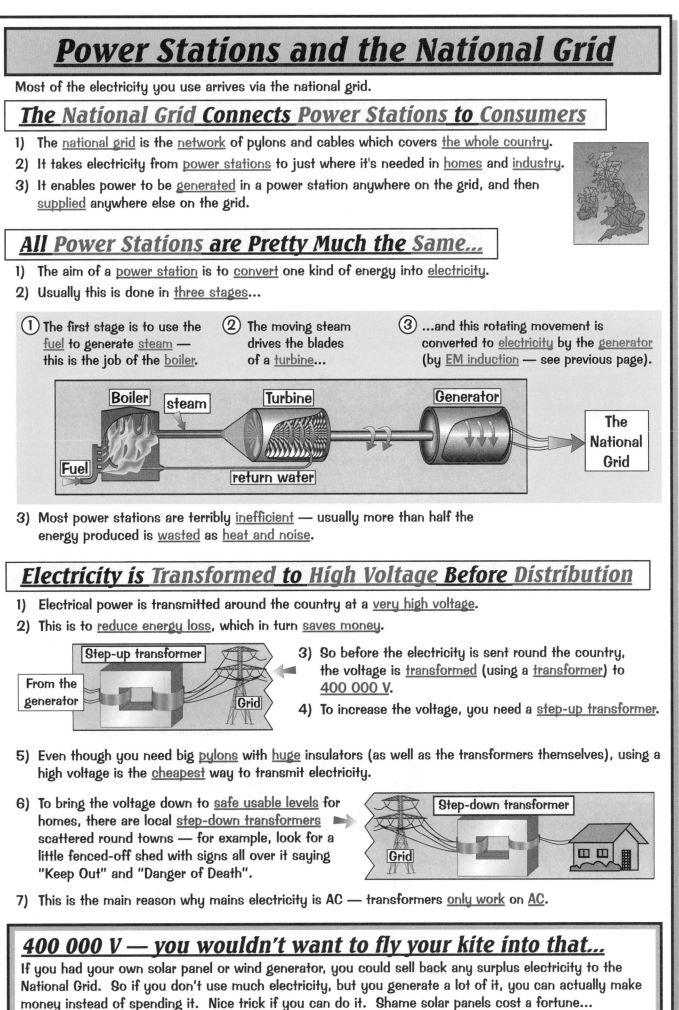

3) Most power stations are terribly <u>inefficient</u> — usually more than half the energy produced is <u>wasted</u> as <u>heat and noise</u>.

Electricity is Transformed to High Voltage Before Distribution

1) Electrical power is transmitted around the country at a <u>very high voltage</u>.
2) This is to <u>reduce energy loss</u>, which in turn <u>saves money</u>.

3) So before the electricity is sent round the country, the voltage is <u>transformed</u> (using a <u>transformer</u>) to <u>400 000 V</u>.
4) To increase the voltage, you need a <u>step-up transformer</u>.

5) Even though you need big <u>pylons</u> with <u>huge</u> insulators (as well as the transformers themselves), using a high voltage is the <u>cheapest</u> way to transmit electricity.

6) To bring the voltage down to <u>safe usable levels</u> for homes, there are local <u>step-down transformers</u> ▶ scattered round towns — for example, look for a little fenced-off shed with signs all over it saying "Keep Out" and "Danger of Death".

7) This is the main reason why mains electricity is AC — transformers <u>only work</u> on <u>AC</u>.

400 000 V — you wouldn't want to fly your kite into that...

If you had your own solar panel or wind generator, you could sell back any surplus electricity to the National Grid. So if you don't use much electricity, but you generate a lot of it, you can actually make money instead of spending it. Nice trick if you can do it. Shame solar panels cost a fortune...

Electrical Power

This page is about the <u>power</u> of electrical appliances.

Electrical Power _is the_ Rate of Transfer _of_ Electrical Energy

1) Electrical appliances take in <u>electrical energy</u> and <u>convert it</u> into <u>other forms of energy</u>, e.g. a light bulb turns <u>electrical</u> energy into <u>light</u> and <u>heat</u> energy.

2) The electrical <u>power</u> of an appliance tells you how <u>quickly</u> it converts (or <u>transfers</u>) electrical energy. The <u>units</u> of power are watts (W) or kilowatts (kW). 1 kilowatt = 1000 watts.

> <u>ELECTRICAL POWER</u> is the <u>Rate of Transfer</u> of <u>Electrical Energy</u>.

3) The <u>higher</u> the power of your appliance, the <u>more energy</u> is transferred every second. So a 3 kW kettle boils water <u>faster</u> than a 2 kW kettle, and a 100 W light bulb is <u>brighter</u> than a 60 W bulb.

Power = Current × Voltage

There's a nice easy equation for the <u>power</u> of an appliance.

> **Power = Current × Voltage**
> (watts, W)   (amps, A)   (volts, V)

or the shorter version

> **P = I × V**

As usual, you need to practise <u>rearranging</u> the equation too.

> You'll need to change the <u>units</u> — in this formula, power has to be in <u>watts</u>, not kilowatts.

<u>EXAMPLE:</u> Anna's hairdrier has a power rating of 1.1 kW. She plugs the hairdrier into the 230 V mains supply. What is the current through the hairdrier?

<u>ANSWER:</u> You're trying to find <u>current</u>, so you need to rearrange the equation. Using the formula triangle, I = P ÷ V = 1100 ÷ 230 = <u>4.8 A</u>.

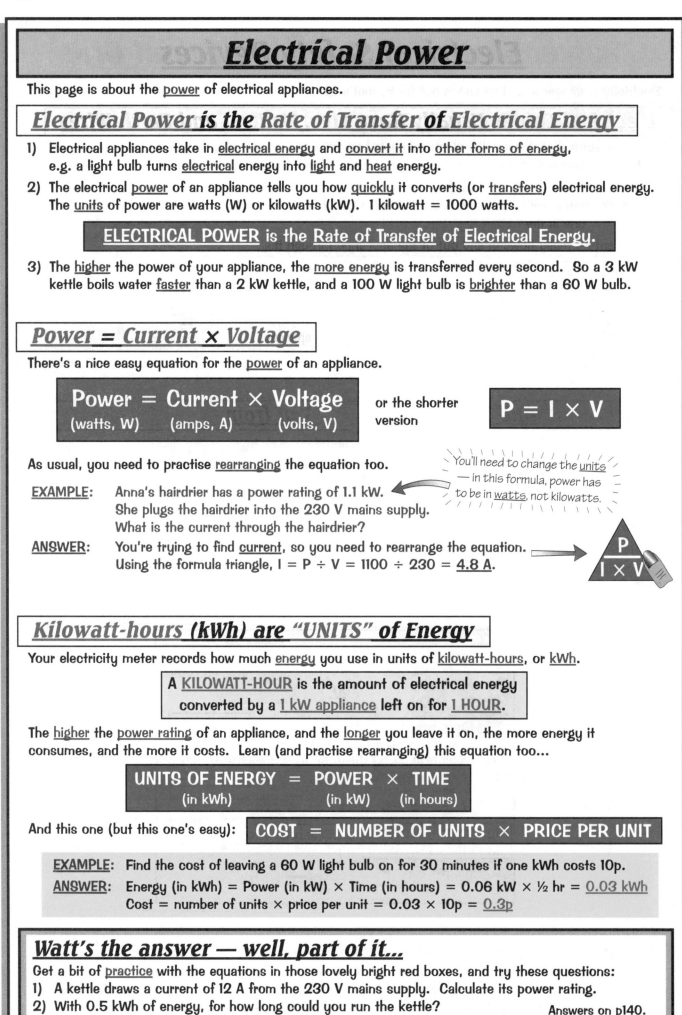

Kilowatt-hours (kWh) are "UNITS" of Energy

Your electricity meter records how much <u>energy</u> you use in units of <u>kilowatt-hours</u>, or <u>kWh</u>.

> A <u>KILOWATT-HOUR</u> is the amount of electrical energy converted by a <u>1 kW appliance</u> left on for <u>1 HOUR</u>.

The <u>higher</u> the <u>power rating</u> of an appliance, and the <u>longer</u> you leave it on, the more energy it consumes, and the more it costs. Learn (and practise rearranging) this equation too...

> **UNITS OF ENERGY = POWER × TIME**
> (in kWh)   (in kW)   (in hours)

And this one (but this one's easy):

> **COST = NUMBER OF UNITS × PRICE PER UNIT**

> <u>EXAMPLE:</u> Find the cost of leaving a 60 W light bulb on for 30 minutes if one kWh costs 10p.
> <u>ANSWER:</u> Energy (in kWh) = Power (in kW) × Time (in hours) = 0.06 kW × ½ hr = <u>0.03 kWh</u>
> Cost = number of units × price per unit = 0.03 × 10p = <u>0.3p</u>

Watt's the answer — well, part of it...

Get a bit of <u>practice</u> with the equations in those lovely bright red boxes, and try these questions:

1) A kettle draws a current of 12 A from the 230 V mains supply. Calculate its power rating.

2) With 0.5 kWh of energy, for how long could you run the kettle?   Answers on p140.

Electrical Safety Devices

Electricity is dangerous. Just watch out for it, that's all.

Electrical Cables Usually Have Live, Neutral and Earth Wires

In most electrical appliances the electrical cable has three copper wires inside it.
Each wire is covered with an insulating sheath — in a different colour for each wire.

1) The brown one is the LIVE WIRE.
   The live wire passes through a fuse (or a trip switch).

2) The blue one is the NEUTRAL WIRE.

3) Current normally flows in and out of the appliance through the
   live and neutral wires.

4) The green and yellow wire is the EARTH WIRE. One end of this
   wire is connected to the earth (it's usually clipped on to your
   cold water pipe, which comes from underground).
   The other end is connected to the metal casing of the appliance
   — so the casing is 'earthed'.

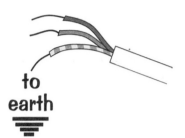

to
earth

Earth Wires and Fuses Can Protect You from Electric Shocks

The earth wire and fuse are just there for safety — and they work together like this:

1) If your toaster develops a fault, the live wire could touch the metal casing of the toaster.

2) The outside of the toaster would then be at high voltage, and potentially dangerous.

3) BUT the metal case is connected to the earth by the earth wire. So a very big current flows in through
   the live wire, through the metal casing and out through the earth wire.

4) This large current quickly melts the fuse in the live wire (or flips the trip switch) — and cuts off the
   high voltage supply.

5) This isolates the whole appliance from the high voltage supply, making it impossible to get an electric
   shock from the case of the appliance. It also prevents the risk of fire.

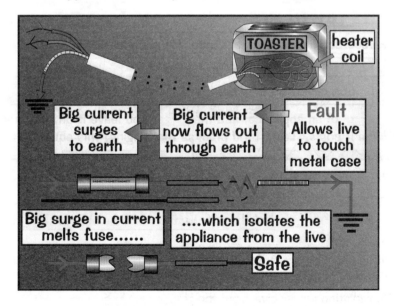

Hurrah for the earth wire — now my toaster won't kill me...

Not all electrical appliances have to be earthed. If the appliance has a plastic casing and no metal parts
exposed, it's said to be double insulated. Anything with double insulation just needs a live and a neutral
wire. Household products like hairdriers and vacuum cleaners usually have double insulation.

Waves — The Basics

Waves transfer <u>energy</u> from one place to another without transferring any <u>matter</u> (stuff).

Waves **Have** Amplitude, Wavelength **and** Frequency

1) The <u>amplitude</u> is the displacement from the <u>rest position</u> to the <u>crest</u> (NOT from a trough to a crest).

2) The <u>wavelength</u> is the length of a <u>full cycle</u> of the wave, e.g. from <u>crest to crest</u>.

3) <u>Frequency</u> is the <u>number of complete waves</u> passing a certain point <u>per second</u>. Frequency is measured in hertz (Hz). 1 Hz is <u>1 wave per second</u>.

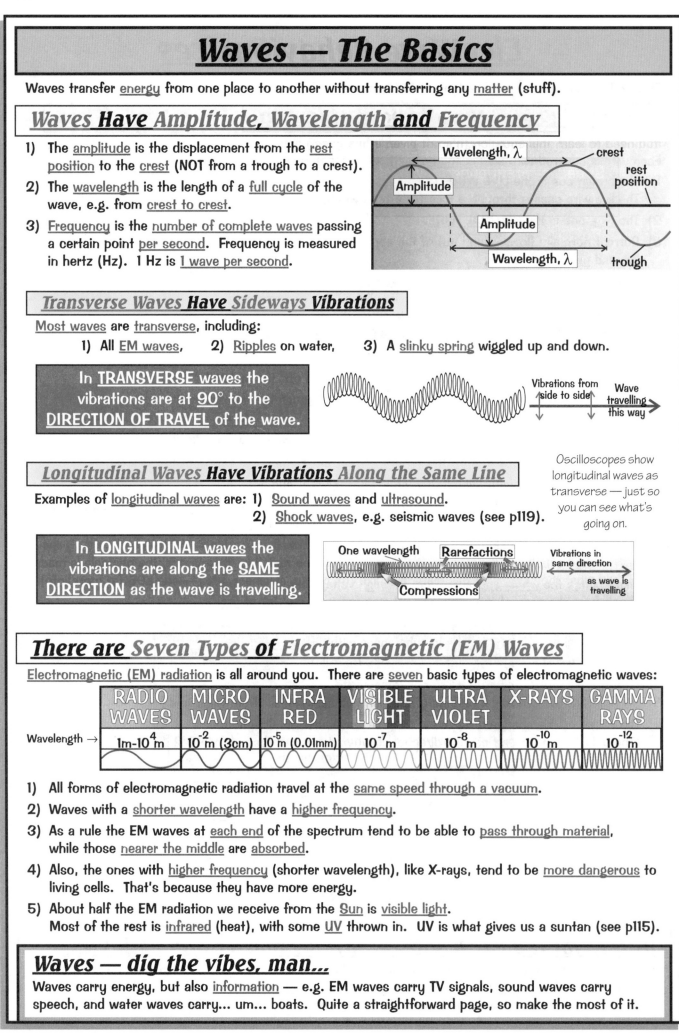

Transverse Waves **Have** Sideways **Vibrations**

<u>Most waves</u> are <u>transverse</u>, including:

1) All <u>EM waves</u>, 2) <u>Ripples</u> on water, 3) A <u>slinky spring</u> wiggled up and down.

> In **TRANSVERSE** waves the vibrations are at <u>90°</u> to the **DIRECTION OF TRAVEL** of the wave.

Longitudinal Waves **Have Vibrations** Along the Same Line

Examples of <u>longitudinal waves</u> are: 1) <u>Sound waves</u> and <u>ultrasound</u>.

2) <u>Shock waves</u>, e.g. seismic waves (see p119).

> In **LONGITUDINAL** waves the vibrations are along the **SAME DIRECTION** as the wave is travelling.

Oscilloscopes show longitudinal waves as transverse — just so you can see what's going on.

There are Seven Types **of** Electromagnetic (EM) Waves

<u>Electromagnetic (EM) radiation</u> is all around you. There are <u>seven</u> basic types of electromagnetic waves:

	RADIO WAVES	MICRO WAVES	INFRA RED	VISIBLE LIGHT	ULTRA VIOLET	X-RAYS	GAMMA RAYS
Wavelength →	$1m\text{-}10^{4}$ m	10^{-2} m (3cm)	10^{-5} m (0.01mm)	10^{-7} m	10^{-8} m	10^{-10} m	10^{-12} m

1) All forms of electromagnetic radiation travel at the <u>same speed through a vacuum</u>.

2) Waves with a <u>shorter wavelength</u> have a <u>higher frequency</u>.

3) As a rule the EM waves at <u>each end</u> of the spectrum tend to be able to <u>pass through material</u>, while those <u>nearer the middle</u> are <u>absorbed</u>.

4) Also, the ones with <u>higher frequency</u> (shorter wavelength), like X-rays, tend to be <u>more dangerous</u> to living cells. That's because they have more energy.

5) About half the EM radiation we receive from the <u>Sun</u> is <u>visible light</u>. Most of the rest is <u>infrared</u> (heat), with some <u>UV</u> thrown in. UV is what gives us a suntan (see p115).

Waves — dig the vibes, man...

Waves carry energy, but also <u>information</u> — e.g. EM waves carry TV signals, sound waves carry speech, and water waves carry... um... boats. Quite a straightforward page, so make the most of it.

Wave Behaviour

This stuff is true for all waves — not just EM ones...

Wave Speed = Frequency × Wavelength

You need to learn this equation (it's not given in the exam) and practise using it.

> **Speed = Frequency × Wavelength**
> **(m/s)   (Hz)   (m)**

OR

> $v = f\lambda$

Speed
(v is for velocity)

Frequency

Wavelength
(that's the Greek
letter 'lambda')

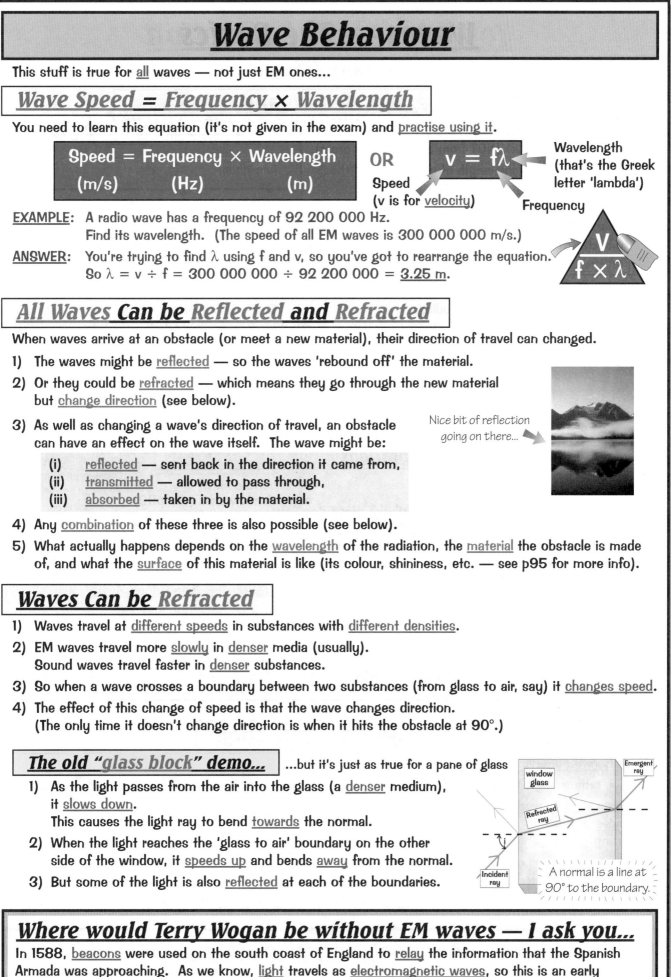

EXAMPLE: A radio wave has a frequency of 92 200 000 Hz.
Find its wavelength. (The speed of all EM waves is 300 000 000 m/s.)

ANSWER: You're trying to find λ using f and v, so you've got to rearrange the equation.
So $\lambda = v \div f = 300\ 000\ 000 \div 92\ 200\ 000 = \underline{3.25\ m}$.

All Waves Can be Reflected and Refracted

When waves arrive at an obstacle (or meet a new material), their direction of travel can changed.

1) The waves might be reflected — so the waves 'rebound off' the material.

2) Or they could be refracted — which means they go through the new material
but change direction (see below).

3) As well as changing a wave's direction of travel, an obstacle
can have an effect on the wave itself. The wave might be:

   (i)   reflected — sent back in the direction it came from,
   (ii) transmitted — allowed to pass through,
   (iii) absorbed — taken in by the material.

Nice bit of reflection going on there...

4) Any combination of these three is also possible (see below).

5) What actually happens depends on the wavelength of the radiation, the material the obstacle is made
of, and what the surface of this material is like (its colour, shininess, etc. — see p95 for more info).

Waves Can be Refracted

1) Waves travel at different speeds in substances with different densities.

2) EM waves travel more slowly in denser media (usually).
Sound waves travel faster in denser substances.

3) So when a wave crosses a boundary between two substances (from glass to air, say) it changes speed.

4) The effect of this change of speed is that the wave changes direction.
(The only time it doesn't change direction is when it hits the obstacle at 90°.)

The old "glass block" demo...

...but it's just as true for a pane of glass

1) As the light passes from the air into the glass (a denser medium),
it slows down.
This causes the light ray to bend towards the normal.

2) When the light reaches the 'glass to air' boundary on the other
side of the window, it speeds up and bends away from the normal.

3) But some of the light is also reflected at each of the boundaries.

Emergent ray

window glass

Refracted ray

Incident ray

A normal is a line at 90° to the boundary.

Where would Terry Wogan be without EM waves — I ask you...

In 1588, beacons were used on the south coast of England to relay the information that the Spanish
Armada was approaching. As we know, light travels as electromagnetic waves, so this is an early
example of transferring information using electromagnetic radiation — or wireless communication.

Total Internal Reflection

Total internal reflection happens when waves "can't bend enough" to refract properly.
Let me explain that a bit better...

Total Internal Reflection Happens Above the Critical Angle

1) Total internal reflection can only happen when a wave travels through a dense substance like glass or water or perspex towards a less dense substance like air.

2) It all depends on whether the angle of incidence (i.e. the angle it hits at) is bigger than the critical angle...

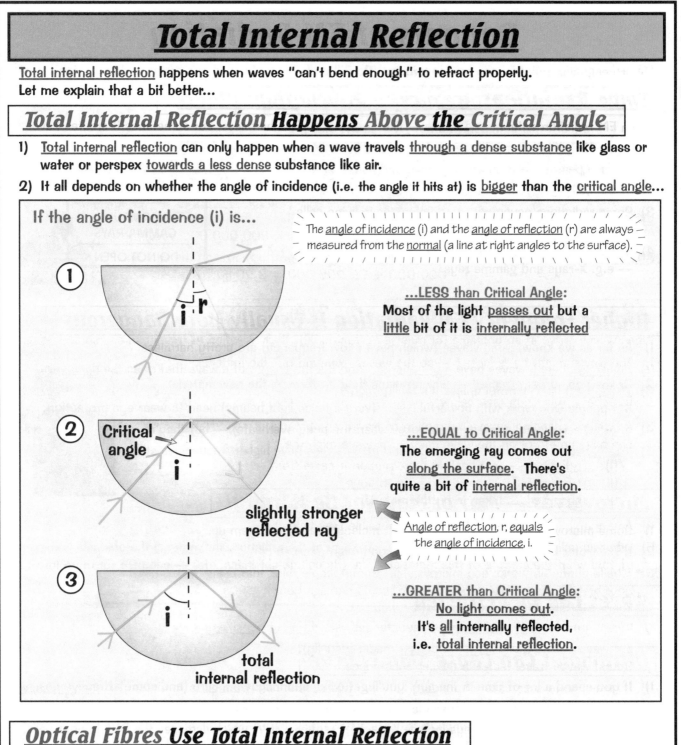

If the angle of incidence (i) is...

The angle of incidence (i) and the angle of reflection (r) are always measured from the normal (a line at right angles to the surface).

①

...LESS than Critical Angle:
Most of the light passes out but a little bit of it is internally reflected

② Critical angle

...EQUAL to Critical Angle:
The emerging ray comes out along the surface. There's quite a bit of internal reflection.

slightly stronger reflected ray

Angle of reflection, r, equals the angle of incidence, i.

③

...GREATER than Critical Angle:
No light comes out.
It's all internally reflected,
i.e. total internal reflection.

total internal reflection

Optical Fibres Use Total Internal Reflection

1) Different materials have different critical angles.

2) The critical angle for glass is about 42°.

3) Optical fibres work by bouncing waves off the sides of a thin inner core of glass or plastic using total internal reflection.

4) The wave enters one end of the fibre and is reflected repeatedly until it emerges at the other end.

5) Optical fibres can be bent, but not sharply, or the angle of incidence might fall below the critical angle.

repeated reflections

inner core

plastic sheath

outer layer

Critical angles — they're always complaining...

Optical fibres are a good way to send data over long distances — the EM waves travel fast, and they can't be tapped into or suffer interference (unlike a signal that's broadcast from a transmitter, like radio).

Dangers of EM Radiation

Electromagnetic radiation can be dangerous. (So it'll probably be banned one of these days... sigh.)

Some Radiations Are More Harmful than Others

When EM radiation enters living tissue — like you — it's often harmless, but sometimes it creates havoc.

1) Some EM radiation mostly passes through soft tissue without being absorbed — e.g. radio waves.

2) Other types of radiation are absorbed and cause heating of the cells — e.g. microwaves.

3) Some radiations cause cancerous changes in living cells — e.g. UV can cause skin cancer.

4) Some types of EM radiation can actually destroy cells — e.g. X-rays and gamma rays.

DANGER
HARMFUL:
GAMMA RAYS
DO NOT OPEN

Higher Frequency EM Radiation Is Usually More Dangerous

1) As far as we know, radio waves (which have a low frequency) are pretty harmless.

2) Higher frequency waves have more energy. And it's the energy of a wave that does the damage.

3) Visible light isn't harmful unless it's really bright.
But people who work with powerful lasers (very intense light beams) need to wear eye protection.

4) Infrared can cause burns or heatstroke (when the body overheats) — but they're easily avoidable risks.

5) X-rays have a really high frequency. And gamma rays have higher frequencies still.

Microwaves — May or May Not Be Harmful

1) Some microwaves are absorbed by water molecules and heat them up.

2) If the water happens to be in your cells, you might start to cook.

3) Mobile phone networks use microwaves. Some people think that using your mobile a lot, or living near a mast, could damage your health.
There isn't any conclusive proof either way yet.

Ultraviolet Can Cause Skin Cancer

1) If you spend a lot of time in the sun, you'll get a tan and maybe sunburn (and some attractive peeling).

2) The more time you spend in the sun, the more chance you also have of getting skin cancer.

3) This is because the Sun's rays include ultraviolet radiation (UV) which damages the DNA in your cells.

4) Dark skin gives some protection against UV rays — it absorbs more UV radiation, stopping it from reaching the more vulnerable tissues deeper in the body.

5) Everyone should protect themselves from overexposure to the Sun, but if you're pale skinned, you need to take extra care, and use a sunscreen with a higher Sun Protection Factor (SPF).

An SPF of 15 means you can spend 15 times as long in the sun as you otherwise could without burning (if you keep reapplying the sunscreen).

Size matters — and my wave's longer than yours...

There's no point being paranoid — a little bit of sunshine won't kill you (in fact it'll probably do you good). But don't be daft... getting cancer from sunbathing for hours on end is just stupid.

Radio Waves and Microwaves

Radio waves and microwaves have fairly long wavelengths (and so low frequencies). X-rays are the opposite — they're short wavelength (and so high frequency). This means their uses are very different...

Radio Waves Are Used Mainly for Communications

1) Radio waves and some microwaves are good at transferring information long distances.

2) This is partly because they don't get absorbed much by the Earth's atmosphere.

3) To receive the radio waves used for TV and FM radio transmissions, and the microwaves used for mobile phone communications, you must be in direct sight of the transmitter.

4) This is why mobile phone transmitters are positioned on hill tops and fairly close to one another.

5) Signals for satellite TV go through the atmosphere and are absorbed by and retransmitted from satellites:

> 1) A transmitter on Earth sends the signal up into space...
> 2) ...where it's picked up by the satellite receiver dish orbiting thousands of kilometres above the Earth. The satellite transmits the signal back to Earth...
> 3) ...where it's picked up by a receiving satellite dish.

Different Frequencies Behave Differently

6) Some radio waves with slightly shorter wavelengths will bounce off a layer in the atmosphere called the ionosphere.

7) And some radio waves with longer wavelengths will actually bend (diffract) around the surface of the Earth.

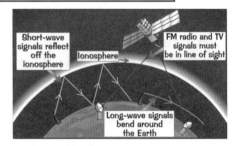

Microwaves in Ovens are Absorbed by Water Molecules

1) The microwaves used in microwave ovens have a different wavelength to those used in communication.

2) These microwaves are actually absorbed by the water molecules in the food.

3) They can penetrate a few centimetres into the food before being absorbed.

4) The energy is then conducted or convected to other parts.

5) If microwaves are absorbed by molecules in living tissue, cells may be burned or killed.

X-Rays are Used to Identify Fractures

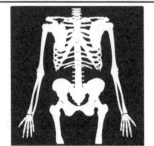

The brighter bits are where fewer X-rays get through. This is a negative image. The plate starts off all white.

1) Radiographers in hospitals take X-ray photographs of people to see if they have any broken bones.

2) X-rays pass easily through flesh but not so easily through denser material like bones or metal.

3) So it's the amount of radiation that's absorbed (or not absorbed) that gives you an X-ray image.

4) X-rays can cause cancer (see p115), so radiographers wear lead aprons and stand behind a lead screen or leave the room to keep their exposure to X-rays to a minimum.

Concentrate — don't get diffracted...

A key point on this page is that the longer the wavelength, the more it diffracts (so long-wave radio bends round the Earth, while microwaves need to be transmitted in the line of sight). But diffraction can also occur at the edges of the dishes used to transmit signals, resulting in signal loss (i.e. weaker signals).

More Uses of Waves

Infrared Radiation Can be Used to Monitor Temperature

1) Infrared radiation (or IR) is also known as heat radiation.
2) Infrared is also detected by night-vision equipment.
3) Heat radiation is given off by all objects, even in the dark of night. The equipment turns it into an electrical signal, which is displayed on a screen as a picture.

Prenatal Scanning Uses Ultrasound to Make a Picture

1) As the ultrasound hits different substances some of the waves are partially reflected.
2) These reflected waves are processed by computer to produce a video image of the foetus.

Advantages

1) As far as we know, it's safe.
2) It can show that the baby's alive and developing normally, determine its sex and show if it's likely to have Down's syndrome.
3) Ultrasound equipment is usually small and cheap.

Disadvantages

1) We can't be totally sure it's safe.
2) Will the parents want an abortion if the foetus is 'the wrong sex' or if it has Down's syndrome.
   Is it right for parents to have this choice?

Iris Scanning Uses Light to Make a Picture

1) Each eye's iris has a unique pattern. This means that iris patterns can be used in security checks to prove a person's identity.
2) A picture is taken of your eye using an iris scanner. A computer then analyses the patterns in your iris to check your identity.

Advantages

1) There's very little chance of mistaking one iris code for another.
2) Your iris won't (usually) change.
3) Iris scanning is quick and easy to carry out.

Disadvantages

1) Some people feel their personal freedom is threatened: who's holding our data, and why?
2) If iris data is assumed to be 'unfakeable', will genuine mistakes or stolen identity be believed?
3) Eye injuries or surgery can occasionally change your iris pattern.

CD Players Use Lasers to Read Information

1) The surface of a CD has a pattern of shallow pits cut into it.
2) A laser is shone onto the CD as it spins around in the player.
3) The beam is reflected from a pit and from the surrounding area slightly differently — this difference can be picked up by a light sensor.
4) These differences in reflected signals can then be changed into an electrical signal, which is converted into sound.

Cross section of CD

Plastic disk

Pit

Laser shines from underneath

IR cameras and iris scanning — wave bye bye to your privacy...

To some people, this identity-checking stuff feels a wee bit too '1984'* — but to others (including the Government) it'll help us cut down on passport forging and is essential for security.

*The book by George Orwell. It's a bit sinister.

Analogue and Digital Signals

Digital technology is gradually taking over. By 2012, you won't be able to watch TV unless you've got a digital version — that's when the Government's planning to switch off the last analogue signal.

Analogue Signals Vary but Digital's Either On or Off

1) Information is being transmitted everywhere all the time.

2) Very often it's sent long distances down telephone wires or carried on EM waves.

3) There are two basic kinds of signal — analogue and digital...

4) An analogue signal can take any value in a particular range.

   Dimmer switches, thermometers, speedometers and old-fashioned watches are all analogue devices.

Analogue

This analogue signal takes every value in this range.

Digital

This digital signal only takes these two values.

5) Digital signals can only take two values (the two values sometimes get different names, but the key thing is that there are only two of them): on or off, true or false, 0 or 1...

6) On/off switches and the displays on digital clocks and meters are all digital devices.

Signals Have to Be Amplified

Both digital and analogue signals weaken as they travel, so they may need to be amplified along their route.

They also pick up interference or noise from electrical disturbances or other signals.

Digital Signals Are Far Better Quality

1) Noise is less of a problem with digital signals. If you receive a noisy digital signal, it's pretty obvious what it's supposed to be.

   This noisy digital signal... ...is obviously supposed to be this.

   But this noisy analogue signal... ...could have started like this... ...or this...

2) But if you receive a noisy analogue signal, it's difficult to know what the original signal would have looked like. And if you amplify a noisy analogue signal, you amplify the noise as well.

3) This is why digital signals are much higher quality — the information received is the same as the original.

4) Digital signals are also easy to process using computers, since computers are digital devices too.

I've got loads of digital stuff — watch, radio, fingers...

Digital signals are great — unless you live in a part of the country which currently has poor reception of digital broadcasts, in which case you get no benefit at all. This is because if you don't get spot-on reception of digital signals in your area, you won't get a grainy but watchable picture (like with analogue signals) — you'll get nothing at all. Except snow.

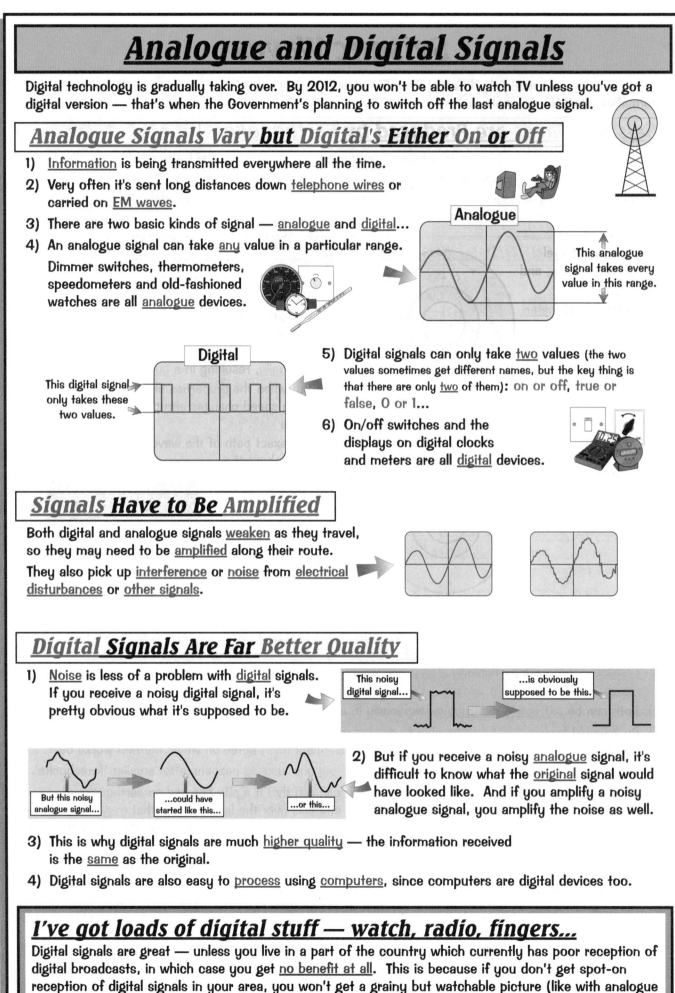

Seismic Waves

Seismic waves are completely different from EM waves (although they're still waves, so all the 'normal wave stuff' still applies).

Seismic Waves are Produced by Earthquakes

1) When there's an earthquake somewhere, it produces seismic waves which travel out through the Earth.
2) We detect these waves all over the surface of the planet using seismographs.
3) There are two different types of seismic waves you need to learn — P-waves and S-waves.

P-Waves are Longitudinal

1) P-waves travel through solids and liquids.
2) They travel faster than S-waves.

S-Waves are TranSverSe

1) S-waves only travel through Solids.
2) They're Slower than P-waves.

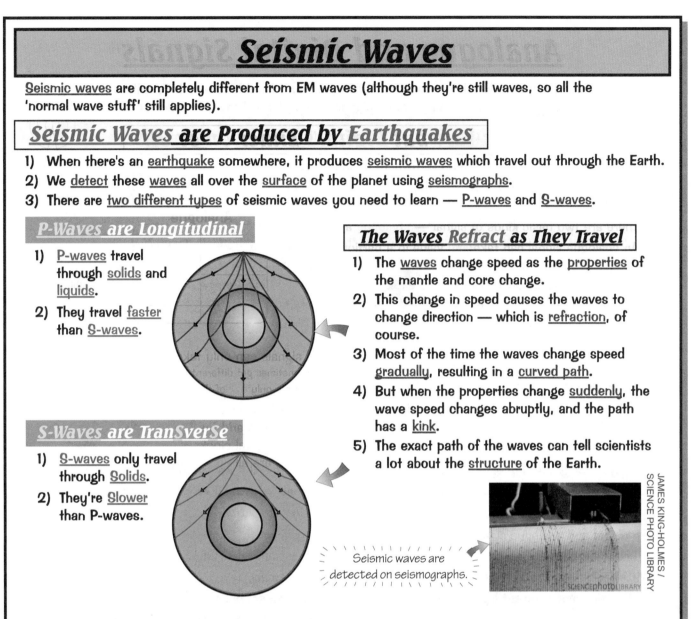

The Waves Refract as They Travel

1) The waves change speed as the properties of the mantle and core change.
2) This change in speed causes the waves to change direction — which is refraction, of course.
3) Most of the time the waves change speed gradually, resulting in a curved path.
4) But when the properties change suddenly, the wave speed changes abruptly, and the path has a kink.
5) The exact path of the waves can tell scientists a lot about the structure of the Earth.

Seismic waves are detected on seismographs.

JAMES KING-HOLMES / SCIENCE PHOTO LIBRARY

It's Difficult to Predict Earthquakes and Tsunami Waves

1) Some countries are particularly susceptible to earthquakes, which can also sometimes cause tsunami waves.
2) Both can be extremely destructive, especially in areas where the housing isn't built to withstand them.
3) So it would be very useful to be able to predict when they're likely to hit. But predicting earthquakes accurately is hard. Scientists don't agree on which method works best.
4) Seismic waves can help predict earthquakes — a 'big one' usually happens after smaller 'foreshocks'.

SPENCER GRANT / SCIENCE PHOTO LIBRARY

5) Or you can say that if a city has had an earthquake at regular intervals over the last century, that trend may continue. This isn't necessarily dead-on accurate, but it still gives the area time to prepare, just in case.
6) Changes in animal behaviour have also been used to try and predict earthquakes.
7) Various methods have been successful, but they have also missed some biggies.

My dog's in the shed and won't stop barking — evacuate the city...

Scientists are still doing lots of research into earthquake prediction — and disasters like the Indian Ocean tsunami in 2004 and the Kashmir earthquake in 2005 have really raised its profile of late.

Revision Summary for Section 8

Try these lovely questions. Go on — you know you want to. It'll be nice.

1) Explain what current, voltage and resistance are in an electric circuit.

2) Do batteries produce AC or DC current? In what units is battery capacity measured?

3) Sketch a voltage-current graph for a resistor.

4)* Calculate the resistance of a wire if the voltage across it is 12 V and the current through it is 2.5 A.

5) Describe how the resistance of an LDR varies with light intensity. Give an application of an LDR.

6) Describe how you can create a current in a coil of wire using a magnet.

7) What are three factors that affect the size of the voltage that you get this way?

8) Sketch a generator with all the details. Explain how it works.

9) Sketch a typical power station, and explain what happens at each stage.
   Describe the useful energy transformations that occur.

10) Why is a very high electrical voltage used to transmit electricity in the national grid?

11) What's the name of the type of transformer that increases voltage? Where are these used?

12) Write down the formula linking voltage, current and power.

13)* Calculate the energy used by a 3.1 kW kettle if it's on for 1½ minutes.

14)* a) How many units of electricity (in kWh) would a kettle of power 2500 W use in 2 minutes?
     b) How much would that cost, if one unit of electricity costs 12p?

15) Explain fully how a fuse and earth wire work together.

16) Draw a diagram of a wave and label a crest and a trough, and the wavelength and amplitude.

17) Sketch the EM spectrum with all the details you've learned. Put the lowest frequency waves first.

18) Electromagnetic waves don't carry any matter. What <u>do</u> they carry?

19) What aspect of EM waves determines their differing properties?

20)* Find the speed of a wave with frequency 50 kHz and wavelength 0.3 cm.

21) Describe what can happen to a wave when it meets an obstacle.

22) Explain what is meant by: a) refraction, b) total internal reflection.

23) Explain why sending data by optical fibre might be better than broadcasting it as a radio signal.

24)* In which of the cases A to D below would the ray of light be totally internally reflected?
     (The critical angle for glass is approximately 42°.)

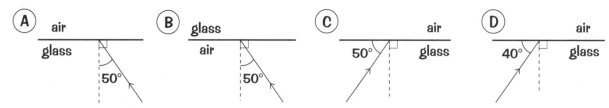

25) Which is generally more dangerous — low frequency or high frequency EM radiation?

26) Describe the main <u>known</u> dangers of microwaves, infrared, visible light, UV and X-rays.

27) Describe the different ways that short and long-wave radio signals can travel long distances.

28) Describe two uses of microwaves, and explain why microwaves are suitable for these uses.

29) Explain how X-rays can be useful in hospitals.

30) Explain how EM waves are used in: a) prenatal scanning, b) iris scanning, c) CD players.

31) Draw diagrams illustrating analogue and digital signals. What advantages do digital signals have?

32) How are P-waves and S-waves different?

33) Why do P-waves and S-waves change direction as they travel through the Earth?

* Answers on page 140

Radioactivity

Nuclear radiation is different from EM radiation. So you do need to read these next few pages. Sorry.

Nuclei Contain Protons and Neutrons

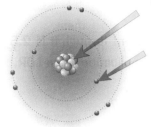

The nucleus contains protons and neutrons. It makes up most of the mass of the atom, but takes up virtually no space — it's tiny.

The electrons are negatively charged and really really small. They whizz around the outside of the atom.

Isotopes Are Atoms with Different Numbers of Neutrons

1) Isotopes are atoms with the same number of protons but a different number of neutrons.
2) E.g. there are two common isotopes of carbon. The carbon-14 isotope has two more neutrons than 'normal' carbon (carbon-12).
3) Some isotopes are unstable, so they decay. When this happens, they emit radiation.
4) These isotopes are radioactive.
5) Carbon-14 is a radioactive isotope of carbon.

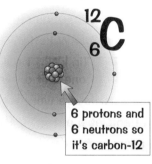

6 protons and 6 neutrons so it's carbon-12

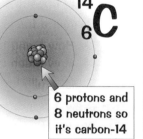

6 protons and 8 neutrons so it's carbon-14

Radioactive Decay Is a Random Process

1) If you have 1000 unstable nuclei, you can't say when any one of them is going to decay, and you can't do anything at all to make a decay happen.
2) Each nucleus just decays in its own good time. It's completely unaffected by temperature or by any sort of chemical bonding.
3) When a nucleus decays, it spits out one or more of the three types of radiation — alpha, beta and gamma (see next page).
4) In the process, the nucleus often changes into a new element.

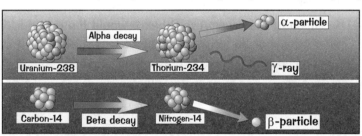

Background Radiation is Everywhere All the Time

There's (low-level) background nuclear radiation all around us all the time. It comes from:
- substances here on Earth — e.g. air, soil, rocks, building materials...
- radiation from space (cosmic rays) — these come mostly from the Sun (see p127),
- living things — there's a little bit of radioactive material in all living things,
- radiation due to human activity — e.g. fallout from nuclear explosions, or nuclear waste (though this is usually a tiny proportion of the total background radiation).

Unstable isotopes — put them in the field...

This isotope business can be confusing at first, as you can have different isotopes which are all the same element. Remember... it's the number of protons which decides what element it is, then the number of neutrons decides what isotope of that element it is. (And it's unstable isotopes which undergo radioactive decay.)

The Three Kinds of Radioactivity

There are three types of radiation — alpha (α), beta (β) and gamma (γ). You need to remember what they are, how well they penetrate materials (including air), and their ionising power.

Nuclear Radiation Causes Ionisation

1) Nuclear radiation causes ionisation by bashing into atoms and knocking electrons off them.

2) There's a pattern: the further the radiation can penetrate before hitting an atom and getting stopped, the less damage it will do along the way and so the less ionising it is.

Alpha Particles Are Helium Nuclei ^4_2He

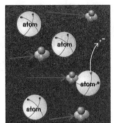

1) Alpha particles are made up of 2 protons and 2 neutrons.

2) They're big, heavy and slow-moving.

3) They don't penetrate far into materials. Because of their size they bash into a lot of atoms and knock electrons off them. So they're heavily ionising.

4) Alpha particles are deflected (their direction changes) by electric and magnetic fields.

Beta Particles Are Electrons $^0_{-1}e$

1) A beta particle is an electron which has been emitted from the nucleus of an atom.

2) Beta particles move quite fast and they are quite small.

3) They penetrate moderately before colliding and are moderately ionising too.

4) Beta particles are also deflected by electric and magnetic fields.

Gamma Rays Are Very Short Wavelength EM Waves

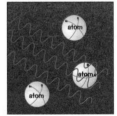

1) Gamma rays are an electromagnetic wave (see p112). They have no mass — they're just energy.

2) They penetrate a long way into materials without being stopped.

3) This means they're weakly ionising because they tend to pass through rather than collide with atoms. But eventually they hit something and do damage.

4) Gamma rays are not deflected by electric or magnetic fields.

You Can Identify the Type by What Blocks It

1) Alpha particles are blocked by paper, skin or a few centimetres of air.

2) Beta particles are stopped by thin metal.

3) Gamma rays are blocked by thick lead or very thick concrete.

4) So if radiation can penetrate metal it could be beta or gamma — you'd have to test it with thick lead to find out which.

Skin or paper stops ALPHA   Thin aluminium stops BETA   Thick lead stops GAMMA

Learn your alphabet-agamma...

Remember: alpha's big, slow and clumsy — always knocking into things. Beta's lightweight and fast, and gamma weighs nothing and moves super-fast. Practise with this: if it gets through paper and is deflected by a magnetic field, it must be _____ radiation. (Answer on page 140.)

Section 9 — Radioactivity and Space

Half-Life

The waste from nuclear power stations is a real pain, because some of it stays radioactive for years and years — it has a long half-life.

The Radioactivity of a Sample Always Decreases Over Time

1) Each time an unstable nucleus decays and emits radiation, that means one more radioactive nucleus isn't there to decay later.

2) As more unstable nuclei decay, the radioactivity of the source as a whole decreases.
   So the older a radioactive source is, the less radiation it emits.

3) How quickly the activity decreases varies a lot.
   For some isotopes it takes just a few hours before nearly all the unstable nuclei have decayed.
   Others last for millions of years.

4) The idea of half-life is used to measure how quickly the activity decreases.
   Learn this important definition of half-life:

> HALF-LIFE is the **TIME TAKEN** for **HALF** of
> the nuclei now present to **DECAY**

5) A short half-life means the activity falls quickly, because lots of the nuclei decay quickly.

6) A long half-life means the activity falls more slowly because most of the nuclei don't decay for a long time — they just sit there, basically unstable, but kind of biding their time.

one half-life   one half-life

Half-Life Is the Time Taken for the Count Rate to Halve

Count rate halves from 400 to 200 in 4 hours. It takes another 4 hours to halve again.

one half-life   one half-life   one half-life

COUNT RATE counts per min.

TIME in hrs.

1) You can work out the half-life of a sample by monitoring its count rate (the number of atoms which decay per minute) using a Geiger counter.

2) Then plot a graph of count rate against time.

- 'Carbon dating' of archaeological specimens uses the idea of half-life.

- Scientists can work out how long dusty bits of bone have been around by looking at the count rate now of certain isotopes.

Half-life — a teenager in the morning...

To measure half-life, you time how long it takes for the number of nuclei (or the count rate) to halve — and this can vary from fractions of a second (you need to be quick with the stopwatch) to thousands of millions of years (which is quite a while to hang around with the Geiger counter and graph paper).

Dangers from Nuclear Radiation

You've got to be really careful with anything radioactive — no mucking about.

Radiation Harms Living Cells...

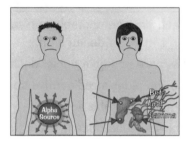

1) Alpha radiation can't penetrate the skin. But if it gets inside your body (by you <u>swallowing</u> or <u>breathing it in</u>, say) — alpha sources will do a lot of damage.

2) <u>Beta</u> and <u>gamma</u> radiation can penetrate the skin and soft tissues to reach the delicate <u>organs</u> inside the body.

3) But <u>inside</u> the body, beta and gamma sources are <u>less dangerous</u> than alpha sources — their radiation mostly <u>passes straight out</u> without doing much damage.

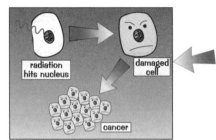

4) If radiation enters your body, it will <u>collide</u> with molecules in your cells, and cause <u>ionisation</u>.

5) This can <u>damage</u> or <u>destroy</u> molecules (which means the cells will also be damaged).

6) <u>Lower</u> doses tend to cause <u>minor</u> damage without <u>killing</u> the cell. But this can eventually cause <u>cancer</u> — <u>mutant</u> cells which <u>divide uncontrollably</u>.

7) <u>Higher</u> doses can <u>kill cells</u> completely, causing <u>radiation sickness</u> if a large part of your body is affected at the same time.

8) The <u>extent</u> of the harmful effects depends on <u>how much exposure</u> you have to the radiation, and its <u>energy</u> and <u>penetration</u>.

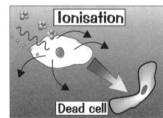

You Should Protect Yourself in the Laboratory...

You should always act to <u>minimise</u> your exposure to radioactive sources.

1) <u>Never</u> allow <u>skin contact</u> with a source. Always handle sources with <u>tongs</u>.

2) Keep the source at <u>arm's length</u> to keep it <u>as far</u> from the body <u>as possible</u>.

3) Keep the source <u>pointing away</u> from the body and <u>avoid looking directly at it</u>.

4) <u>Always</u> keep the source in a <u>labelled lead box</u> and put it back in <u>as soon</u> as the experiment is <u>over</u>, to keep your <u>exposure time</u> short.

...and If You Work with Nuclear Radiation

1) Industrial nuclear workers wear <u>full protective suits</u> to prevent <u>tiny radioactive particles</u> being <u>breathed in</u> or getting <u>on the skin</u> or <u>under fingernails</u> etc.

2) <u>Lead-lined suits</u> and <u>lead/concrete barriers</u> and <u>thick lead screens</u> are used to prevent exposure to <u>gamma rays</u>.
(α and β radiation are stopped <u>much more easily</u>.)

3) Workers use <u>remote-controlled robot arms</u> to carry out tasks in highly radioactive areas.

Revision sickness — never mind, only a few pages to go...

It's quite difficult to do research on how radiation affects humans. This is partly because it would be very <u>unethical</u> to do <u>controlled experiments</u>, exposing people to huge doses of radiation just to see what happens. We rely mostly on studies of populations affected by <u>nuclear accidents</u> or nuclear <u>bombs</u>.

Uses of Nuclear Radiation

Nuclear radiation can be very <u>dangerous</u>. But it can be very <u>useful</u> too. Read on...

Alpha Radiation *is Used in Smoke Detectors*

1) Smoke detectors have a <u>weak</u> source of <u>α-radiation</u> close to <u>two electrodes</u>.
2) The radiation <u>ionises</u> the air, and a <u>current</u> flows between the electrodes.
3) But if there's a fire, the <u>smoke absorbs</u> the <u>radiation</u> — the <u>current stops</u> and the <u>alarm sounds</u>.

Beta Radiation *is Used in Tracers and Thickness Gauges*

1) Radioactive substances have <u>medical</u> uses.

   For example, if a radioactive source is <u>injected</u> into a patient (or <u>swallowed</u>), its progress around the body can be followed using an <u>external radiation detector</u>.

   These '<u>tracers</u>' can show if the body is working properly.

   Doctors use <u>beta</u> or <u>gamma</u> emitters as <u>tracers</u> because this radiation <u>passes out</u> of the body. They also choose things that are only radioactive for a <u>few hours</u>.

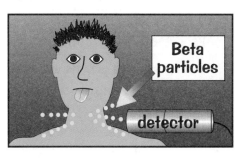

2) <u>Beta radiation</u> is also used in <u>thickness control</u>.

   You direct radiation through the stuff being made (e.g. paper or cardboard), and put a detector on the other side, connected to a control unit.

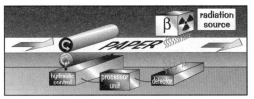

   When the amount of <u>detected</u> radiation goes <u>down</u>, it means the paper's coming out <u>too thick</u>, so the control unit pinches the rollers up a bit to make it thinner.

   If the reading goes <u>up</u>, the paper's <u>too thin</u>, so the control unit opens the rollers out a bit.

   For this use, your radioactive substance mustn't decay away <u>too quickly</u>, otherwise its strength would gradually fall (and the control unit would keep pinching up the rollers trying to compensate).

   You need to use a <u>beta</u> source, because then the paper or cardboard will <u>partly block</u> the radiation. If it <u>all</u> goes through (or <u>none</u> of it does), then the reading <u>won't change</u> at all as the thickness changes.

Gamma Radiation *Has Medical and Industrial Uses*

1) High doses of <u>gamma rays</u> can be used to treat <u>cancers</u>.

   The gamma rays have to be <u>directed carefully</u> at the cancer, and at just the right <u>dosage</u> so as to kill the <u>cancer</u> cells <u>without</u> damaging too many <u>normal</u> cells.

2) Gamma rays are also used to <u>sterilise</u> medical instruments — by <u>killing</u> all the microbes.

   You need to use a strongly radioactive source that lasts a long time, so that it doesn't need replacing too often.

3) Gamma radiation is also used in <u>non-destructive testing</u>.

   For example, <u>airlines</u> can check the turbine blades of their jet engines by directing gamma rays at them. If <u>too much</u> radiation reaches the <u>detector</u> on the other side, they know the blade's <u>cracked</u> or there's a fault in the welding. It's so much better to find this out before you take off than in mid-air.

Thickness gauges — they're called 'exams' nowadays...

Knowing the detail is important here. For instance, swallowing an alpha source as a medical tracer would be very foolish — alpha radiation would cause all sorts of chaos inside your body but couldn't be detected outside, making the whole thing pointless. So learn <u>what</u> each type's used for <u>and why</u>.

The Solar System

Our Solar System consists of a star (the Sun) and lots of stuff orbiting it in elongated circles.

Planets Reflect Sunlight and Orbit the Sun in Ellipses

- Closest to the Sun are the inner planets — Mercury, Venus, Earth and Mars.
- Then the asteroid belt — see below.
- Then the outer planets, much further away — Jupiter, Saturn, Uranus, Neptune and Pluto.

You need to learn the order of the planets, which is made easier by using the little jollyism below:

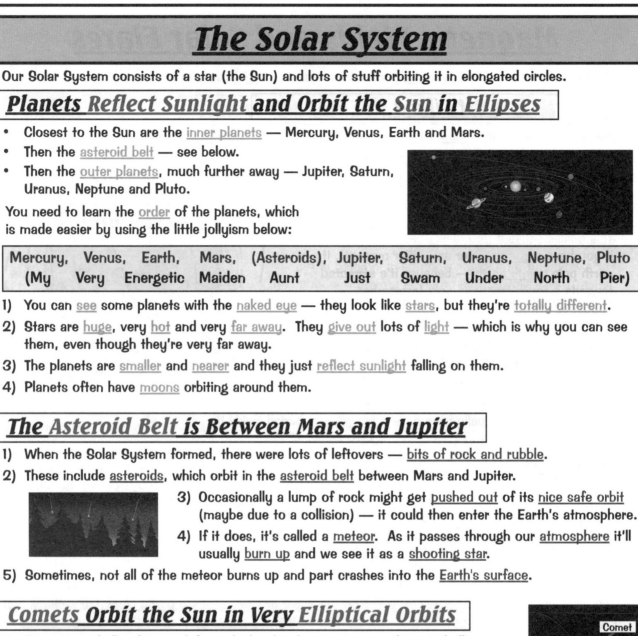

Mercury,	Venus,	Earth,	Mars,	(Asteroids),	Jupiter,	Saturn,	Uranus,	Neptune,	Pluto
(My	Very	Energetic	Maiden	Aunt	Just	Swam	Under	North	Pier)

1) You can see some planets with the naked eye — they look like stars, but they're totally different.

2) Stars are huge, very hot and very far away. They give out lots of light — which is why you can see them, even though they're very far away.

3) The planets are smaller and nearer and they just reflect sunlight falling on them.

4) Planets often have moons orbiting around them.

The Asteroid Belt is Between Mars and Jupiter

1) When the Solar System formed, there were lots of leftovers — bits of rock and rubble.

2) These include asteroids, which orbit in the asteroid belt between Mars and Jupiter.

3) Occasionally a lump of rock might get pushed out of its nice safe orbit (maybe due to a collision) — it could then enter the Earth's atmosphere.

4) If it does, it's called a meteor. As it passes through our atmosphere it'll usually burn up and we see it as a shooting star.

5) Sometimes, not all of the meteor burns up and part crashes into the Earth's surface.

Comets Orbit the Sun in Very Elliptical Orbits

1) Comets are balls of ice and dust which orbit the Sun in very elongated ellipses — taking them very far away and then back in close — which is when we see them.

2) The Sun is near one end of the orbit, not at its centre.

3) As a comet approaches the Sun, it speeds up. Also, its ice melts, leaving a bright tail of gas and debris which can be millions of kilometres long.

Near-Earth Objects (NEOs) Could Collide with Earth

1) Some asteroids and comets have orbits that pass very close to the orbit of the Earth.

2) They're called Near-Earth Objects (NEOs). Astronomers keep a close eye on the orbits of NEOs, since they might collide with us in the future.

3) A huge collision is unlikely in our lifetimes, but it's possible — there have been big impacts in the past. Evidence for this includes:

   i) big craters, ii) layers of unusual elements in rocks — these must have been 'imported' by an asteroid or comet, iii) sudden changes in fossil numbers between adjacent layers of rock, as species suffer extinction.

Asteroids... my dad had those — very nasty...

It's serious business, this NEO stuff. In 2002, an asteroid narrowly missed us, and we only found it 12 days beforehand — not very much time to put a plan together. Even if Bruce Willis had been on hand.

Magnetic Fields and Solar Flares

The Earth can protect us from a lot of nasties from space — e.g. cosmic rays. Hurrah.

The Earth _is a Bit Like a_ Big Magnet

1) The Earth is surrounded by a magnetic field.
   Basically, this means the Earth acts like a big bar magnet.

2) Like all magnets, it has north and south poles.

3) But... (concentrate now) the Earth's south magnetic pole is actually at the North Pole.

   This makes sense if you think about it...
   if you have a compass (or any other magnet), its north pole points north — because it's attracted towards a south magnetic pole (remember, opposites attract).

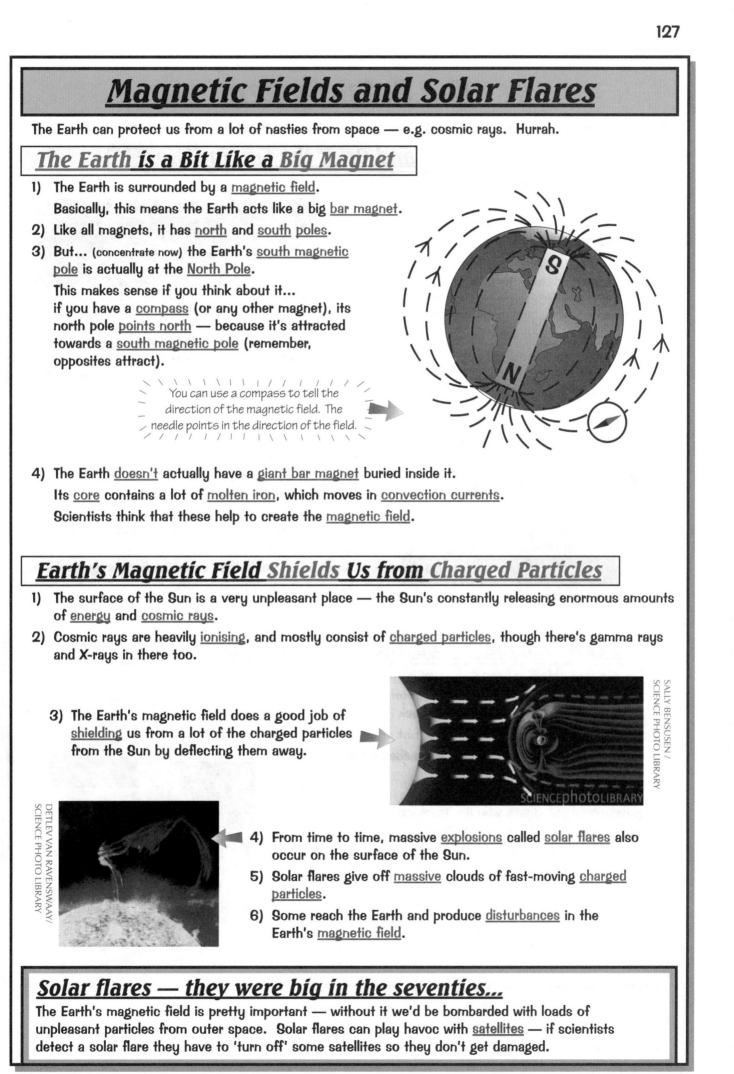

> You can use a compass to tell the direction of the magnetic field. The needle points in the direction of the field.

4) The Earth doesn't actually have a giant bar magnet buried inside it.
   Its core contains a lot of molten iron, which moves in convection currents.
   Scientists think that these help to create the magnetic field.

Earth's Magnetic Field _Shields_ Us from _Charged Particles_

1) The surface of the Sun is a very unpleasant place — the Sun's constantly releasing enormous amounts of energy and cosmic rays.

2) Cosmic rays are heavily ionising, and mostly consist of charged particles, though there's gamma rays and X-rays in there too.

SALLY BENSUSEN / SCIENCE PHOTO LIBRARY

3) The Earth's magnetic field does a good job of shielding us from a lot of the charged particles from the Sun by deflecting them away.

sciencephotolibrary

DETLEV VAN RAVENSWAAY / SCIENCE PHOTO LIBRARY

4) From time to time, massive explosions called solar flares also occur on the surface of the Sun.

5) Solar flares give off massive clouds of fast-moving charged particles.

6) Some reach the Earth and produce disturbances in the Earth's magnetic field.

Solar flares — they were big in the seventies...

The Earth's magnetic field is pretty important — without it we'd be bombarded with loads of unpleasant particles from outer space. Solar flares can play havoc with satellites — if scientists detect a solar flare they have to 'turn off' some satellites so they don't get damaged.

Section 9 — Radioactivity and Space

Beyond the Solar System

There's all sorts of exciting stuff in the Universe... Our whole Solar System is just part of a huge galaxy. And there are billions upon billions of galaxies. You should be realising now that the Universe is huge...

We're in the Milky Way Galaxy

1) Our Sun is just one of many billions of stars which form the Milky Way galaxy. Our Sun is about halfway along one of the spiral arms of the Milky Way.

2) The distance between neighbouring stars in the galaxy is usually millions of times greater than the distance between planets in our Solar System.

3) The force which keeps the stars together in a galaxy is gravity, of course. And like most things in the Universe, galaxies rotate — a bit like a Catherine wheel.

You are here

You are here

The Whole Universe Has More Than a Billion Galaxies

1) Galaxies themselves are often millions of times further apart than the stars are within a galaxy.

2) So even the slowest among you will have worked out that the Universe is mostly empty space and is really really BIG.

Stars Can Explode — and They Sometimes Leave Black Holes

1) When a really big star has used up all its fuel, it explodes.

2) What's left after the explosion is really dense — sometimes so dense that nothing can escape its gravitational pull. It's now called a black hole.

3) Black holes have a very large mass but their diameter is tiny in comparison.

4) They're not visible — even light can't escape their gravitational pull (that's why it's 'black', d'oh).

5) Astronomers have to detect black holes in other ways — e.g. they can observe X-rays emitted by hot gases from other stars as they spiral into the black hole.

See p129 for more about the death of stars.

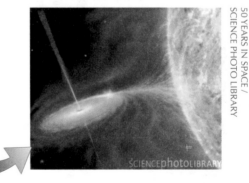

DAVID A. HARDY, FUTURES: 50 YEARS IN SPACE / SCIENCE PHOTO LIBRARY

This is what a black hole might look like (it's in the centre of the disc on the left). It's quite pretty really... but you probably wouldn't want to stand too close. This one's 'hoovering up' matter from a nearby star.

Spiral arms — would you still need elbows...

A lot of people say it's a small world. I'm not sure... it's always seemed pretty big to me. Anyway... you never hear anybody say the Universe is small. Not nowadays, anyway. Weirdly though, the Universe used to be tiny (see p130). That was a while ago though.

The Life Cycle of Stars

Stars go through <u>many traumatic stages</u> in their lives — just like teenagers.

Clouds of Dust and Gas

1) Stars <u>initially form</u> from clouds of <u>DUST AND GAS</u>.

Protostar

2) The <u>force of gravity</u> makes the gas and dust <u>spiral in together</u> to form a <u>protostar</u>. <u>Gravitational energy</u> has been converted into <u>heat energy</u>, so the <u>temperature rises</u>.

Main Sequence Star

3) When the <u>temperature</u> gets <u>high enough</u>, <u>hydrogen nuclei</u> undergo <u>nuclear fusion</u> to form <u>helium nuclei</u> and give out massive amounts of <u>heat and light</u>. A star is born. It immediately enters a <u>long stable period</u> where the <u>heat created</u> by the nuclear fusion provides an <u>outward pressure</u> to <u>balance</u> the <u>force of gravity</u> pulling everything <u>inwards</u>. In this stable period it's called a <u>MAIN SEQUENCE STAR</u> and it lasts <u>several billion years</u>. (The Sun is in the middle of this stable period — or to put it another way, the <u>Earth</u> has already had <u>half its innings</u> before the Sun <u>engulfs</u> it.)

4) Eventually the <u>hydrogen</u> begins to <u>run out</u> and the star then <u>swells</u> into a <u>RED GIANT</u>. It becomes <u>red</u> because the surface <u>cools</u>.

5) A <u>small star</u> like our Sun will then begin to <u>cool</u> and <u>contract</u> into a <u>WHITE DWARF</u> and then finally, as the <u>light fades completely</u>, it becomes a <u>BLACK DWARF</u>. (That's going to be really sad.)

Red Giant

Small stars → White Dwarf → Black Dwarf

Big stars

6) <u>Big stars</u>, however, start to <u>glow brightly again</u> as they undergo more <u>fusion</u> and <u>expand and contract several times</u>, forming <u>heavier elements</u> in various <u>nuclear reactions</u>. Eventually they'll <u>explode</u> in a <u>SUPERNOVA</u>.

new planetary nebula... ...and a new solar system

Supernova

Neutron Star...

...or Black Hole

7) The <u>exploding supernova</u> throws the outer layers of <u>dust and gas</u> into space, leaving a <u>very dense core</u> called a <u>NEUTRON STAR</u>. If the star is <u>big enough</u> this will become a <u>BLACK HOLE</u> (see p128).

8) The <u>dust and gas</u> thrown off by the supernova will form into <u>SECOND GENERATION STARS</u> like our Sun. The <u>heavier elements</u> are <u>only</u> made in the <u>final stages</u> of a <u>big star</u> just before and during the final <u>supernova</u>, so the <u>presence</u> of heavier elements in the <u>Sun</u> and the <u>inner planets</u> is <u>clear evidence</u> that our beautiful and wonderful world, with its warm sunsets and fresh morning dews, has all formed out of the snotty remains of a grisly old star's last dying sneeze.

Red Giants, White Dwarfs, Black Holes, Green Ghosts...

Erm. Now how do they know that exactly... Anyway, now you know what the future holds — our Sun is going to fizzle out, and it'll just get <u>very very cold</u> and <u>very very dark</u>. Great.

The Origins of the Universe

Once upon a time, there was a really Big Bang — that's the most convincing theory we've got for how the Universe came into existence.

Light From Other Galaxies is Red-Shifted

1) When we look at light from distant galaxies we find the frequencies are all lower than they should be — they're shifted towards the red end of the spectrum. This is called the red-shift.

2) It's kind of the same effect as a car's noise sounding lower-pitched when the car's moving away from you.

3) Now then... all galaxies seem to be moving away from us very quickly — and it's the same result whichever direction you look in.

4) Also, more distant galaxies have greater red-shifts than nearer ones... which means that more distant galaxies are moving away faster than nearer ones.

5) All these findings indicate that the whole Universe is expanding.

There's a Uniform Microwave Radiation From All Directions

1) Scientists have detected low frequency electromagnetic radiation coming from all parts of the Universe.

2) This radiation is in the microwave part of the EM spectrum. It's known as the cosmic microwave background radiation.

3) For complicated reasons this background radiation is strong evidence for an initial Big Bang (see below).

It All Started Off with a Very Big Bang (Probably)

1) Right now, all the galaxies are moving away from each other at great speed. But something must have got them going in the first place.

2) That 'something' was probably a big explosion — so they called it the Big Bang.

3) According to this theory, all the matter and energy in the Universe was compressed into a very small space. Then it exploded and started expanding.

4) The expansion is still going on. We can use the current rate of expansion of the Universe to estimate its age.

5) Our best guess is that the Big Bang happened about 14 billion years ago (though that might not be very accurate, as it's hard to tell how much the expansion has slowed down since the Big Bang).

The Future of the Universe...

Depending on how much mass there is in the Universe, there are two ways it could go...

Either a Big Crunch...

If there's enough mass, the Universe will eventually stop expanding — and then begin contracting. This would end in a Big Crunch.

...or Just Cold Lonely Oblivion

If there's too little mass in the Universe to stop the expansion, it could expand forever with the Universe becoming more and more spread out into eternity.

In the beginning, there was — well, nobody knows, actually...

Most scientists accept the idea of the Big Bang — it's the best way to explain the evidence we have at the moment. But if new evidence turns up, the theory could turn out to be rubbish. After all, there wasn't anyone around 14 billion years ago, taking photos and writing things down in a little notebook.

Gravity, Mass and Weight

The only thing that stops you flying off the planet into space is gravity. You'd be <u>very lost</u> without it.

Gravity is the Attraction Between All Masses

1) <u>Gravity</u> is what <u>attracts masses</u> to each other.
All masses attract each other, but the <u>bigger the mass</u>, the <u>stronger its gravity</u> is.

2) The attraction is only noticeable when one of the masses is <u>really really big</u>, e.g. a planet or star.
Gravity keeps <u>planets</u>, <u>moons</u> and <u>satellites</u> in their <u>orbits</u> around stars and planets.

The Resultant Force is the Overall Unbalanced Force

1) The force of gravity acts on pretty much everything.

2) But there's usually <u>more than one force</u> acting on any <u>object</u>, and they <u>don't always balance</u>...
Unbalanced forces cause <u>objects</u> to <u>accelerate</u>.

3) How it <u>accelerates</u> depends on its <u>mass</u> and the <u>force</u>:

$$\text{Resultant Force} = \text{Mass} \times \text{Acceleration}$$

$$F = ma \quad \text{or} \quad a = F/m$$

Make sure you use the right units:
<u>Force</u> in <u>newtons, N</u>; <u>Mass</u> in <u>kg</u>; <u>Acceleration</u> in <u>m/s²</u>

$$\frac{F}{m \times a}$$

Weight and Mass are Not the Same

1) <u>Mass</u> is the <u>amount of 'stuff'</u> in an object.
It's measured in <u>kilograms</u>.

2) <u>Weight</u> is caused by the <u>pull of gravity</u>.
<u>Weight</u> is a <u>force</u>, and has units of <u>newtons</u>.

Weight is measured with a
spring balance or newton meter.

3) An object has the <u>same mass</u> whether it's on <u>Earth</u> or on the <u>Moon</u>,
but its <u>weight</u> will be <u>different</u>.
This is because the Moon has <u>weaker</u> gravity.

4) This is why astronauts seem to be bouncing when they walk
on the Moon — they weigh less (i.e. their weight is smaller).

Weight = Mass × Acceleration of Free-Fall

To work out the <u>weight</u> of an object, you'll need this equation:

1) Hopefully it's obvious what W and m stand for.

2) The letter "g" represents the <u>strength of the gravity</u>, in N/kg.
The value of g is <u>different</u> for <u>different</u> planets.
On <u>Earth</u> g ≈ 10 N/kg. On the <u>Moon</u>, it's just 1.6 N/kg.

$$W = m \times g$$
(in <u>N</u>) (in <u>kg</u>) (in <u>N/kg</u>)

3) This formula is <u>hideously easy</u> to use:

<u>EXAMPLE:</u> On the Earth, what is the weight, in newtons, of a 5 kg mass?
<u>ANSWER:</u>   W = 5 × 10 = <u>50 N</u>

See... easy.

I hate gravity — it really gets me down...

Apparently the whole point of Newton trying to explain gravity was to work out the <u>motion of the planets</u>.
I always thought his theory of gravity just came out of nowhere and hit him on the head, so to speak.

Exploring the Solar System

If you want to know what it's like on another planet, you have three options — peer at it from a distance, get in a spaceship and go there yourself, or send a robot to have a peek...

Scientists Explore the Universe from a Distance...

The easiest way to find out about the Universe is to use remote sensing (i.e. looking from a distance). The idea is to detect EM radiation, but it's best if you can detect different kinds of EM wave...

- Radio telescopes are the very large dishes — they detect radio waves from space.
- Optical telescopes detect visible light.
- X-ray telescopes are a good way to 'see' violent, high-temperature events in space, like exploding stars.

Part of the reason for exploring other planets is to try and find out if there's life out there.

1) Scientists look for chemical changes in a planet's atmosphere.

2) Some changes in an atmosphere could be caused by things like volcanoes.

3) But others are a clue that there might be life there (e.g. changing levels of oxygen and carbon dioxide in an atmosphere could be due to respiration or photosynthesis).

...but Sometimes Manned Spacecraft are Used...

1) Sending a manned spacecraft to Mars would take at least a couple of years (for a round trip).

2) The spacecraft would need to carry a lot of fuel, making it heavy — and expensive.

3) And it would be difficult keeping the astronauts alive and healthy for all that time...
   - the spacecraft would have to carry loads of food, water and oxygen,
   - you'd need to regulate the temperature and remove toxic gases from the air,
   - the spacecraft would have to shield the astronauts from cosmic rays from the Sun,
   - long periods in low gravity causes muscle wastage and loss of bone tissue,
   - spending ages in a tiny space, with the same people, is psychologically stressful.

Space travel can be very stressful.

...but Sending Unmanned Probes is Much Easier

Build a spacecraft. Pack as many instruments on board as will fit. Launch. That's the basic idea here.

Advantages of Unmanned Probes	Disadvantages of Unmanned Probes
• They don't have to carry food, water and oxygen (or people) — so more instruments can be fitted in. • They can withstand conditions that would be lethal to humans (e.g. extreme heat, cold or radiation levels). • They're cheaper — they carry less, they don't have to come back to Earth, and less is spent on safety. • If the probe does crash or burn up unexpectedly it's a bit embarrassing, and you've wasted lots of time and money, but at least no one gets hurt.	• Unmanned probes can't think for themselves (whereas people are very good at overcoming simple problems that could be disastrous). • A spacecraft can't do maintenance and repairs — people can (as the astronauts on the Space Shuttle 'Discovery' had to do when its heat shield was damaged during take-off).

Probes — a popular feature of alien abduction stories...

When people first sent things into space, we began cautiously — in October 1957, Russia sent a small aluminium sphere (Sputnik 1) into orbit around the Earth. A month later, off went Sputnik 2, carrying the very first earthling to leave the planet — a small and unfortunate dog called Laika.

Revision Summary for Section 9

And that's the end of Physics — but it's not quite over yet. You've got to check that what you think you learned actually stuck in your brain. The best way to do that is by answering all these lovely questions. There are a couple of formulas to learn to use in this section. Watch out for units though — before you bung your numbers into the formulas you have to make sure they're in the right units. It's a big pitfall, so don't fall head first into it. Anyway, enough gasbagging — off you go.

1) Sketch an atom, showing its protons, neutrons and electrons.

2) Explain what isotopes are. What does 'unstable' mean?

3) Oxygen atoms contain 8 protons. What is the difference between oxygen-16 and oxygen-18?

4) Radioactive decay is a totally random process. Explain what this means.

5) List three sources of background radiation.

6) Describe in detail the nature and properties of the three types of radiation: α, β and γ.

7) What substances could be used to block: a) α-radiation   b) β-radiation   c) γ-radiation?

8) Describe what is meant by the term 'half-life'.

9) Explain how radiation damages the human body: a) at low doses, b) at high doses.

10) Explain what precautions you should take to protect yourself from:
    a) alpha radiation, in a school laboratory,
    b) gamma rays, if you work at a nuclear reprocessing plant.

11) Explain which types of radiation are used, and why, in each of the following:
    a) medical tracers,   b) treating cancer,   c) detecting faults in aeroengine turbine blades,
    d) sterilisation,   e) smoke detectors,   f) thickness control.

12) What's the difference between a star and a planet? What and where are asteroids?

13) What and where are comets? What are they made of? Sketch a diagram of a comet orbit.

14) What does NEO stand for? What are they and why do scientists lose sleep over them?

15) Sketch the magnetic field of the Earth. What do scientists think causes the Earth's magnetic field?

16) What's the Milky Way?

17) How big is the Universe?

18) Why would a black hole form? Why's it called 'black'? How can you spot one?

19) What happens inside a star to make it so hot?

20) What is a 'main sequence' star? How long does it last? What happens after that?

21) Why will our Sun never form a black hole?

22) What's the main theory for the origin of the Universe? Give two important bits of evidence for it.

23) How long ago do we think the Universe began?

24) What are the two possible futures for the Universe, and what do they depend on?

25) What force keeps planets and satellites in their orbits?

26)*What force would be needed to give a 50 kg buggy an acceleration of 1.5 m/s²?

27)*I weigh 600 N on Earth. Find: a) my mass, and b) my weight on the Moon.

28) How could scientists investigate Neptune's atmosphere without actually sending someone there?

29) Explain four possible problems with going on a really long space journey.

30) Give two advantages and two disadvantages of manned space travel, compared to unmanned probes.

* Answers on page 140

Thinking in Exams

In the old days, it was enough to learn a whole bunch of <u>facts</u> while you were revising and just spew them onto the paper come exam day. But nowadays there's a bit more to it than that. Rats.

Remember — You Might Have to Think During the Exam

1) In the exam, they might expect you to read an article and <u>apply</u> your science knowledge to it. Eeek.

2) The trick is <u>not</u> to <u>panic</u>. They're <u>not</u> expecting you to show Einstein-like levels of scientific insight.

3) They're just expecting you to <u>use</u> the stuff you <u>know</u> in a <u>practical setting</u> — and usually it's <u>not as bad as it looks</u>.

So to give you an idea of what to expect come exam-time, use the new <u>CGP Exam Simulator</u> (below). Read the article, and have a go at the questions. It's <u>guaranteed</u> to be just as much fun as the real thing.

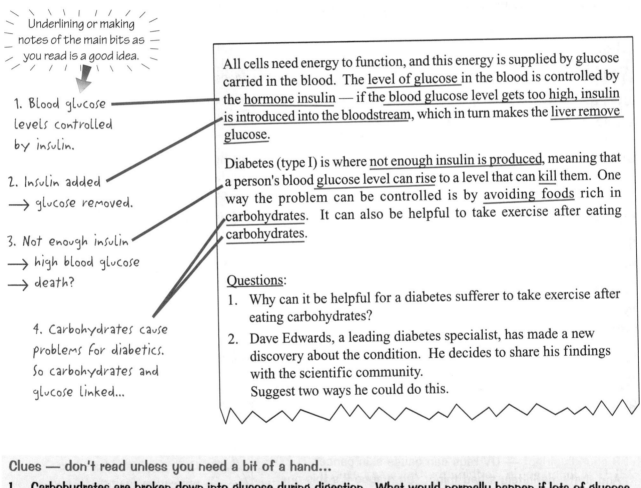

Underlining or making notes of the main bits as you read is a good idea.

1. Blood glucose levels controlled by insulin.

2. Insulin added → glucose removed.

3. Not enough insulin → high blood glucose → death?

4. Carbohydrates cause problems for diabetics. So carbohydrates and glucose linked...

All cells need energy to function, and this energy is supplied by glucose carried in the blood. The <u>level of glucose</u> in the blood is controlled by the <u>hormone insulin</u> — if the <u>blood glucose level gets too high, insulin is introduced into the bloodstream</u>, which in turn makes the <u>liver remove glucose</u>.

Diabetes (type I) is where <u>not enough insulin is produced</u>, meaning that a person's blood <u>glucose level can rise</u> to a level that can <u>kill</u> them. One way the problem can be controlled is by <u>avoiding foods</u> rich in <u>carbohydrates</u>. It can also be helpful to take exercise after eating <u>carbohydrates</u>.

<u>Questions</u>:
1. Why can it be helpful for a diabetes sufferer to take exercise after eating carbohydrates?

2. Dave Edwards, a leading diabetes specialist, has made a new discovery about the condition. He decides to share his findings with the scientific community.
Suggest two ways he could do this.

Clues — don't read unless you need a bit of a hand...

1. Carbohydrates are broken down into glucose during digestion. What would normally happen if lots of glucose is suddenly put into the blood? How would this normally be controlled? And how is it different in a diabetic?

2. This isn't a trick question — think of how you'd expect to read or hear about scientific discoveries.

Answers

1. Eating carbohydrates puts a lot of glucose into the blood. Exercising can use up extra glucose, which helps stop blood glucose levels getting too high.

2. Any two sensible means of communication, e.g. conference, internet, book, journal, phone, meeting.

Thinking in an exam — it's not like the old days...

It's a bit scary, being expected to <u>think</u> in the exam. But then, a lot of people would rather that than have to learn shedloads of facts and formulas, so I guess there's something for everyone now. Anyway — just <u>take your time</u> and <u>think things through</u>. Nearly always the <u>answer</u> will be there, <u>hidden in the question</u>... or if it's not, there'll probably be a big hint to remind you of something you'll have learnt.

Dealing with Tricky Questions

<u>Most</u> of the questions you'll get in the exam will be <u>straightforward</u>, as long as you've <u>learnt your stuff</u>. But there are a few things you need to be aware of that could <u>catch you out</u>...

Some Questions Could be Based on a Real-Life Situation...

...so learn to live with it.

All they do is show you how <u>the science you've learnt</u> fits into the <u>real world</u> — that's all.

<u>That equation</u> you learnt <u>still works</u>... and <u>that graph</u> is still the <u>same shape</u>.

<u>Don't</u> go worrying, just because it's set in a practical situation, that the <u>theory might not apply</u>. IT WILL.

Hmmm... all very entertaining. But at the end of the day, all you need to know is:

Force = mass × acceleration

Lina and Magnus go on holiday to Shanghai. They take the Shanghai Maglev train from Pudong Airport to the city.

The train has a mass of 80 000 kg, and accelerates at 5 m/s².

1. What is the force on the train?

Some Multiple Choice Questions Can Be Tricky — DON'T PANIC

In the exam, there's <u>always the risk</u> you'll run into a stumper. A question that looks confusing... maybe 3 of the answers look like they could be right, or maybe there's an option that you've no idea about.

Don't panic.

If you've learnt something about the topic, it's bound to come in handy.

1) Flick through your options and use what you know to <u>rule out the wrong 'uns</u>:

Well, <u>A is wrong</u> for starters. I'm sure you won't have read anywhere about UV rays giving you digestive problems — that's clearly nonsense. ✗

<u>B, C and D look like possibles</u>. All of them seem true on first read, so they can stay in the running for now.

2) Look at what's left. They can't all be right, so check which one <u>answers the question best</u>.

<u>B sounds alright</u> — UV rays can cause skin cancer. And that's definitely a bad thing. So maybe it's this one...

<u>C sounds possible</u> — it could be true maybe, but vitamin production is a good thing, and the question is asking about the <u>dangers</u> of UV. So I don't reckon it's this one, even if it is true. ✗

Lina finds an article in a newspaper:

In 2005, China broke the record for the world's highest railway, as it completed the **Golmud to Lhasa railway**. At its highest point, the track reaches 5072 m above sea level. Due to the high altitude, the railway will use special carriages that provide enough oxygen for passengers and special windows to protect against UV rays.

2. Why are UV rays dangerous? Choose the best explanation:

A UV rays can cause digestion problems.

B UV rays can cause skin cancer.

C UV rays can help the body produce vitamin D.

D Dark skin provides some protection against UV rays.

<u>D is true</u> — but again, it's not a reason for it being dangerous. ✗

So <u>B looks like your best bet</u> — it's true AND it answers the question well.

If at first you don't succeed — come back to it later...

It's true — you might get a stinker in the exam. And it's not easy to stay calm and think things through when you're under pressure. So <u>remember</u> — <u>most</u> questions will be <u>straightforward</u>. <u>Do those first</u>. Come back to the tricky ones only when you've done your best with the rest of the paper.*

* And I know I shouldn't say this, but at least if it's multiple choice you can always have a last-minute guess.

Exam Skills

Answering Experiment Questions

You're guaranteed to get <u>at least one</u> question on an <u>experiment</u>, nay <u>SEVERAL questions</u> on experiments. The good news is — the examiners are pretty <u>limited</u> as to what they can ask you. More than likely it'll be either <u>writing down facts</u> you've learnt, or it'll be about <u>fair testing</u> and <u>reading graphs</u>. (Or a mixture.)

Make Sure You Read Graphs Carefully

Melissa did an experiment comparing the rates of reaction of magnesium ribbon with two different concentrations of dilute hydrochloric acid, labelled Concentration A and Concentration B.

For each test she put the ribbon in the flask and every 10 seconds she measured the mass of gas that had been given off. She used the same volume of acid and the same length of magnesium ribbon for each test.

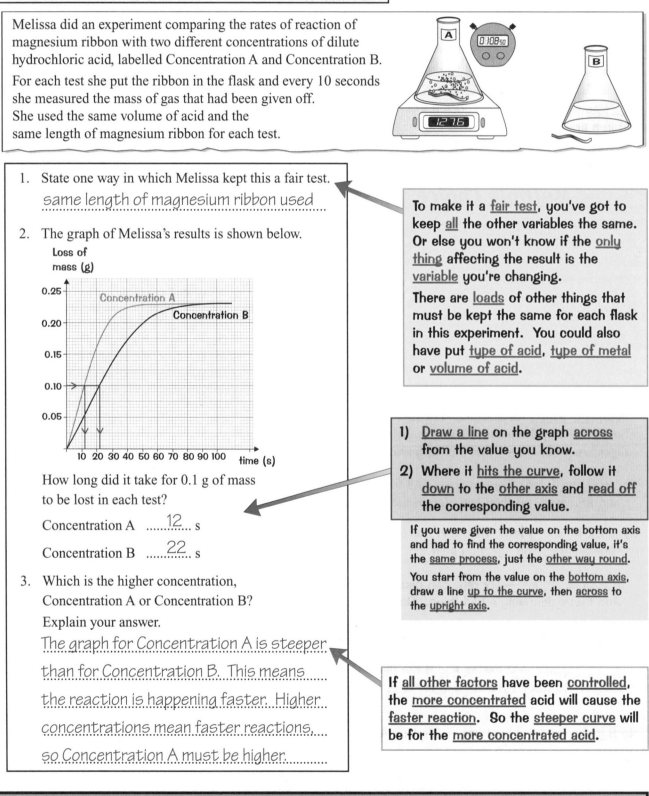

1. State one way in which Melissa kept this a fair test.

   <u>same length of magnesium ribbon used</u>

2. The graph of Melissa's results is shown below.

   Loss of mass (g)

   How long did it take for 0.1 g of mass to be lost in each test?

   Concentration A ....12.... s

   Concentration B ....22.... s

3. Which is the higher concentration, Concentration A or Concentration B? Explain your answer.

   <u>The graph for Concentration A is steeper</u>
   <u>than for Concentration B. This means</u>
   <u>the reaction is happening faster. Higher</u>
   <u>concentrations mean faster reactions,</u>
   <u>so Concentration A must be higher.</u>

To make it a <u>fair test</u>, you've got to keep <u>all</u> the other variables the same. Or else you won't know if the <u>only thing</u> affecting the result is the <u>variable</u> you're changing.

There are <u>loads</u> of other things that must be kept the same for each flask in this experiment. You could also have put <u>type of acid</u>, <u>type of metal</u> or <u>volume of acid</u>.

1) <u>Draw a line</u> on the graph <u>across</u> from the value you know.

2) Where it <u>hits the curve</u>, follow it <u>down</u> to the <u>other axis</u> and <u>read off</u> the corresponding value.

If you were given the value on the bottom axis and had to find the corresponding value, it's the <u>same process</u>, just the <u>other way round</u>.

You start from the value on the <u>bottom axis</u>, draw a line <u>up to the curve</u>, then <u>across</u> to the <u>upright axis</u>.

If <u>all other factors</u> have been <u>controlled</u>, the <u>more concentrated</u> acid will cause the <u>faster reaction</u>. So the <u>steeper curve</u> will be for the <u>more concentrated acid</u>.

GCSE Science — a graph a minute...

...and there you have it. That's about all I can do for you — you're on your own now. (<u>Good luck</u> ☺)

Index

Index

Index

Index and Answers

Answers

Revision Summary for Section 1 (page 13)
11) a) Response A   b) Response B
Revision Summary for Section 2 (page 27)
5) Professional runner, mechanic, secretary
18) a) 6 pm   b) 8 pm   c) No
Revision Summary for Section 4 (page 56)
7) 2 sodium atoms, 1 carbon atom and 3 oxygen atoms
8) a) bottom-left   b) top-right   c) top-left   d) bottom-right
9) calcium
10) a) $CaCO_3 + 2HCl \rightarrow CaCl_2 + H_2O + CO_2$
    b) $Ca + 2H_2O \rightarrow Ca(OH)_2 + H_2$
Revision Summary for Section 6 (page 91)
32) When using the concentrated acid it will take less time to produce the same amount of gas than when using the dilute acid — the rate of reaction is faster. The slope of the graph (time vs volume of gas) will be steeper for the acid which produces the faster rate of reaction.

Revision Summary for Section 7 (page 105)
8) A: 2 years, B: 1.5 years
14) 0.7 (or 70%)
Top tip for page 110
1) Power = voltage × current = 230 × 12 = 2760 W
                                          = 2.76 kW
2) Time = energy ÷ power = 0.5 ÷ 2.76 = 0.181 h = 11 min
Revision Summary for Section 8 (page 120)
4) 4.8 ohms
13) 279 kJ
14) a) Units = power × time = 2.5 × (2/60) = 0.08 kWh
    b) 0.96p
20) 150 m/s
24) A and D (which are identical)
Top tip for page 122
beta
Revision Summary for Section 9 (page 133)
26) 75 N
27) a) 60 kg   b) 96 N